NOV 2006

The 150 Best American Recipes

*Indispensable Dishes from
Legendary Chefs
and Undiscovered Cooks*

The 150 Best American Recipes

Edited by Fran McCullough and Molly Stevens

Foreword by Rick Bayless   Photography by Ben Fink

 Houghton Mifflin Company · BOSTON NEW YORK 2006

Copyright © 2006 by Houghton Mifflin Company

Foreword copyright © 2006 by Rick Bayless

Introduction and text copyright © 2006
by Fran McCullough and Molly Stevens

Photographs copyright © 2006 by Ben Fink

Visit our Web site: www.houghtonmifflinbooks.com.

Library of Congress Cataloging-in-Publication Data

The 150 best American recipes : indispensable dishes from legendary
chefs and undiscovered cooks / edited by Fran McCullough and
Molly Stevens ; foreword by Rick Bayless ; photography by Ben Fink.

    p. cm.

    Includes index.

    ISBN-13: 978-0-618-71865-8

    ISBN-10: 0-618-71865-6

    1. Cookery, American. I. Title: One hundred fifty best American
recipes. II. McCullough, Frances Monson. III. Stevens, Molly.

    TX715.A1126 2006

    2006005604 641.5973 — dc22

Book design by Melissa Lotfy

Typefaces: Paperback by House Industries, Akzidenz Grotesk by Adobe

Food styling by Megan Fawn Schlow

Prop styling by Barb Fritz

PRINTED IN THE UNITED STATES OF AMERICA

QWT 10 9 8 7 6 5 4 3 2 1

To the many loyal fans of *The Best American Recipes* —
especially Darlene, Dennis, and Sarah.

You inspire us and bring us much delight.

acknowledgments

We're always asked how on earth we've been able to put together these collections year after year, given the overwhelming number of recipes generated all over the country. The answer is that we couldn't without the advice of dozens of trusty helpers and the good work of our terrific collaborators at Houghton Mifflin. We owe them all a huge debt.

To begin at the beginning, thanks to Houghton's former publisher Wendy Strothman, for having the bright idea of this series one morning in the shower. To Rux Martin, our beloved one-of-a-kind editor, for immediately "getting it" and encouraging us to make the series into a good deal more than just a collection of recipes. To Suzanne Hamlin, co-editor for the first two books in the series, who contributed a distinctive sensibility that still informs our approach. To Doe Coover and Irene Skolnick, the literary agents who made sure we were all happy. And to Rux's series of superb assistants—Lori Galvin, Susan Warhover, and Elizabeth Goffin—all of whom performed superhuman tasks as a routine matter. And especially to Mimi Assad, who never fails to tell us when she's cooked something wonderful, and who took on the enormous task of getting permissions for this book in addition to all her other duties. Because we're testing recipes up to the last minute, there's always a mad rush to get the edited manuscript into presentable type; this year, as always, it's Jacinta Monniere who magically types it perfectly in just a few days.

Deborah DeLosa, our savvy publicity director, immediately starts cooking as soon as the books leave our computers and manages to get everyone excited in advance about her favorite recipes. Challenging as it is to promote annual books in a series, somehow she manages to pull a new rabbit out of the hat each time.

When we combed through all the editions, we were shocked to discover that a number of our favorite cooks had died, all of them much too young. And all of them had contributed recipes that were instantly obvious as Best of the Best. Making their delicious food is a good way to honor Bill Devin, Heather Ho, Raji Jallepali, Leslie Revsin, Michael Roberts, and Pat Tillinghast.

We're grateful to the remarkable string of chefs and waiters who have graced the series with their lively forewords — Paul Theroux, Marcus Samuelsson, Anthony Bourdain, Alan Richman, Bobby Flay, Mario Batali, and Rick Bayless.

Our huge thanks to the following people, who have been our tipsters and testers, our facilitators, and our trusted advisers: Pat Adrian, Gene Burns, Annie Copps, Darian Cork, Barbara Fairchild, Roy Finamore, Janet Fletcher, Millissa Frost, Maria Guarnaschelli, Elizabeth Gurney, Lynn Hildebrandt, Jennifer Josephy, Susan Costner Kenward, Niloufer Ichaporia King, Bill LeBlond, Katy McCullough, Susie Middleton, Sydny Miner, Kemp Minifie, Julie Monson, Jan Newberry, Deborah Orrill, James O'Shea, Sara Perry, Chris Prosperi and Courtney Febbroriello, Pat and Cindy Puglio, Judith Riven, Dana Rogers, Alice Rosengard, Robin Schempp, Arthur Schwartz, Marlena Spieler, Zanne Stewart, John Martin Taylor, Tina Ujlaki, Patty Unterman, Hugh Van Dusen, Nach Waxman, Eileen Weinberg, Ari Weinzweig, Paula Wolfert, and John Willoughby.

We're especially grateful for the good-hearted enthusiasm with which everyone embraced this project, which has been a great joy for us.

contents

foreword

BY RICK BAYLESS

I was standing at my stove recently, cooking up the classic salmon with butter, lemon, and chives, an unfailing family favorite, when the salmon asked for something else to be added to the pan. "Can't you just add a little basil from the garden?" it pined, in the same way I might crave a punchy new necktie to dress up my black suit. "At least snip garlic chives this time, or add some cilantro. Did you ever think of stirring in a little chopped green chile? Wouldn't lime instead of lemon give a breath of fresh air here?"

I suspect something similar has happened to you? You've been cooking along, putting together ingredients the way you have, time and again, when some of them start talking to you, asking to spend some time with the new playmates who've moved into the kitchen. Or with new playmates who may have lived there for a good long time, but with whom they've never become acquainted. And the next thing you know, you're serving up a dish that seems even more perfect — a dish that you'll want to make just that way from then on. (Take a look at page 124 for a very delicious, Asian-accented version of this very conversation.)

Sometimes we just have to stay out of the way and let creativity happen. Occasionally, it's sparked by bringing new flavors and cooking techniques into the kitchen, other times it's by visits to far-off cultures (or their outpost restaurants in our land) or by flights of fancy, dreams, or accidents. Like the Sunday morning when, in an embarrassingly distracted moment, I ground a bunch of black pepper into my French toast batter. In an attempt to cover over my mistake, I added some allspice (I'd discovered in Mexico that cooks there think of allspice as the "sweet" version of black pepper), which helped some, but the batter needed something more. It needed sour cream and honey, too. That morning's French toast, cooked up in nutty browned butter, turned out to be a whole new kind of delicious. Bayless's Black Pepper French Toast was born, all because I was trying to cover up having made a mistake no professional chef should ever have made. (Try it topped with fig jam.)

As I was getting to know the recipes in the delectable volume you've got in your hands, I wondered about all the stories behind each list of ingredients, each step-by-step procedure. Even more than a collection of happy accidents, I sense that these recipes represent a happy evolution—dishes welcoming flavors and cooking techniques that are just right for the moment, dishes we can't wait to make—again and again.

And exactly what are we wild about eating right now? Roasty flavored things, I'd say, with textures from voluptuous to crispy-crunchy. Bacony flavored things—well, anything flavored with cured pork to be exact, whether pancetta or prosciutto, aged ham or standard-issue bacon. Mushroomy flavored things, or any dish flavored with the ever-satisfying richness of soy or balsamic vinegar or Worcestershire. The Japanese would tell us that our love affair with all these flavors celebrates the fact that we've discovered the glories of *umami,* that super-delicious "fifth flavor" that is concentrated in everything I've just mentioned. (If you've never made Leslie Revsin's *umami*-charged braised beef short ribs with soy and brown sugar, page 166, go straight to the kitchen and get cooking.)

As seductive as *umami* may be, we have to admit that we're in love with bright flavors, too, and we're taking them where bright flavors have never gone before. Perky chiles, pungent cilantro, and springy citrus—why, you could almost say we've adopted them as the salt and pepper of the twenty-first century.

I could go on and on about our infatuation with the playful, sweet-savory teeter-totter of crunchy bacon baked with brown sugar (page 250) and Malaysian Noodle Soup (page 57), but suffice it to say that our American taste buds have come alive to more possibilities than any other collective set of taste buds on the planet.

Now, like many of you, I read more cookbooks in bed than in the kitchen. More often than not, I'll admit, I use the recipes as starting points for fantasies of perfect dinner parties, family meals, and restaurant dishes I'll create. (Of course, there are always prolonged ovations in my fantasies, too—this is, after all, my bedtime reading.) I dream of the afternoons I'll set aside to slow-roast duck (the recipe on page 142 is my *favorite* way to prepare duck) or turkey or onions for a salad. As much as we've all come to appreciate a quick and tasty weeknight dish, I still treasure the restorative quality of unrushed weekend time in the kitchen. That's when I can truly create culinary alchemy for friends and family.

While savoring the captivating freshness and variety of the recipes between these covers, I was reminded of the nutritional wisdom Julia Child shared at a culinary conference years ago. Never one to suffer the restrictive tyranny of fad diets, she said — in so many words — that a person needs to know only three nutritional truths for healthy living: don't eat too much, eat a little of everything, and make sure every bite is so delicious that it truly satisfies your hunger.

Though Julia's advice may fly in the face of conventional wisdom (haven't we grown up with the rather puritanical notion that really good food leads to gluttony and weight gain?), maybe she knew something that the flip-flopping nutritionists are just coming to: a wonderfully varied collection of really good recipes just may be our first line of defense when it comes to health and happiness.

bayless's black pepper french toast
(serves 6)

Whisk together 1 cup milk, 2 eggs, a heaping 1/2 teaspoon freshly ground black pepper, a heaping 1/2 teaspoon freshly ground allspice, 1/2 cup sour cream, and 2 tablespoons very aromatic honey.

Cut each of six ¾-inch-thick slices of brioche or other rich egg bread (challah, for instance) in half diagonally, then lay them in a baking dish. Pour the custard evenly over them, pressing lightly on the bread to encourage quick absorption of the custard. After 15 minutes, flip the brioche slices, nestle them back into the custard, and press lightly again. When another 15 minutes have passed, the bread should have absorbed most of the custard and be soaked through. Heat 2 table-spoons butter in a large (12-inch) skillet, prefer-ably nonstick. When the butter begins to brown, lay half the slices in the pan. Cook until richly browned underneath, about 5 minutes, then flip and brown the other side. Repeat with 2 more ta-blespoons of butter and the rest of the slices. Lay 2 slices of French toast on each plate, sprinkle with powdered sugar, and serve with fig jam. Oc-casionally, I'll serve a bowl of crème fraîche or vanilla yogurt alongside the jam.

introduction

Initially, it seemed like an impossible idea—compile a cookbook of the best recipes to appear in print during the course of an entire year. We balked. How could anyone read the many hundreds of cookbooks published every year, plus all the food magazines and newspaper sections, scan the Internet, and search through all the other surprising places recipes turn up? And even if two of us could, how on earth would we find the best among them?

The more we thought about it, though, the more we realized that our fellow home cooks were confronted with the same hopeless task—and the very fact that it was so daunting might be the best reason to try. We started to imagine a book we wanted to have ourselves, so we gulped and said yes. And so began our journey into the amazing world of American recipes, where we've read tens of thousands of them and cooked many thousands in our home kitchens, all in search of the best.

From the beginning, we wanted to find recipes that excited our own palates but also brought something else to the party: a new way of looking at a dish, a terrific trick, a solution to a kitchen problem, the ultimate version of a much-beloved classic. We wanted to have a kind of conversation with our readers, telling them what we discovered as we cooked the dish and how to take it in other directions, as well as which steps they could safely shortcut and which ones were absolutely essential. Our goal was to create an up-to-date cookbook for ourselves, full of those keeper dishes we were always meaning to serve again.

We knew there were many others who needed the book: time-challenged food lovers with sophisticated palates who can never find the extra hours to cook from all the magazines they get, who can't keep track of the recipes they clip from newspapers, and who have barely enough room on their shelves for another cookbook, but who always—always—are in the market for good new recipes. We also knew that many men and women needed a book to get them through the holidays, especially Thanksgiving, when most people feel obligated to cook, even if they don't make so much as a baked potato the rest of the year.

It didn't take us long to develop a kind of radar for the truly great recipes, the ones we immediately wanted to make again for our friends, forgetting momentarily that we were supposed to be finding still more dishes. Most of the recipes we saw were familiar (some of them filched word for word from other cooks). But now and again a little bell went off in our heads as we encountered something truly new and exciting.

We soon learned to our dismay that plenty of recipes that sound great just don't work; testing is key. We never got the big staff that we originally thought it would take to accomplish the project. We made all the dishes ourselves, sometimes with the help of a couple of game family members and the occasional friend. Since we cook in ordinary home kitchens, with regular home stoves—and no special restaurant equipment—we know how each recipe performs in real life. For starters, if we can't find the ingredients within ten miles of home, we don't make the dish (or we figure out a viable substitution and tell you about it). Since our goal is to be recipe sleuths, not recipe doctors, if the recipe is flawed, we ditch it and move on.

Cooking aficionados often say that if you find three good recipes in a book, your money has been well spent. Our first job was to zoom in on those and then sort out which one stood above the rest—the most delicious, the most useful for a busy cook, the most unusual for one reason or another. Sometimes we ended up cooking our way through many candidates (often from highly touted cookbooks), without finding anything worth passing along. At other times, it was torture to choose between two or three favorites.

Although cookbooks and major magazines are the most obvious sources of new recipes, the real thrills came when we found recipes in obscure places and discovered genius cooks no one had heard of before. Cooking talent is scattered like salt over the whole population. We've learned of

Best recipes from newspaper contests, supermarket flyers, restaurant press releases, and radio and TV shows. More than a few have come from the back of the box. Good recipes really are everywhere. As jaded as we may get after reading thousands and thousands of recipes every year, we're still excited to see a new one. Nothing makes us happier than finding something brilliantly simple that any fool can make without a moment's anxiety—a dead-easy, accessible, knock-your-socks-off dish that appeals to tenderfoot cooks as well as old hands in the kitchen.

As the number of books in this series stacked up, we often found ourselves calling each other frantically trying to recall in what year a favorite had appeared. Yes, we love all the recipes in all the books, but inevitably there are some that we turn to again and again. So we got to thinking—what if we assembled a Best of the Best and put them together in one grand edition?

With nearly 1,000 recipes to choose from, restricting ourselves to an essential 150 was a great deal more difficult than we had imagined. Often we had to stage cook-offs, testing the many turkey recipes or chocolate cakes or chocolate chip cookies to select the best. Just as the series began with a book we wanted to have ourselves, we now have the ultimate resource we need, with the recipes we absolutely can't live without, along with the tips we've gathered over the years that have changed the way we cook. And we're betting that you, too, will want to make every single one of these recipes again and again.

— Fran McCullough
and Molly Stevens

Starters

Starters

charred tomatillo guacamole with seeded tortilla triangles 4

sweet and spicy pecans 7

cheddar walnut crisps 9

phyllo cheese straws 10

pancetta crisps with goat cheese and pear 12

salsa-baked goat cheese 13

parsi deviled eggs 15

vodka-spiked cherry tomatoes with pepper-salt 16

crimped shrimp 18

smoked salmon rolls with arugula, mascarpone, chives, and capers 19

roasted asparagus with panko bread crumbs 22

mini frittatas with wild mushrooms 24

manly meatballs 25

savory fig tart 27

charred tomatillo guacamole with seeded tortilla triangles

charred tomatillo guacamole with seeded tortilla triangles

SOURCE *Gourmet*

COOK **Mary Sue Milliken and Susan Feniger**

If there's a more beloved dip in America than guacamole, we don't know about it. So a new twist on our old favorite is an enticing prospect, and this delicious version, by one of the *Two Hot Tamales* team of TV chef-restaurateurs, completely delivers. Acidy little tomatillos are charred and then mashed into the basic seasonings before the avocados are added to create a whole new taste.

Chef Milliken has taken the tortilla chips for a spin as well. These crunchy scoops come crusted with all kinds of seeds. The tortilla scoops don't have a particularly Mexican taste, so you can use them with any dip that would be good with the seeds. They're also delicious all by themselves.

For a party, you can make the tortilla triangles a day ahead and the guacamole up to 8 hours ahead. Just be sure to bring it to room temperature before serving. ❧

seeded tortilla triangles

❈

- ¼ **cup flaxseeds (see note)**
- ¼ **cup sesame seeds**
- ¼ **cup poppy seeds**
- 4 **10- to 12-inch flour tortillas**
- 1 **large egg, beaten with 2 tablespoons cold water and 1 teaspoon salt**

makes about 32 triangles

Preheat the oven to 350 degrees and set the racks in the upper- and lower-middle levels.

Stir together the three kinds of seeds. Put 1 tortilla on each of two baking sheets and brush with some of the egg mixture. Sprinkle with seeds to coat, then cut each tortilla into long, thin triangles with a sharp knife.

Bake, switching the position of the sheets halfway through, until the tortillas are crisp and lightly golden, 15 to 20 minutes total.

Transfer the triangles to wire racks to cool. Repeat with the remaining tortillas.

- Flaxseeds are delicate and best bought at a natural food store that restocks frequently. If you can't find them, just replace them with 2 more tablespoons each of the other seeds.
- Try other seeds, such as cumin.
- If the triangles lose their crispness, recrisp them in a 350-degree oven for about 5 minutes.

charred tomatillo guacamole

❄

6 ounces tomatillos (6–7), husked and rinsed
¹/₂ small red onion, finely chopped
3–4 fresh serrano chiles, seeded and finely chopped
¹/₂ cup finely chopped fresh cilantro
1 teaspoon salt
¹/₂ teaspoon freshly ground black pepper
2 large California avocados (about 1 pound)

makes about 3¹/₂ cups

Preheat the broiler.

Broil the tomatillos in a shallow flameproof baking pan about 4 inches from the heat until the tops are charred, 7 to 10 minutes. Turn the tomatillos over with tongs and broil until charred, about 5 minutes more.

Combine the onion, chiles, cilantro, salt, and pepper in a large bowl. Add the tomatillos two at a time, mashing with a fork or pestle to form a coarse paste.

Pit and peel the avocados. Add to the bowl and continue mashing until incorporated but still chunky. If you're making the guacamole ahead, press a piece of plastic wrap directly on top and store it in the fridge. Let come to room temperature before serving. Serve with the Seeded Tortilla Triangles.

sweet and spicy pecans

SOURCE *New Tastes from Texas* by Stephan Pyles
COOK Stephan Pyles

We have to admit, we're suckers for a great batch of homemade spiced nuts. Over the years, we've had a spiced nut recipe in almost every edition of our book, so choosing a single favorite for this collection was tough. But these Texas pecans are like no others — snappy, buttery, spicy, a little sweet, a little zingy. You taste them at the front, back, sides, and roof of your mouth. They're as rich as pralines, with a chile heat as deep as the sweet.

The pecans are also amazingly easy to make in large batches, so they're a good choice for holiday parties or gift giving. ❧

tip

TO MAKE CHILE POWDER, use either a mixture or a single type of dried chiles, such as anchos, chipotles, and guajillos. Preheat the oven to 300 degrees. Slit the chiles open and remove the seeds. Place the split chiles in a single layer on a baking sheet and roast until they are thoroughly dry and stiff, 3 to 5 minutes.

Crumble the chiles into a bowl. Put the pieces in a spice grinder and grind them to a powder. Store in an airtight container in a cool, dry place for up to 1 month or in the freezer for up to 3 months.

2 **tablespoons unsalted butter**

3 **cups pecan halves**

1/2 **cup firmly packed light brown sugar**

1 **tablespoon ground cumin**

2 **teaspoons pure chile powder (see tip)**

1 **teaspoon paprika**

1/4 **cup cider vinegar**

Salt

makes 3 cups

Preheat the oven to 350 degrees and set a rack in the middle level.

Melt the butter in a large skillet over medium heat. Add the pecans and sauté, stirring, until lightly browned, about 3 minutes. Stir in the brown sugar and cook, stirring, until lightly caramelized. Stir in the cumin, chile powder, and paprika. Add the vinegar and cook, stirring, until all the liquid has evaporated. Season to taste with salt.

Spread the pecans in a single layer on a baking sheet and bake until crisp, 3 to 5 minutes. Let cool, then store in an airtight container at room temperature until ready to serve.

note from our test kitchen

These nuts are Texas-sweet. If you don't have a big sweet tooth, use a level 1/3 cup brown sugar. They'll still have a sweet-tart edge.

cheddar walnut crisps

SOURCE *Sainsbury's Magazine*

COOK Lorna Wing

Of all the variations we've seen on the *frico* — the crispy cheese wafer from the Friuli region of Italy — this version, from ace food writer Lorna Wing, is our favorite. And it's simplicity itself: the cheeses can be quickly grated in a food processor, they are ones you usually have on hand, a batch can be made in less than 10 minutes, and the crisps can be made up to 4 days ahead. The only trick is to use parchment paper, available in most supermarkets. 🍂

note from our test kitchen

Store the crisps layered with parchment paper in an airtight tin.

2$^1/_2$ **ounces aged cheddar cheese, grated (about 1 cup)**

2$^1/_2$ **ounces Parmesan cheese, grated (about 1$^1/_4$ cups)**

2 **ounces walnuts, coarsely chopped ($^1/_2$ cup)**

2 **tablespoons finely chopped fresh thyme or 1 tablespoon dried**

makes about 60 crisps

Preheat the oven to 400 degrees and set a rack in the middle level. Line two baking sheets with parchment paper.

Combine the cheeses in a small bowl. Drop the mixture by rounded teaspoonfuls onto the lined baking sheets, leaving about an inch between them. Flatten the cheese mixture with the back of a spoon. Sprinkle the top of each cheese circle with a little of the chopped nuts and thyme.

Bake, one sheet at a time, for 5 minutes, or until the crisps are bubbling and the edges are golden brown. Let stand for several minutes, then slide off the paper with a spatula. Blot the crisps gently with paper towels and serve at room temperature.

phyllo cheese straws

***

SOURCE *Patrick O'Connell's Refined American Cuisine* by Patrick O'Connell
COOK Patrick O'Connell

Cheese straws — thin, elegant pastry twists — are nothing new, but these are the first we've seen made with phyllo dough in place of ordinary puff pastry. The idea comes from Patrick O'Connell, the much-admired chef-co-owner of the Inn at Little Washington, where elegance is the watchword. Rather than being twisted and baked, the phyllo is rolled scroll-like to form fragile, slender straws. With nothing more than a dusting of Parmesan, they're more crunch than substance, making them addictive without being filling.

The delicate pastries make a handsome little nibble to serve with drinks, especially when you're pouring something bubbly and bright, such as champagne or Prosecco. We also love the fact that you can assemble them several days ahead, then refrigerate and bake before serving, or bake and store in a closed tin for several days. ❧

2 **sheets phyllo dough (12 x 18 inches each; see note)**
6 **tablespoons clarified butter (see tip)**
2½ **tablespoons finely grated Parmesan cheese**

makes 36 crisps

Preheat the oven to 375 degrees.

On a cutting board, lay out 1 sheet of phyllo, brush it lightly with clarified butter, and sprinkle evenly with the cheese. (Keep the remaining phyllo covered with a moistened tea towel.) Place the other sheet of phyllo on top of the cheese and brush with more clarified butter.

Using a sharp knife, cut the phyllo lengthwise into thirds. (You will have 3 long strips, each about 4 inches wide and 18 inches long.) Next cut these strips crosswise into 1½-inch-wide rectangles. Wrap each rectangle lengthwise around a pencil or skewer. Remove the pencil or skewer and place the rolled phyllo straws on a baking sheet. Continue until all the phyllo has been rolled.

Refrigerate the phyllo straws on the baking sheet for at least 10 minutes, or until they become firm.

Bake for about 9 minutes, or until golden brown. Remove from the oven and, using a spatula, slip the straws onto paper towels to cool. The straws may be kept in a sealed tin for several days.

THE 150 BEST AMERICAN RECIPES

10

tip

TO MAKE CLARIFIED BUTTER, melt 1 stick (8 tablespoons) unsalted butter over medium-low heat. When the butter is thoroughly melted, turn off the heat and skim the creamy foam from the surface. Pour the butter into a small bowl, leaving any white sediment behind. One stick will yield about 6 tablespoons clarified butter. (We sometimes simply use melted butter. The phyllo may brown a little unevenly, but the taste is the same.)

notes from our test kitchen

- Some phyllo comes in 9-x-12-inch sheets and not the 12-x-18-inch sheets called for here. In this case, you'll need to use 4 sheets and make 2 batches of straws. For each batch, follow the directions by sandwiching half the grated cheese between 2 buttered sheets of phyllo, then cutting the sheets lengthwise into thirds so you have long strips that are each about 3 inches wide and 12 inches long. Next cut these strips crosswise into 1½-inch-wide rectangles.

- Unless you're very quick with rolling and shaping, the phyllo may start to dry out as you go. Use any extra clarified butter to brush the edges, which will keep them from becoming brittle.

- Place the rolls seam sides down on the baking sheet to prevent them from unfurling as they chill or bake.

pancetta crisps with goat cheese and pear

SOURCE *Bon Appétit*

COOK Sarah Tenaglia

Prepare to be ambushed at the kitchen door when you emerge with a tray of these elegant crisps. Happily, they take little time to prepare, so you may want to make double the amount you think you'll need. We find that each guest can easily devour two or three without pause. ❧

note from our test kitchen

These crisps are best served soon after making, while the pancetta is still warm. Take care that it's not piping hot, however, or the cheese will melt.

16 **thin slices pancetta**
   Freshly ground black pepper
16 **teaspoons fresh goat cheese (from a 5-ounce log), at room temperature**
 2 **very ripe small pears, halved, cored, and cut into ¼-inch-thick slices**
   Fresh thyme leaves for garnish

makes 16 crisps

Preheat the oven to 450 degrees.

Place the pancetta slices in a single layer on a large rimmed baking sheet. Sprinkle with pepper. Bake until golden, about 10 minutes. Using a spatula, slide the pancetta crisps onto a platter. Top each with 1 teaspoon of the goat cheese and 1 pear slice. Sprinkle with thyme and serve.

salsa-baked goat cheese

SOURCE *El Mundo de Frontera* newsletter
COOK Rick Bayless

Here's a great idea for Super Bowl Sunday, from the newsletter of Chicago's terrific Mexican restaurant twins, Frontera Grill and Topolobampo. This spread/dip fulfills all imaginable requirements: it's quick, it's easy, it's delectable, you eat it with tortilla chips, and it goes with guacamole — and beer or margaritas or whatever else you're serving. It's one of those vanishing dishes — no leftovers.

It's not just a snack, though. It also works very well as a first course to serve with drinks. The chips can be Frontera's flavored chips (available at gourmet markets), pita crisps, or just crisp toasts. You can spread it or dip it, as you like. ❧

notes from our test kitchen

- If the salsa is very chunky, you might want to strain it or chop it in a food processor so the pieces won't fall off the chips.
- We like to heat the chips, too — just a few minutes in the hot oven.

¹/₄ **cup pine nuts or coarsely chopped walnuts or pecans**

1 **4-ounce log plain fresh goat cheese (or you can just use more cream cheese)**

1 **3-ounce package cream cheese, at room temperature**

1 **cup salsa, such as Topolo Classic Salsa Veracruzana**

1 **tablespoon chopped fresh cilantro for garnish**

Tortilla chips or pita crisps for serving

serves 4 to 6

Preheat the oven to 350 degrees.

Spread the nuts on a baking sheet and toast them in the oven until lightly browned and very fragrant, 7 to 8 minutes. Transfer to a medium bowl.

Add the cheeses to the bowl and combine thoroughly with the nuts. Scoop the cheese mixture into the center of a baking dish, such as a decorative 9-inch pie plate, and form into a 5-inch disk. Spoon the salsa over and around the cheese.

Bake until heated through, 10 to 15 minutes. Sprinkle with the cilantro and serve as a dip or a spread with tortilla chips or pita crisps.

parsi deviled eggs

***

SOURCE *San Francisco Examiner* STORY BY Patricia Unterman
COOK Niloufer Ichaporia King

San Francisco food writer Patricia Unterman calls Bay Area culinary expert Niloufer Ichaporia King "one of the best cooks on the planet." Certainly, her deviled eggs are the most addictive we've yet tasted, and you wouldn't easily guess the secret ingredient (honey).

Despite its name, this isn't a classic Parsi recipe. Niloufer—as everyone calls her—found it in a book published in Bombay in the 1940s, under the mysterious heading "Italian Eggs."

These deviled eggs, more Parsi than Italian, have all the virtues of their genre plus something else: they're very sophisticated, with zingy flavors that go well with contemporary food. These are great for picnics and also with drinks before an Indian-flavored or spicy meal. We guarantee a lively cocktail hour when you serve these. ❧

notes from our test kitchen

- It's important to let the deviled eggs season a bit for the best flavor. Two hours will do it, but overnight is better.
- You can play with the seasonings, using more butter, lime, and/or jalapeño, as you like.

6 large eggs, hard-cooked (see tip)
1½ teaspoons fresh lime juice, or more to taste
1 teaspoon honey
¼ teaspoon salt, or more to taste
½ jalapeño pepper, seeded and minced
1 tablespoon minced fresh cilantro
1 tablespoon unsalted butter, softened
¼ cup mayonnaise

serves 6

Shell the eggs, cut them in half lengthwise, and put the egg yolks in a small bowl. Set the egg whites aside. Add all of the remaining ingredients except the mayonnaise to the yolks, mashing well with a fork. Be sure the honey is well distributed. Stir in the mayonnaise and taste for lime and salt.

Spoon the mixture into the egg whites, cover, and refrigerate for at least 2 hours or overnight. Let come to room temperature before serving.

tip

TO HARD-COOK EGGS, set them in a saucepan just big enough to hold them, then cover with water. Slowly bring the water to a boil. Cover the pan and remove from the heat. Let the eggs sit in the pan for 14 minutes. For picture-perfect eggs, use the French trick Julia Child used and Jacques Pépin favors: plunge the eggs into a bowl of ice water and let them sit for 20 minutes. No green rings around the yolks, and the eggs will be a cinch to peel.

vodka-spiked cherry tomatoes with pepper-salt

SOURCE *Gourmet*

COOK Katy Massam

Peeling cherry tomatoes might seem to be in the category of peeling grapes — life is too short — but it's such a cinch and the results are so astoundingly good that we beg you to indulge us and give these a try. It's a good mindless job you can do while watching TV — or get the kids to do, because it's actually kind of fun. If peeling little tomatoes is out of the question, see the tip for a simpler variation.

In recent years, we're hearing more and more about how certain flavor compounds are released only by alcohol, and this recipe is a brilliant example. Vodka brings out a new dimension in tomatoes — an indescribable zing with a sweet, lemony kick. One guest we served these tomatoes to called four days later to say she couldn't get them out of her mind. We can't either. ❧

3 pints firm, small, red and yellow cherry tomatoes
1/2 cup vodka
3 tablespoons white wine vinegar
1 tablespoon superfine sugar
1 teaspoon finely grated lemon zest
3 tablespoons kosher salt
1 1/2 tablespoons coarsely ground black pepper

serves 12

Cut a small X in the skin of the blossom end of each tomato. Have ready a bowl of ice water. Drop the tomatoes, five at a time, into a saucepan of boiling water for 3 seconds, then immediately scoop them out and transfer them to the bowl of ice water so they don't cook. Drain and, with a paring knife, peel the tomatoes. Place them in a large shallow dish.

In a small bowl, stir together the vodka, vinegar, sugar, and lemon zest until the sugar is dissolved. Pour over the tomatoes, gently tossing to coat. Marinate, covered, in the refrigerator for at least 30 minutes or up to 1 hour.

In a small bowl, stir together the salt and pepper. Serve with the tomatoes on toothpicks for dipping into the seasoned salt.

tip

FOR THOSE WHO refuse to peel cherry tomatoes, make James Beard's Drunken Cherry Tomatoes, which Arthur Schwartz resurrected in the *New York Times Magazine*. All you need is a bowl of cherry tomatoes, some small bowls of vodka or gin, and some even smaller bowls of salt, pepper, and ground cumin or cayenne pepper—with some toothpicks, of course. Guests dip the tomatoes in the vodka or gin, then into the seasonings as they please.

notes from our test kitchen

- Be sure the tomatoes are firm and not too ripe, or they'll be mushy.
- You can prepare the tomatoes and the vodka marinade the day before you plan to serve them and combine them 30 minutes to 1 hour before serving. Place the vodka mixture in a screw-top jar, cover the tomatoes with plastic wrap, and store both in the refrigerator.

crimped shrimp

SOURCE *Los Angeles Times*

COOK Michael Roberts

The late, great French-trained California chef Michael Roberts discovered an incredibly easy, superb way of cooking fish, which the English call "crimping." One day Roberts accidentally turned off the burner under a poaching salmon. Later he found a reference to the technique in a book by the French culinary giant Madeleine Kamman, who'd learned about crimping from a British friend.

The idea is to make a flavored broth, bring it to a boil, turn down the heat, add the fish, cover, and cook for 1 minute without boiling. Then the fish comes off the heat in its pot, still covered, and sits for a few minutes, until the temperatures of the fish and the liquid are equal. The texture is perfect, the oils in the fish aren't heated enough to release any smell, and the fish picks up the flavor of the broth and vice versa. The steeping time is about 6 minutes for each half-inch thickness of fish, but of course it all depends on the fish and the pot.

Here's how it works for shrimp—no more mushy shrimp! ❧

3 cups water
1 cup dry white wine
1/4 cup rice or malt vinegar
1 carrot, coarsely diced
1 celery rib, coarsely diced
1/2 onion, coarsely diced
2 teaspoons salt
1 teaspoon dried thyme
2 bay leaves
6 black peppercorns
24 jumbo shrimp (about 2 pounds), peeled, with tails on

serves 6

Bring everything but the shrimp to a boil in a medium heavy pot, covered. Reduce the heat and simmer for 5 minutes. Add the shrimp, cover again, and simmer for 1 minute.

Remove from the heat and steep, covered, for 4 minutes. Remove the shrimp from the liquid and refrigerate for at least 1 1/2 hours. Serve with your favorite cocktail sauce.

---

notes from our test kitchen

- If you're defrosting shrimp, do it in the refrigerator, placing the frozen shrimp in a bowl of salted water to improve their flavor.
- You can freeze the poaching liquid to use again or to make a sauce. Just strain it before freezing.

smoked salmon rolls
with arugula, mascarpone, chives, and capers

SOURCE *In the Hands of a Chef* by Jody Adams and Ken Rivard
COOK Jody Adams

This is one of those divine combinations that Adams, a prominent Boston chef, credits to Peck, the Milanese gourmet emporium. It was at Peck that Adams saw a display of torta cheeses — soft, rich layered creations. One of them, featuring stripes of mascarpone and smoked salmon, struck her as an inspired idea. Indeed it is. The sweet, fresh mascarpone doesn't take over the delicacy of smoked salmon the way other cheeses do; it's the perfect partner. Adams has contributed a few other key flavor elements: capers, lemon, and chives are classic. The arugula provides a nice, biting contrast.

Smoked salmon rolls can be charming little hors d'oeuvres or a more substantial appetizer, with several rolls placed over an arugula salad. We think this makes a pretty great breakfast or lunch, too. 🍤

5 ounces mascarpone cheese (about 2/3 cup)

2 tablespoons capers, rinsed and drained

2 tablespoons minced fresh chives

1 teaspoon fresh lemon juice

Kosher salt and freshly ground black pepper

12 ounces smoked salmon, cut into 24 thin slices, 2–3 inches on the short side (presliced salmon is fine)

48 small, tender arugula leaves

serves 6 as an appetizer,
12 as an hors d'oeuvre

Mix the mascarpone with 1 tablespoon of the capers, 1 tablespoon of the chives, and the lemon juice in a small bowl. Season with salt and pepper.

Lay the salmon slices out on a cutting board with one of their short sides facing you and with plenty of space above and below each slice. (You can do this in batches.)

Put a spoonful of the mascarpone mixture on the narrow end of a slice. Lay 2 arugula leaves, fanned slightly, across the mascarpone, so that the leaves will extend several inches from one end of the roll. Roll up the salmon slice and stand it upright, leaves pointed up, on a serving

tip

CAPER CONNOISSEURS often tout the virtues of plump salt-packed capers, but these fashionable capers can often be unbearably salty. California chef Jeremiah Tower has come up with a brilliant way to tame and flavor them so we can taste what all the fuss is about. Begin by rinsing the capers thoroughly. Then soak them in cold water for 20 minutes. Repeat two more times. Drain and transfer to a jar. Cover with 1 part dry white wine and 2 parts olive oil. Add a sprig of fresh thyme, basil, or both. Cover and refrigerate for up to 2 weeks. Serve on smoked salmon, deviled eggs, sandwiches, or salads. You'll vow to always have a jar at the ready in the fridge.

platter (see note). Repeat with the remaining slices. Cover with plastic wrap and refrigerate until ready to serve.

Remove from the refrigerator, sprinkle with the remaining 1 tablespoon chives and 1 tablespoon capers, and serve.

notes from our test kitchen

- Presliced smoked salmon doesn't always neatly fall into slices that can be cut for the rolls. Sometimes it's very ragged. In that case, just spread the salmon slices thinly with the mascarpone mixture (chop the capers before you mix them in), roll, and trim them into shapes you can spear with a toothpick. Serve on a bed of baby arugula.

- If you have trouble getting the rolls to stand upright, arrange them on their sides on the serving platter. Less dramatic, but just as delicious.

- We beg you to make these with Jeremiah Tower's marinated capers (chop them first), described in the tip at the left. Sensational!

roasted asparagus with panko bread crumbs

SOURCE *The Way We Cook* by Sheryl Julian and Julie Riven
COOK Arlene Jacobs

Creative cooks are forever coming up with ways to prepare asparagus, but here's one we've never seen before. Coat thick spears of fresh asparagus with a lemony mustard-mayonnaise mixture, then roll them in the super-crunchy Japanese bread crumbs known as panko and bake until tender and golden. Besides being a cinch to assemble, the asparagus can be made ahead and cooked once your guests arrive. If you're looking for a unique hors d'oeuvre that takes almost no time to put together and will be the hit of your party, here it is. Don't be surprised if these crunchy spears disappear in seconds flat.

We sometimes like to arrange a few spears on a plate and top them with a poached or fried egg and call it supper. In that case, the recipe will serve only four. ❧

- 1/4 **cup mayonnaise**
- 2 **tablespoons Dijon mustard**
- 1 **teaspoon fresh lemon juice**
  Coarse salt (kosher or sea salt)
- 1/4 **teaspoon freshly ground black pepper**
- 1 **cup Japanese panko bread crumbs (see notes)**
- 2 **tablespoons olive oil, plus more for the baking sheet**
- 1 **pound thick asparagus spears, fibrous stems snapped off (see notes)**

serves 6

Preheat the oven to 450 degrees.

In a large shallow bowl wide enough to hold the asparagus, whisk together the mayonnaise, mustard, lemon juice, 1/2 teaspoon salt, and pepper. Put the bread crumbs in another shallow bowl.

Lightly oil a large rimmed baking sheet. Roll the asparagus in the mayonnaise mixture to coat, then in the bread crumbs so the spears are well breaded. Transfer the asparagus to the prepared baking sheet and sprinkle with the oil. The asparagus can be covered and refrigerated for several hours before roasting.

Roast the asparagus, turning halfway through, for 12 to 18 minutes, or until the crumbs are golden brown and the spears are tender but have some bite. Sprinkle with salt and serve at once.

notes from our test kitchen

- Japanese panko bread crumbs are lighter, flakier, and crisper than ordinary bread crumbs, and they've become popular in the United States as a coating and breading. You can find panko in Asian markets, health food and gourmet stores, and increasingly in the international section of many large supermarkets. Use leftover panko as a coating for fish or as a topping for gratins.

- If you can't find panko, substitute unseasoned dry bread crumbs.

- When shopping for fresh asparagus, don't be tempted by the skinny spears that are so often in the market. The coating won't stick to thin asparagus. Besides, the thicker spears are tender and sweet and give you more surface for the crunchy coating.

- To remove the fibrous ends from the asparagus, hold a spear with both hands and bend gently until the end snaps off. It will break naturally. Pare off any stringy ends with a small knife.

mini frittatas with wild mushrooms

SOURCE Macy's De Gustibus recipe handout

COOK Eileen Weinberg

Manhattan caterer-to-the-stars Eileen Weinberg, of Good & Plenty to Go, is famous for elegant food that tastes entirely homemade, and in fact she ghost-chefs for some of the biggest names in the food world. This divine recipe is one of her trademarks: it's as popular at wedding receptions as it is for cocktail parties—and brunch.

This amount is calculated to feed a small crowd for cocktails, but you can easily cut the recipe in half.

You can also make one large skillet frittata for lunch, dinner, or brunch. Just bake it for 1 hour and run it under the broiler to brown just before serving. ❧

tip

REAL SIMPLE magazine points out that oiling the holes of a grater makes cheese less likely to stick.

notes from our test kitchen

- You can also use a regular muffin pan and increase the cooking time slightly.
- The frittatas can be made up to 1 day ahead and reheated at the last minute.

1/4 cup olive oil

2 cups cleaned, minced wild mushrooms or a combination of shiitakes and portobellos

8 large eggs

Pinch of salt

Pinch of freshly ground black pepper

1/2 cup cream cheese, cut into small pieces

3/4 cup grated Muenster cheese

3/4 cup grated mozzarella cheese

3/4 cup grated Swiss cheese

3/4 cup freshly grated Parmesan cheese

3/4 cup grated white cheddar cheese

1/2 cup heavy cream

serves 12; makes 3 dozen

Preheat the oven to 350 degrees. Rub two mini-muffin pans with olive oil.

Heat the 1/4 cup olive oil in a small skillet over medium-high heat. Add the mushrooms and sauté until they begin to brown and reabsorb some of the cooking juices. Set aside.

In a large bowl, beat the eggs well and add the salt and pepper. Stir in the cheeses, cream, and mushrooms. Pour the egg mixture into the muffin pans.

Bake for 30 to 40 minutes, or until the tops are light golden brown and firm. Serve warm or at room temperature.

manly meatballs

*

SOURCE **Thefoodmaven.com by Arthur Schwartz**

COOK **Alan Richman**

Alan Richman, food and wine critic of *GQ* magazine, is responsible for the public launching of these unabashedly macho (not to mention retro) appetizers, which he brought to a Manhattan party. The guests demanded the recipe, and the obliging party giver, cookbook author Arthur Schwartz, obliged by e-mailing it to dozens and dozens of meatball fans, both manly and not.

Serve these pop-in-your-mouth hors d'oeuvres at just about any gathering — from a Super Bowl party to an elegant uptown dinner — and watch people swoon. With a big green salad, Manly Meatballs can become dinner for four. 🖎

notes from our test kitchen

- Avoid extra-lean ground beef. The meatballs won't hold together and will dry out. Don't use anything leaner than 85 percent.

- Add a rounded teaspoon of brown sugar if you use regular soy sauce instead of dark soy sauce.

- Kids love to shape the little meatballs, and like adults, they are fascinated by how each meatball and bread slice glue together.

2 **long, slim loaves of crusty bread (baguettes), about 2½ inches in diameter**

1 **pound ground chuck (not leaner beef; see note)**

¼ **cup dark soy sauce, tamari, or low-sodium soy sauce**

1 **teaspoon firmly packed dark brown sugar (see note)**

5–6 **scallions, white and light green parts only**

makes 36 meatballs

Preheat the oven to 450 degrees and set a rack in the middle level, or set the racks in the upper and lower levels if you plan to use two baking sheets.

Slice off and discard the heels of the baguettes and cut them into 36 slices about ½ inch thick. (Depending on the length of the baguettes, there may be leftover bread for another use.) Lay the slices side by side on one or two baking sheets.

Mix together the meat, soy sauce or tamari, brown sugar, and scallions in a large bowl with your hands. Knead thoroughly until you have a fine paste. Make 36 meatballs about the size of a walnut. Put one in the middle of each bread slice, pressing down slightly.

Bake for 7 to 9 minutes, or until the meatballs and bread have become one and you can no longer hold back the hungry hordes.

savory fig tart

SOURCE *Whole Foods Holiday Entertaining Guide*
COOK Heather Ramsdell

If you'd like to present your guests with a professional-looking savory tart warm from the oven with a minimum of fuss, this is your recipe. Puff pastry is the key ingredient here—golden brown and barely covered with a fig spread. The top accents are crumbled goat cheese, ribbons of prosciutto, and fresh thyme.

The tart is perfect for entertaining, since you can do the initial baking early in the day, then top and broil the tart at the last minute.

It can be rustic-looking or more formal, with the ribbons of prosciutto forming an elegant lattice pattern and the cheese scattered in between. Either way, the tart looks irresistible. ❧

note from our test kitchen

Fig spread isn't the same thing as fig jam; it's quite a bit less sweet. You'll find it in gourmet stores and cheese shops.

   All-purpose flour for dusting
 7 ounces frozen puff pastry, thawed
 1/2 cup fig spread (see note)
 4 ounces crumbly fresh goat cheese
 4 slices prosciutto, cut into thin strips
   Freshly ground black pepper
   Fresh thyme leaves

serves 8

Preheat the oven to 375 degrees and set a rack in the middle level. Line a baking sheet with parchment paper.

Lightly dust the work surface and the pastry with flour. Roll the pastry out to a 7-x-15-inch rectangle. Brush the perimeter with water. Fold all four edges over, creating a 1/2-inch overlapping "frame" around the pastry. Transfer to the baking sheet.

Poke the pastry all over with a fork. Bake until firm and golden brown all over, 25 to 30 minutes. Remove from the oven and let cool for 5 minutes. The tart can be made ahead up to this point and kept in a cool, dry place for 8 to 10 hours.

Preheat the broiler. Fill the pastry with the fig spread. Crumble the goat cheese over the top and drape strips of prosciutto over the cheese. Broil for about 4 minutes, or until the prosciutto starts to brown and the cheese melts. Let cool for 15 minutes.

Cut into 8 bars, sprinkle with black pepper and thyme leaves, and serve warm.

Soups

Soups

pea soup with crispy pancetta, bread, and sour cream 31

carrot ginger soup with lime crème fraîche 34

yellow pepper and pine nut soup 36

fresh corn soup 37

italian pumpkin soup 38

roasted butternut squash soup with bacon 41

garlic soup with ham and sage butter 43

senegalese peanut soup 44

crab soup with sweet spices and ginger juice 46

tortilla soup with chicken and avocado 48

roasted mushroom-leek soup with crispy pancetta 52

the lentil soup 54

malaysian noodle soup 57

smoky shrimp and halibut stew 59

wild rice and turkey soup 62

pea soup with crispy pancetta, bread, and sour cream

SOURCE *Jamie's Kitchen* by Jamie Oliver

COOK Jamie Oliver

This is an unusual soup you'll come to crave. It's not the sludgy kind made from dried peas, but a fresh-tasting baby pea soup with the zing of mint and a crunchy crouton-and-bacon topping. It's both subtle and hearty, and although it's not heavy, it can easily be a meal in itself.

Oliver used to make it with fresh spring peas, but he quickly realized that frozen peas (he likes Birds Eye) work perfectly and make it possible to have the soup on the table speedily. Using frozen peas also means you can serve it year-round, not just in the spring.

The rustic croutons and pancetta (unsmoked Italian bacon, usually available at the deli counter) are great on other soups, too, such as lentil or potato. You can also use other herbs instead of mint, such as basil or oregano. ✎

1/2 **loaf stale white bread**

Extra-virgin olive oil

1 **large handful of fresh mint, leaves stripped**

Sea salt and freshly ground black pepper

12 **thin slices pancetta or bacon**

1 **bunch scallions, trimmed and coarsely chopped**

2 **pats butter**

1 **pound 2 ounces frozen peas (see note)**

4 **cups chicken broth**

7 **tablespoons heavy cream**

4 **teaspoons sour cream**

serves 4 to 6

Preheat the oven to 350 degrees.

Take the crust off the bread and pinch off irregular dice-size pieces. Put these in a roasting pan and drizzle with a little olive oil, scatter over some of the mint leaves, and season with salt and pepper. Chop the pancetta, add it to the roasting pan, and bake, stirring occasionally, until the bread and pancetta are crunchy and golden, 15 to 20 minutes.

Meanwhile, in a medium to large saucepan, slowly fry the scallions and remaining mint in the butter for about 3 minutes, or until soft. Turn up the heat, add the frozen peas and

notes from our test kitchen

- The size of pea packages varies. Just come as close as you can to the amount specified here. Petite peas are the best-tasting.
- To have everything ready at the same time, put the bread in the oven when you begin to fry the scallions.
- Chilling the pancetta makes it a bit easier to chop.
- Oliver likes to use spinach and asparagus in the soup, too.

chicken broth, and bring to a boil. Lower the heat, add the heavy cream, and simmer gently for 15 minutes.

Puree the soup until it's very smooth. (You may want to do this in batches.) Correct the seasoning very carefully to taste — really think about this and get it just right. Remember: add, taste, add, taste. By this time, the bread and pancetta should be nice and crisp. Ladle the soup into bowls and sprinkle with the bread, mint, and pancetta. Add a little sour cream, drizzle with some peppery extra-virgin olive oil, and serve.

carrot ginger soup with lime crème fraîche

SOURCE *Simply Elegant Soup* by George Morrone with John Harrisson
COOK George Morrone

Over the years, we've tried a number of recipes highlighting carrots and ginger, a made-in-heaven couple, and this exhilarating version is clearly the best. George Morrone, a San Francisco chef with a passion for soup, created it in Los Angeles in the 1980s, when he was trying to entice beautiful people to the table with exciting food that wouldn't expand their waistlines. Two elements make Morrone's soup different from other carrot ginger soups: ginger oil with turmeric, which is both an ingredient and a garnish, and lime crème fraîche, which pulls all the flavors together. This is possibly the most gorgeous soup we've ever seen, as well as one of the most delectable.

   You can serve the soup hot or cold. Note that you need to make the ginger oil the day before you prepare the soup; it will take less than 5 minutes. 🐟

ginger oil

- 1 cup canola oil
- 2 tablespoons ground ginger
- 1½ tablespoons ground turmeric

carrot ginger soup

- 2½ tablespoons olive oil
- 1 white onion, thinly sliced
- 1 small garlic clove, minced
- 1 small jalapeño pepper, seeded and thinly sliced
- 1 teaspoon peeled, grated fresh ginger
- 4 large carrots (about 1 pound), peeled and sliced
- 4 cups chicken or vegetable broth
- Salt and cayenne pepper

lime crème fraîche

- ½ cup crème fraîche
- Zest and juice of 1 lime
- 1 tablespoon minced fresh cilantro
- Salt

garnish

- 12 cilantro sprigs
- Freshly cracked black pepper

notes from our test kitchen

- The ginger oil is a wonderful condiment to have on hand, and since it keeps forever in the fridge, you might want to consider making a double batch. It's great over grilled fish, chicken, or vegetables.
- Confession: we didn't strain our smooth puree, and the consistency was fine.

serves 4

To make the ginger oil: Combine all the ingredients in a small bowl. Carefully whisk together and pour into a small saucepan. Bring to a simmer over medium-high heat and then return to the bowl. Refrigerate overnight to infuse the oil with the flavors. The following day, carefully ladle off the yellow ginger oil and store in a bottle or other airtight container. Discard the solids. The oil will keep in the refrigerator almost indefinitely.

To make the soup: Heat the olive oil and 1 tablespoon of the ginger oil in a saucepan over medium heat. Add the onion, garlic, jalapeño, and ginger and cook for about 5 minutes, or until translucent; do not let brown. Add the carrots and cook for 5 minutes more. Add 3 cups of the broth and simmer for 20 minutes, or until the carrots are tender. Transfer the soup to a blender or food processor and puree in batches until smooth. Pass through a fine-mesh strainer into a clean saucepan. Reheat the soup, adjusting the consistency with the remaining 1 cup broth as needed, and season to taste with salt and cayenne.

To make the crème fraîche: Put the crème fraîche in a small bowl. Mince the lime zest and add to the crème fraîche with the lime juice and cilantro. Season to taste with salt and whisk until combined. Refrigerate.

To serve, pour the soup into warm bowls and drizzle each serving with 1 teaspoon of the ginger oil. Diagonally drizzle about 1 tablespoon of the crème fraîche across each bowl in the opposite direction (you'll have some left over). Place 3 cilantro sprigs across each bowl and sprinkle with pepper.

yellow pepper and pine nut soup

SOURCE *Marie Claire* STORY BY Gillian Duffy

COOK Han Feng

Eating this golden soup is a bit puzzling: you can't quite figure out why it's so delicious (our notes say, simply, "fabulous!"); you only know that it is. The combination of tender yellow peppers and sweet, fleshy pine nuts, highlighted by just a little fresh thyme, is an unexpected alchemy.

The soup was the first course of a dinner party menu cooked by Han Feng, a fashion designer from China's Hangzhou province. Now designing in New York, she has developed a passion for cooking, she says, and for refining Western dishes with Eastern flavors. ❧

6 **cups chicken broth**

3 **pounds yellow bell peppers (8–10), halved, cored, and seeded**

1 **cup pine nuts**

  Salt and freshly ground black pepper

8 **small thyme sprigs**

serves 8

Bring the chicken broth to a boil in a large heavy pot. Add the pepper halves, pushing them down into the broth. Cover and simmer, turning the peppers once or twice, for about 30 minutes, or until the peppers are soft.

Meanwhile, toast the pine nuts in a dry skillet over medium-low heat for 3 to 4 minutes, or until golden, stirring almost constantly to prevent burning. Immediately transfer to a small bowl.

With a slotted spoon, remove the softened peppers from the broth. Put them in a blender or food processor and add the pine nuts. Blend until smooth. Do this in batches, if necessary, adding a little broth if it makes blending easier.

Stir the puree back into the broth, season with salt and pepper, and heat gently. The soup can be made up to 1 day in advance; reheat before serving.

To serve, ladle the soup into bowls and place a thyme sprig in the center of each.

fresh corn soup

* * *

SOURCE *The Essential Cuisines of Mexico* by Diana Kennedy

COOK Diana Kennedy

This is, in our opinion, one of the great soups of the world. It's a delicate soup, with the little piquant touch of poblano chiles and the crunch of crisp fried tortillas. It's also a very easy soup to make if you have a food mill, and it allows you to use one of the great convenience foods, frozen corn kernels. Anyone who still thinks Mexican food is coarse and fiery will be stunned by the elegance of this simple soup.

Because the soup freezes well, you can make lots and keep it on hand for a quick bowlful anytime. ❧

note from our test kitchen

The quality of queso fresco, a Mexican cheese, is iffy in the United States, except for the excellent product made by the Mozzarella Company: mozzco.com or (800) 798-2954. To substitute, use a fresh crumbly cheese that has a little acid, such as ricotta salata or feta.

4 **cups corn kernels (about 1½ pounds), fresh or frozen**

1 **cup water**

4 **tablespoons (½ stick) butter**

3½ **cups milk or light chicken broth**

½ **teaspoon salt**

2 **poblano chiles, charred, peeled, and seeded, then diced and briefly fried in a little oil**

6 **tablespoons crumbled queso fresco (see note)**

6 **small tortillas, cut into small squares, then fried in oil until crisp**

serves 6

If you're using frozen corn, measure it frozen and then let it defrost. Blend the corn with the water at high speed until you have a smooth puree. Put the puree through the medium disk of a food mill or a coarse strainer.

Melt the butter in a large saucepan, but do not let it get too hot. Add the corn puree and let it cook over medium heat for about 5 minutes, stirring all the time.

Add the milk or broth and salt to the mixture and bring to a boil. Lower the heat and let the soup simmer for about 15 minutes, stirring it from time to time to prevent sticking. It will thicken slightly.

Put about ½ tablespoon diced chiles and 1 tablespoon crumbled cheese in each bowl. Pour the soup over them, top with the crisp tortilla squares, and serve.

italian pumpkin soup

SOURCE Palio press release

COOK Maria Pia

This spectacular soup was originally served at Manhattan's glamorous Palio restaurant, where it had a puff pastry top — but that's a flourish home cooks can safely pass up. The soup is perfect for Christmas dinner or any other celebration for which you want to pull out all the stops.

At some point during the cooking process, you'll suddenly understand what an absolutely stunning combination of ingredients we have here. The amaretto liqueur and the amaretti cookies are key elements in this divine chemistry: they add a distinct almond flavor and an enriching texture without making the soup sweet. The result is very unusual and very delicious. ❧

1 sugar pumpkin or butternut squash (about 2 pounds)

1/3 cup extra-virgin olive oil

4 tablespoons (1/2 stick) butter

1 large onion, finely chopped

Salt

6–8 cups vegetable broth

1 cup heavy cream

1/3 cup amaretto, such as Disaronno

1/3 cup crushed amaretti cookies (without sugar on top)

serves 6 to 8

Preheat the oven to 450 degrees and set a rack in the middle level. Line a baking sheet with aluminum foil, grease it, and set aside.

Peel the pumpkin or squash and cut it into small (about 1-inch) pieces. Remove and discard the seeds. Spread the pieces on the baking sheet in a single layer and roast, stirring once, for 10 to 20 minutes, or until almost tender.

Meanwhile, heat the olive oil and butter in a large pot over medium heat. Add the onion and a pinch of salt and cook, stirring frequently, for about 7 minutes, or until totally wilted.

note from our test kitchen

The soup can be made up to 1 day ahead, covered, and refrigerated. Just before serving, reheat it gently, stirring frequently, until hot. It freezes well, so don't worry about making too much.

Add the pumpkin or squash and 4 cups of the vegetable broth to the onion mixture. Simmer over medium heat until the pumpkin or squash is completely soft, 15 to 20 minutes. Reduce the heat to low and stir in the cream, amaretto, and amaretti. Remove from the heat and let cool for 15 minutes.

Transfer the soup to a food processor and puree. Return to the pot and stir in 2 cups broth, or more to taste. Taste and add a bit more salt, if desired.

roasted butternut squash soup with bacon

———————————————————— ✳ ————————————————————

SOURCE *Tom Valenti's Soups, Stews, and One-Pot Meals*
by Tom Valenti and Andrew Friedman
COOK Tom Valenti

Most ordinary squash soup recipes begin by instructing you to simmer the squash in broth until tender, but roasting the squash in a very hot oven concentrates its flavor and sweetness. And roasting it under a blanket of sliced bacon infuses it with an appealing smoky, savory dimension. Before serving, the crisp bacon is crumbled and scattered onto each bowlful of this voluptuous cold-weather soup.

The recipe comes from Tom Valenti, the New York City chef considered by many to be the grand master of comfort food. He points out that it's equally good with other winter squash, such as acorn and Hubbard.

The soup can be held for a few days in the refrigerator or frozen for up to a month. ❧

6 **pounds butternut squash**

6 **tablespoons (¾ stick) unsalted butter**
   Coarse salt and freshly ground black pepper

8 **slices smoked bacon (see note)**

2 **tablespoons olive oil**

1 **large Spanish onion, cut into small dice**

3 **thyme sprigs, plus extra leaves for garnish**

1 **bay leaf**

6 **cups chicken broth**

2 **tablespoons heavy cream (optional; see note)**
   Sugar, if needed
   Extra-virgin olive oil for drizzling

serves 8

Preheat the oven to 400 degrees.

Cut the squash in half lengthwise. Scoop out and discard the seeds. Place the squash halves cut sides up on a rimmed baking sheet. Divide the butter among the hollowed-out seed cavities and generously season the squash with salt and pepper. Lay 1 or 2 slices of bacon lengthwise along the surface of each half. Roast, basting a few times by scooping the butter out of the cavity and spooning it over the bacon and squash, until the squash is tender and easily pierced by a sharp knife, 35 to 40 minutes (see notes).

Remove the baking sheet from the oven. Transfer the bacon to a paper towel–lined plate to drain. Once cool, mince or

notes from our test kitchen

- Tom Valenti uses double-smoked slab bacon and slices it himself. You can also use good-quality medium- to thick-sliced bacon here.

- Depending on the season, the squash may take as much as an hour to cook to tenderness. The longer the squash has been in storage, the more time it will take to cook.

- If the bacon gets crisp before the squash is tender, remove the strips and set aside on paper towels to drain.

- There may be a fair amount of fat drippings on the baking sheet after roasting the squash. Discard or save for another use.

- This is one instance where an immersion blender is not recommended. Stick with the food processor or regular blender.

- Even though the cream is listed as optional, it goes a long way toward pulling together the various flavors. We wouldn't dream of leaving it out.

crumble into small bits and set aside. Once the squash halves have cooled slightly, scoop out the flesh with a tablespoon. Discard the skins.

Heat the olive oil in a large heavy pot over medium-high heat until hot but not smoking. Add the onion, season with salt and pepper to taste, and cook, stirring, until softened but not browned, about 5 minutes. Stir in the thyme sprigs and bay leaf, then add the squash. Cook, stirring to integrate the flavors and keep the squash from scorching, for 1 to 2 minutes.

Add the broth to the pot, stirring to incorporate. Bring to a boil over high heat. Lower the heat and simmer for 15 minutes.

Using tongs or a slotted spoon, fish out and discard the thyme sprigs and bay leaf. Transfer the soup to a food processor. (You can also use a regular blender, working in batches.) Add the cream, if using, and process for several minutes until uniformly thick and creamy. Be careful not to overblend, which will turn the soup thin. If not serving immediately, let cool, cover, and refrigerate for a few days or freeze for up to a month.

Return the soup to the pot and gently reheat. Taste and adjust the seasonings with salt, pepper, and sugar, if necessary.

To serve, ladle the soup into bowls and scatter some of the bacon bits over the surface. Sprinkle with thyme leaves and drizzle with extra-virgin olive oil. Serve at once.

tip

TOM VALENTI suggests using the same technique to make a richly flavored butternut squash puree. Follow the recipe for the soup, omitting the broth and adding 2 tablespoons cold unsalted butter to the puree as it's blended in the food processor. (A blender won't work for the puree.) Season with a few pinches of light brown sugar, a dash of maple syrup, and ground cinnamon, allspice, or nutmeg, according to your taste. Serves 8 as a side dish.

garlic soup with ham and sage butter

SOURCE *Between Bites* by James Villas

COOK Jeremiah Tower

Every year we used to try a garlic soup or two, until we discovered this simple knockout. Now this is our garlic soup, the one we crave every winter. It has a deep garlic flavor and a satiny quality. We especially like the ham and sage butter that's swirled into the soup just before serving. Country ham is best, but prosciutto is fine. ❧

note from our test kitchen

If you have big, fat garlic cloves, they won't soften in the 30 minutes of cooking time, so peel them first. One whole head of garlic is about the right amount.

15 garlic cloves, unpeeled (see note)

3 cups chicken broth

¼ cup diced cured country ham or prosciutto

5 fresh sage leaves

3 tablespoons butter, softened

Salt and freshly ground black pepper

½ cup heavy cream

3 large egg yolks

serves 6

Combine the garlic and broth in a large heavy saucepan. Simmer over low heat until the garlic is soft, about 30 minutes. Let the mixture cool slightly, then puree, using the fine disk of a food mill or a food processor. Press the mixture through a sieve back into the saucepan and set aside.

Meanwhile, chop the ham and sage together very finely and place in a bowl. Add the butter and salt and pepper to taste and mix until well blended. Set aside.

Whisk together the cream and egg yolks in a small bowl. Set aside.

Bring the soup to a boil, remove it from the heat, and gradually whisk in the cream mixture until the soup is thickened slightly. (If the soup doesn't thicken, return it to the heat for 1 minute, whisking constantly; do not let it boil.) Ladle the soup into warm soup plates and spoon an equal amount of the ham and sage butter onto the center of each serving.

senegalese peanut soup

SOURCE *The Daily Soup Cookbook* by Leslie Kaul, Bob Spiegal,
Carla Ruben, and Peter Siegal with Robin Vitetta-Miller
COOKS Leslie Kaul, Bob Spiegal, and Peter Siegel

It was Manhattanites who first became obsessed with soup. At the many outposts of Daily Soup, the staggeringly good take-out shop empire that now stretches well beyond the borders of New York, people do indeed line up every day for their favorite meal-in-a-bowl.

Among the chain's signature soups is this charmer from Senegal. You'd swear it's a complex brew with coconut milk, perhaps a little cilantro, some chiles, and possibly some exotic spices — but in fact it contains none of these things, unless you consider curry powder exotic. The soup couldn't be simpler. The secret ingredient is peanuts — a whole pound of them — simmered slowly in a fragrant base of onion, celery, and tomatoes. As it cooks, the fragrance becomes almost overwhelming, and the finished soup delivers the full taste its aroma promises.

This soup is at once consoling, intriguing, and invigorating — and now that we have a taste for it, we try to keep some in the freezer for a rainy day. ❧

1 **pound dry-roasted salted peanuts (about 3 cups)**

2 **tablespoons peanut oil**

1 **large Spanish onion, chopped**

2 **celery ribs, chopped**

2 **leeks, washed well and chopped**

2 **teaspoons sugar**

2 **teaspoons curry powder**

2 **teaspoons ground cumin**

1/2 **teaspoon cayenne pepper**

1/2 **teaspoon salt**

1 **28-ounce can whole tomatoes, drained and diced**

6 **cups water**

1/2 **cup chopped scallions**

1/2 **cup heavy cream**

1 **teaspoon minced garlic**

serves 8

Chop 1/2 cup of the peanuts into small pieces and set aside to use as a garnish. Puree the remaining 2 1/2 cups peanuts in a blender or food processor until a thick paste forms; set aside.

In a large pot over medium heat, heat the oil. Add the onion, celery, and leeks and cook gently, without browning, for about 4 minutes, or until tender.

notes from our test kitchen

- If you like, you can use regular roasted salted peanuts instead of the dry-roasted ones.
- This soup freezes beautifully.

Stir in the sugar, curry powder, cumin, cayenne, and salt. Add the tomatoes, water, and peanut paste. Bring to a boil, reduce the heat to low, and simmer, uncovered, for 1 hour.

Stir in the scallions, cream, and garlic and simmer for 2 minutes more, or until heated through.

To serve, ladle the soup into bowls and sprinkle with the reserved chopped peanuts.

⊰ VARIATION ⊱

For a more sustaining soup, add cubes of tofu (vegetarian version) or cooked chicken (poach 1 pound boneless, skinless chicken breasts in simmering water for 10 minutes, let cool, and dice). Add the chicken or tofu to the soup along with the scallions and cream.

crab soup with sweet spices and ginger juice

❋

SOURCE *Raji Cuisine* by Raji Jallepalli

COOK Raji Jallepalli

This sensational soup is hands down one of the best we've ever tasted. It's also one of the richest, jammed with crab and luxurious with cream and saffron. You might want to serve very small cups of it — but then your guests may feel deprived if they can't have more. So save this for a very special occasion, such as New Year's Eve, or serve it as the centerpiece of an otherwise sparse meal when you need a big treat. It's actually a quick recipe to put together once you have the ginger juice on hand.

Raji Jallepalli, the late chef-owner of Raji's in Memphis, Tennessee, based the soup on one from her childhood in India, then gave it a push into the style of a French bisque. Everything about this soup is delicate and elegant, from its use of ginger juice instead of the harsher chopped ginger to its tiny bit of garlic, blanched first to remove its bite. The saffron, the cream, the crab, the sweet spices with a touch of chile — everything comes together perfectly. All it needs is an accompanying glass of champagne. ❧

12 ounces jumbo lump crabmeat, picked over for cartilage and shell bits

1 fresh cayenne chile

3 tablespoons canola oil

1 large garlic clove, blanched and minced

1 tablespoon finely chopped onion

2 teaspoons garam masala

2 tablespoons fresh ginger juice (see notes)

1 teaspoon saffron powder

4 cups heavy cream

Coarse salt, if needed

serves 6

Set aside ¼ cup of the crabmeat for garnish.

Wash the chile and remove the stem. Cut it in half crosswise and mince the top half. (Save the lower half for another purpose.)

Heat the oil in a large heavy saucepan over medium heat. Add the garlic, onion, and minced chile. Sauté for about 3 minutes, or just until the vegetables begin to brown. Stir in the garam masala. When well combined, add the ginger juice and stir well again.

Add the crabmeat and bring to a simmer. Simmer for 5 minutes, stirring gently from time to time. Stir in the saffron and stir for 1 minute more. Add the cream and bring to a simmer again.

notes from our test kitchen

- To make ginger juice, combine 1 cup chopped fresh ginger and 3 table-spoons warm water in a blender and blend to a paste. Strain the ginger in a sieve over a glass measure. Discard the ginger. Ginger juice is more delicate than chopped ginger and freezes well, so it's worth making a double batch.

- You can buy bottled ginger juice at specialty stores and Whole Foods Markets, and by mail from the Ginger People: gingerpeople.com or (800) 551-5284.

Lower the heat and allow the soup to just barely simmer for about 15 minutes, or until it is slightly reduced. Taste and season with salt, if necessary.

Pour an equal portion into six shallow bowls. Divide the reserved crabmeat among the bowls and serve immediately.

tortilla soup with chicken and avocado

SOURCE *Fine Cooking*

COOK Martha Holmberg

We love the complexity and comfort of a bowl of real tortilla soup, but we aren't always up for the toasting, soaking, and grinding of chiles that's required. So we were excited to find this recipe for a streamlined version made from ordinary ingredients that delivers extraordinary results. Sure, our traditionalist friends will turn up their noses, but we can't get over how well this recipe works. In place of dried chiles, Martha Holmberg, the food editor at the *Oregonian,* has devised a mix of finely chopped onion, tomato paste, and supermarket chili powder that serves as the flavor base. To this she adds skinless chicken thighs and canned chicken broth (although you certainly could use homemade) and gently simmers until the chicken is tender and the broth is flavorful.

Finishing each bowl with a few spoonfuls of canned black beans, corn kernels (canned or frozen work well), fresh tomato, avocado, and tortilla strips turns this soup into a substantial meal-in-a-bowl. ❧

1 tablespoon vegetable or olive oil
1/4 cup finely chopped onion (about 1/2 small onion)
1 tablespoon chili powder, or more to taste
1 tablespoon tomato paste
2 skinless chicken thighs (bone-in or boneless)
Salt
4 cups canned low-sodium or homemade chicken broth
6 2-inch stems fresh cilantro
Crispy Tortilla Strips (recipe follows)
3/4 cup diced fresh tomato
1/2 cup corn kernels (fresh, canned, or frozen)
1/2 cup canned black beans, rinsed and drained

garnish

1 ripe avocado, diced and tossed with a squeeze of lime juice
1/4 cup crumbled queso fresco (see note, page 37), feta, or ricotta salata cheese
2 dollops of sour cream
1/4 cup coarsely chopped fresh cilantro leaves
Lime wedges for serving

serves 2

Heat the oil in a large saucepan over medium heat. Add the onion and cook until softened but not browned, about 3 minutes. Add the chili powder and tomato paste and stir with a wooden spoon to mix and cook briefly; take care not to let the chili powder scorch.

tip

REAL HOMEMADE chicken broth is better than canned, of course, but sometimes there's just no time. That's where Michael Chiarello's Cheater's Chicken Stock (from his book *Michael Chiarello's Casual Cooking*) comes in handy. Combine two 14-ounce cans low-sodium chicken broth with 1½ cans water in a large saucepan. Add 1 small celery rib (chopped), 1 small carrot (chopped), ½ cup cleaned and coarsely chopped mushrooms, 1 bay leaf (crumbled), ¼ teaspoon black peppercorns, and a few stems flat-leaf parsley. Bring to a simmer over medium heat, adjust the heat to maintain a gentle simmer, and cook for 30 minutes. Let cool briefly, then strain.

Season the chicken thighs lightly with salt and nestle them in the tomato-chili paste, turning them once so they're entirely coated. Add about ½ cup of the broth and adjust the heat to a simmer. Cover and cook the chicken, turning once, until it's extremely tender when pierced with a knife, 30 to 40 minutes. Add a little more broth if the pan starts to dry out. When the chicken is done, remove it from the pan, let it cool a bit, and then cut or shred it into bite-size pieces, discarding any bones or bits of fat or gristle. Set the shredded meat aside.

If there is any visible grease in the pan, spoon it off. Add the remaining broth and the cilantro stems and stir. Simmer, uncovered, until the broth is reduced by about one third, 20 to 30 minutes.

Meanwhile, prepare the tortilla strips.

Divide the shredded chicken, tomato, corn, black beans, and tortilla strips between two large soup bowls. Reheat the broth, if necessary, so it's piping hot and pour it into the bowls. Serve immediately. Garnish with the avocado, cheese, sour cream, chopped cilantro, and a big squeeze of lime juice at the table.

notes from our test kitchen

- Although the soup is best with all the ingredients, you can eliminate either the corn or the beans—but not both. Whatever you do, don't forget the squeeze of lime juice.
- The soup can be made ahead and kept overnight in the refrigerator. The avocado and chopped cilantro leaves are best prepared right before serving.

The crispy tortilla strips can be made up
to 1 day ahead and kept in a dry spot. If
you don't have time to fry the strips, go
ahead and use broken store-bought tortilla chips. They won't be quite the same,
but the soup will still be plenty good.

crispy tortilla strips

4 6-inch fresh corn tortillas
¹/₂–1 cup vegetable oil for frying

Cut the tortillas into ¼-inch-wide strips. Line a plate or
tray with two layers of paper towels. In a small high-sided
saucepan, heat about 1 inch of oil over medium heat. When
it reaches 375 degrees, or when a strip of tortilla sizzles immediately when dipped in the oil, add 6 to 8 tortilla strips.
With tongs or a long fork, "scrunch" the strips for a second
or two so they take on a wavy shape. Fry until the strips
aren't bubbling much and are pale brown, about 1 minute.
Transfer to the paper towels to drain. Repeat with the remaining tortilla strips.

roasted mushroom-leek soup
with crispy pancetta

SOURCE *Stonewall Kitchen Harvest* by Jim Stott, Jonathan King, and Kathy Gunst
COOKS Jim Stott, Jonathan King, and Kathy Gunst

The soup is the creation of the owners and founders of Stonewall Kitchen in York, Maine, the well-known producer of first-rate preserves and condiments. They know a thing or two about fresh, seasonal ingredients. They suggest a mix of mushrooms—including shiitake, cremini, button, and portobello—but they encourage you to go with what looks best in your market. If you choose a different assortment, no problem; just be sure to use a variety and a total of about 1½ pounds. The better the mushrooms are, the better the soup will taste. ❧

8 ounces button mushrooms, wiped clean, stem ends trimmed, and caps cut in half if large

6 ounces cremini mushrooms, wiped clean and stem ends trimmed

6 ounces portobello mushrooms, wiped clean and coarsely chopped to match the size of the other mushrooms

3½ ounces shiitake mushrooms, wiped clean and stems discarded (see note)

3 leeks, white parts only, cut in half lengthwise, washed well, and cut into 1-inch pieces

1 large red or Vidalia onion, cut into 1-inch pieces

1½ tablespoons chopped fresh thyme or ½ teaspoon dried, crumbled

3 tablespoons olive oil

Salt and freshly ground black pepper

¼ cup dry red or white wine (see note)

5 cups chicken or vegetable broth (see note)

About ¼ cup heavy cream (optional)

6 thin slices (about 2 ounces) pancetta

serves 8

Preheat the oven to 400 degrees and set a rack in the middle level.

In a large roasting pan, toss the mushrooms, leeks, onion, thyme, 2 tablespoons of the oil, and salt and pepper to taste until well combined. Roast for 45 minutes, tossing the veg-

IN HER BOOK *Wild Mushrooms*, Cynthia Nims reminds us that mushrooms are "like delicious little sponges" and rinsing causes them to soak up quantities of water, which in turn dilutes their flavor and ruins their texture. Nims wisely suggests better methods: a soft-bristled pastry brush to flick away dirt and debris or (our favorite) a paper towel, dry or damp, depending on how dirty the mushrooms are. Only as a last resort should you use water, and then only for the quickest rinse or dip. If you like having single-use gadgets in your kitchen, cookware stores do sell baby-soft mushroom brushes. We also know some cooks who use the softest-bristled toothbrushes.

etables once or twice as they cook. Transfer to a large bowl and immediately deglaze the hot roasting pan with the wine and then the broth (see note).

Working in batches, puree the vegetables with the broth in a food processor or blender. Pour the pureed soup into a large soup pot and add the cream, if using. Taste for seasoning and add salt and pepper, if needed. The soup can be made 1 day ahead up to this point.

Heat the remaining 1 tablespoon oil in a medium skillet over low heat. Add the pancetta and cook, turning frequently, until crisp, 5 to 10 minutes. Drain on paper towels and, using your hands, break the pancetta into 1-inch pieces.

To serve, reheat the soup until simmering. Serve sprinkled with several pieces of crisp pancetta.

notes from our test kitchen

- When trimming shiitake mushrooms, be sure to remove and discard the entire stem, flush with the cap. Shiitake stems remain tough and fibrous even when cooked and pureed.

- You can easily make this vegetarian — even vegan — if you wish by using vegetable broth and omitting the cream. Obviously, you'll need to skip the pancetta garnish. If you miss the crunch, sauté a few handfuls of small croutons in olive oil and scatter them over each bowl.

- Red wine will give the soup a deeper, meatier profile. White wine will keep it lighter and sharper. If you're using vegetable broth, stick with white wine.

- If the roasting pan cools too much to deglaze (meaning there's no sizzle when you add the wine and broth), put the pan over one or two burners to reheat. The idea is to have the liquid simmer so you can scrape up any browned bits remaining from roasting the mushrooms.

the lentil soup

❋

SOURCE *A Mediterranean Feast* by Clifford A. Wright

COOK Nawja al-Qattan

This must be the original lentil soup, the biblical Esau's pottage, the essence of sustenance—arguably the most satisfying soup in the world. This version, known as *shurbat al-'Adas* and popular in Lebanon and Egypt, is from Clifford Wright's estimable compendium of Mediterranean dishes, and the recipe is from his former wife, Nawja al-Qattan, a Palestinian.

Don't be put off by the lack of showy ingredients or the earth brown hue of the finished soup. The elegance of this particular recipe comes from a unique technique applied to the humble ingredients. The lentils and onion are simmered without stirring and then passed through a food mill, leaving the thin lentil skins behind; the resulting puree is as smooth as velvet. Don't be tempted to use a blender or food processor, which will change the texture as well as the taste of this divine soup. And whatever you do, don't skip the fried pita squares and olive oil drizzle. These elevate the soup heavenward. ❧

2 cups dried brown lentils

8 cups chicken broth (see note)

1 large onion, grated

2 teaspoons ground cumin, preferably freshly ground

Salt and freshly ground black pepper

2 tablespoons fresh lemon juice

2 cups olive oil for frying

1 large pita bread, cut into ½-inch squares

Extra-virgin olive oil for drizzling

serves 8

Rinse the lentils in a colander under cold running water, picking out any stones. In a large saucepan, bring the broth to a boil and add the lentils and onion. When the broth returns to a boil, reduce the heat to low, cover, and simmer for 1 hour. Do not stir.

Pass the lentils and broth through a food mill set over a large bowl. Add the cumin and season with salt and pepper to taste. Return the soup to the saucepan over medium heat. Taste to check the seasonings. Stir in the lemon juice and heat until the soup begins to bubble slightly. The soup will start to thicken very quickly. If it becomes too thick, thin it with some broth or water. Taste again to check the seasonings and add whatever it needs.

notes from our test kitchen

- By substituting vegetable broth for the chicken broth, you could make this into a vegetarian soup.

- This will look like any old bowl of thick brown soup. Don't worry about that; just close your eyes and taste. If you like, you can garnish each bowl with minced fresh parsley to add a little color.

Meanwhile, in a medium saucepan or skillet, heat the 2 cups olive oil to 375 degrees, or until a cube of bread turns golden in 30 seconds. Fry the pita squares until golden, about 1 minute. Serve the soup with the fried pita squares and extra-virgin olive oil passed at the table.

malaysian noodle soup

❋

SOURCE Ramekins Sonoma Valley Culinary School handout

COOK John Ash

The heady, delectable Malaysian soup called *laksa* is unforgettable. Whether you eat it in Singapore, Australia, or even the United States, there are several constants: a fragrant spice paste; a luscious, slightly sweet broth made with coconut milk, which ends up a creamy apricot color; and chicken (or shrimp), cooked rice noodles, and a vegetable or two, which are put into the soup bowl before you add the broth. The bowls are topped with cilantro, scallions, and perhaps a little mint. If the seasoning is just right, one bowl won't be enough — this is a habit-forming soup — so you might as well make a lot of *laksa* paste (or acquire some; see note), since it freezes well. Don't be scared off by the long list of ingredients — the prep goes quickly. ❧

laksa paste

- ⅓ **cup chopped shallots**
- ⅓ **cup chopped toasted macadamia nuts or blanched almonds**
- ¼ **cup peeled, finely chopped fresh ginger**
- 2 **tablespoons coriander seeds, crushed**
- 2 **teaspoons sugar**
  Zest and juice of 2 limes
- 2 **tablespoons fish sauce (nam pla)**
- 2 **tablespoons chili garlic sauce, or to taste (Lee Kum Kee is a good brand that's widely available.)**
- 2 **tablespoons vegetable oil**
- 1 **teaspoon toasted sesame oil**
- ½ **cup canned unsweetened coconut milk, well stirred**

serves 4 to 6

To make the laksa paste: In a blender, combine all the ingredients except the coconut milk and blend for 1 to 2 minutes, or until very smooth. Transfer the paste to a small saucepan and cook over medium heat for 4 to 5 minutes, stirring constantly. The paste will be very fragrant. Stir in the coconut milk and cook for 2 to 3 minutes more. Store, covered, in the refrigerator for up to 1 week or in the freezer for up to 3 months.

notes from our test kitchen

- If you're as crazy about *laksa* as we are, you can make it almost instantly if you have some of Reuben Solomon's excellent Singapore Laksa Paste in your pantry. Order it from Charmaine's Kitchen: charmainesolomon.com or find it at Dean & DeLuca shops.

- Play around with this soup: try adding bean sprouts, fresh green chiles, or even diced cucumber. John Ash's version of *laksa* is gorgeous, but this is the sort of soup you make with what's on hand in the Asian kitchen.

- And what would you do with leftover *laksa* paste? John Ash uses it as a base for a vinaigrette or as a marinade for chicken, fish, or pork.

soup

1 pound boneless, skinless chicken breasts

2 tablespoons soy sauce

2 tablespoons rice wine or sake

3 1/2 cups canned unsweetened coconut milk, well stirred

3 cups chicken broth

1 cup <u>laksa</u> paste, or to taste

2 cups peeled and diced butternut or other hard squash

2 tablespoons vegetable oil

2 small zucchini, trimmed and cut into long julienne

4 ounces thin rice vermicelli or somen, cooked

Fresh lime juice

Salt and freshly ground black pepper

Fresh cilantro leaves and scallions, cut on the diagonal, for garnish

To make the soup: Cut chicken in half lengthwise. At a steep angle, cut it crosswise into 1/8-inch-thick slices. In a medium bowl, combine the soy sauce and rice wine or sake. Add the chicken and toss to coat. Marinate for up to 30 minutes.

In a large saucepan, heat the coconut milk and broth over medium-high heat. Whisk in the *laksa* paste. Add the squash and simmer for 5 minutes, or until tender.

Meanwhile, in a wok or large skillet, heat the oil over high heat. Add the chicken and stir-fry until just cooked through and the slices separate. Transfer the chicken to a plate.

Divide the zucchini and noodles among warm bowls and top with the chicken. Taste the broth and add the lime juice and salt and pepper to taste. Ladle the hot soup into the bowls and garnish with the cilantro and scallions. Serve hot.

smoky shrimp and halibut stew

SOURCE *Bon Appétit*
COOK Bruce Aidells

Bruce Aidells is the famous sausage and meat king, so we were curious to see his take on fish—which starts with bacon, a good sign. It rarely occurs to us to make fish stews, but this recipe called to us. This gratifying dish is also relatively light. There's no fuss here: bottled clam juice, canned chicken broth, and canned diced tomatoes speed things along. You can also make the stew ahead up to the point where you add the fish, which is just 3 minutes before serving, so it's a great last-minute supper. Just add some coleslaw and warm biscuits. ❧

8 ounces smoked bacon slices, coarsely chopped
²⁄₃ cup chopped onion
1 medium fennel bulb, trimmed and coarsely chopped, with 2 tablespoons chopped fronds
1 6-ounce red-skinned potato, unpeeled, cut into ¹⁄₂-inch pieces (see note)
1¹⁄₄ cups dry white wine
1 cup canned low-sodium chicken broth
1 8-ounce bottle clam juice
1 14¹⁄₂-ounce can diced tomatoes, with their juice
1 teaspoon chopped fresh thyme
1¹⁄₂ pounds halibut fillets, cut into 2¹⁄₂-inch pieces (see note)
1 pound large shrimp, peeled and deveined
Salt and freshly ground black pepper
¹⁄₄ cup chopped fresh flat-leaf parsley

serves 4

Sauté the bacon in a large pot over medium-high heat until crisp, about 10 minutes. Transfer one third of the bacon to a bowl and set aside.

Add the onion to the remaining bacon and drippings in the pot and sauté for 5 minutes. Add the fennel bulb and potato and sauté for 5 minutes more. Add the wine and bring to a boil. Add the broth, clam juice, tomatoes with their juice, fennel fronds, and thyme and return to a boil. Reduce

IN A LETTER to *Fine Cooking* magazine, southern food author John Martin Taylor passed on a great tip about eliminating cooking odors from the kitchen, such as those from cooking fish and frying food. Place a shallow dish of bleach near the cooking area. For some reason, the bleach attracts the particles of whatever it is that creates the odor, and they deposit on the surface as a cloudy film. It's a good idea to label the dish of bleach so that no one mistakenly adds it to the food.

the heat and simmer until the potato is tender, about 5 minutes.

Add the halibut and shrimp to the pot. Cover and cook until the halibut is opaque in the center, about 3 minutes. Season with salt and pepper. Stir in the parsley and reserved bacon and serve.

notes from our test kitchen

- We found that thinner potato pieces, about ⅛ inch thick, cooked through more reliably.
- Our favorite canned tomatoes are Muir Glen organic.
- Halibut isn't always available and is sometimes expensive. You can substitute scrod or use a mix of halibut, scrod, and shrimp.

wild rice and turkey soup

SOURCE *Atlanta Journal-Constitution*
COOK Kathie Jenkins

As much as we enjoy serving roast turkey for the holidays and other big gatherings, what we really look forward to, long after the guests have gone, is transforming the leftovers into turkey soup. Usually the soup comes together according to what we find in the fridge and pantry, and until we discovered this recipe, we never even considered following a formula. We'll admit that curiosity inspired us to try something new. What's turmeric doing in turkey soup? And what's with the chopped dill? Now we can't imagine making it any other way. The end result is neither exotic nor bland. It's simply the best turkey soup we've ever tasted — and very restorative after a holiday binge. The two kinds of rice (wild and white) thicken the soup so it becomes a whole meal.

Kathie Jenkins left the *Los Angeles Times* food section to become food editor of the *Pioneer Press* in St. Paul, Minnesota, her home state. And her recipe for post-Thanksgiving wild rice soup was published in the *Atlanta Journal-Constitution* — proving that good things have no regional boundaries.

broth

- 1 turkey carcass, with some meat still on it (see notes)
- 2 celery ribs, cut into 1-inch pieces
- 1 large carrot, cut into 1-inch pieces
- 1 small onion, quartered

soup

- 4 tablespoons (½ stick) butter
- 2 celery ribs, diced
- 2 carrots, peeled and diced
- 2 onions, diced
- ½ cup sliced scallions, including some of the greens
- ½ cup slivered almonds (see note)
- 2 tablespoons chopped fresh dill (see note)
- 2 bay leaves
- ¼ teaspoon ground turmeric
- 1½ cups wild rice, rinsed
- ½ cup white rice
- 3 cups cleaned and sliced mushrooms
- Salt and freshly ground black pepper

serves 8 to 12

To make the broth: Put the turkey carcass in a large soup pot. Cover with cold water and bring to a boil. Reduce the heat and simmer for 30 minutes, skimming off any foam that rises to the top. Add the celery, carrot, and onion and simmer, uncovered, for 1½ hours. Add more water, if neces-

notes from our test kitchen

- Rarely do we have the energy to make soup immediately after the feast. Instead, we wrap the carcass tightly in plastic and refrigerate it for up to 3 days. You can also freeze it for several weeks.

- If you make the broth with the leftover meat still on the carcass as directed, the meat will become dried out and tasteless. Instead, before making the broth, trim and tear off as much of the turkey meat as possible. Shred or chop it into small bits, set it aside, and add it back to the soup at the end. Also, it helps to break the turkey carcass in half before adding it to the soup pot. It will fit in the pot better, and you will extract more flavor.

- We've made this soup both with and without the almonds, and we think they can easily be omitted.

- To brighten the flavor and appearance, scatter a little chopped dill on each bowl before serving.

- This makes a vat: plan on freezing some, or sending leftovers home with your houseguests. The soup can be refrigerated for a couple of days or frozen for several months.

- The soup will thicken as it cools. You will need to add more broth or water when you reheat it.

sary, to keep the carcass covered. Remove from the heat and let cool.

Remove the carcass from the broth and discard the skin and bones. Shred the meat. Reserve 4 cups of the meat for the soup and refrigerate until ready to use.

Strain the broth into a large bowl, discarding the vegetables. There should be about $3\frac{1}{2}$ quarts. If time allows, refrigerate the broth, uncovered; the fat will congeal on the top, making it easy to remove.

To make the soup: Melt the butter in a large heavy skillet over medium heat. Add the celery, carrots, onions, scallions, and almonds and cook for 5 minutes, or until the vegetables are slightly softened. Stir in the dill, bay leaves, and turmeric. Remove from the heat.

Bring 3 quarts of the broth, the wild rice, and white rice to a boil in a large pot. Reduce the heat, add the vegetable mixture, and simmer for 30 minutes, adding more broth if the soup becomes too thick. Discard the bay leaves.

Add the reserved shredded turkey and the mushrooms to the soup and simmer for 10 minutes, or until the turkey is heated through and the mushrooms are cooked. Season with salt and pepper to taste and serve.

tip

KATHIE JENKINS says, "If you are going to make this soup, buy true wild rice, the kind that grows in shallow lakes and streams and is hand-harvested. The other variety, paddy rice — cultivated in artificially seeded ponds and machine-harvested — bears no comparison to hand-harvested, which is softer in texture and much milder, with a far more subtle flavor." Check the label before buying.

Salads

Salads

alice waters's coleslaw 67

crunchy cucumber, celery, and red bell pepper salad with cumin
and fresh mint 69

green bean salad with cream 71

heirloom tomato and watermelon salad 73

carrot, parsley, and pine nut salad with fried goat cheese 74

cherry tomato salad with olives 76

tomato, avocado, and roasted corn salad 77

tomato salad with cumin 80

beet salad with horseradish and fried capers 82

sicilian slow-roasted onion salad 84

fennel, red pepper, and mushroom salad 87

wild rice and chickpea salad 88

sugar snap pea and prosciutto salad 90

corn bread salad with grilled sausage and spicy chipotle dressing 91

alice waters's coleslaw

***

SOURCE *New York Times Magazine*   STORY BY Jason Epstein
COOK Alice Waters

Coleslaw is something we can't imagine living without. What would we serve at cookouts, with slow-cooked barbecue, or with anything fried — especially chicken? But sadly, too many recipes slather on the mayonnaise and spoon in so much sugar that the slaw ends up a goopy, overly sweet mess. Leave it to Alice Waters to come up with a formula that highlights the refreshing spicy-sweet flavor of the cabbage. The accents of jalapeño, lime juice, and cilantro add a sophisticated zip, but this is still just the thing to serve with fish sticks. ❧

note from our test kitchen

Maldon sea salt from England, the darling of many cooks and chefs, is esteemed for its bright taste and soft, flaky crystals, which add a pleasing crunch to many dishes. It's available in specialty shops and some supermarkets. The texture of course dissipates when the salt dissolves into a dish. When making this coleslaw, we use any clean-tasting, coarse-grain sea salt. Kosher salt also will do.

1 medium green cabbage (about 3 pounds), outer leaves removed

1/2 small red onion, cut in half through the stem and thinly sliced

1 cup loosely packed fresh cilantro leaves, coarsely chopped

1 large jalapeño pepper, seeded and finely chopped

1/4–1/3 cup olive oil

3–4 tablespoons fresh lime juice

3–4 tablespoons red wine vinegar

Maldon or other sea salt (see note)

Freshly ground black pepper

Large pinch of sugar, or more to taste

serves 8 to 12

Quarter the cabbage through the core; cut out the core. Cut the quarters crosswise in half and, using a sharp knife, finely shred. Place the shredded cabbage in a very large bowl or pot (you'll have about 5 1/2 quarts). Add the onion, cilantro, and jalapeño and toss to mix. Sprinkle with the oil, lime juice, vinegar, 1 1/2 teaspoons salt, 1/2 teaspoon pepper, and the sugar and toss to coat.

Let the slaw sit for 1 hour, tossing occasionally. Drain. Taste and adjust the seasonings. Wait another hour before serving at room temperature.

crunchy cucumber, celery, and red bell pepper salad with cumin and fresh mint

---

SOURCE *Once Upon a Tart . . .* by Frank Mentesana and Jerome Audureau
with Carolynn Carreño

COOKS Frank Mentesana and Jerome Audureau

This colorful and refreshing salad from Once Upon a Tart . . . , a popular café and bakeshop in New York City, is one of those fail-safe party dishes that we make year-round. It's best, of course, in the summer, with fresh local peppers and cucumbers, but we also rely on it in the winter when we want something crunchy and bright. The dash of cumin and mint in the dressing provides just the right note.

If you're asked to bring a salad to a potluck, combine all the vegetables in a pretty bowl. Bring along the dressing in a little jar; just before serving, give it a shake and toss the salad.

Feel free to exercise your creativity with the elements here. For instance, thinly sliced mushrooms, shaved radishes, or even julienned sticks of jicama are good additions. ❧

salad

6 celery ribs, cut into 1/4-inch-thick slices

3 cucumbers, peeled, halved, seeded, and cut on the diagonal into 1/4-inch-thick slices

3 scallions, white and green parts, cut into 1/4-inch-thick slices

1 red bell pepper, halved, cored, seeded, and julienned

1/2 red onion, halved again and thinly sliced

vinaigrette

1/4 cup white wine vinegar

1 tablespoon Dijon mustard

1 garlic clove, minced

1 teaspoon ground cumin, preferably freshly ground (see note)

Salt

Freshly ground black pepper

1/4 cup olive oil

2 tablespoons finely chopped fresh flat-leaf parsley

2 tablespoons finely chopped fresh mint

serves 6

To make the salad: Toss the vegetables into a big bowl as you cut them.

SPARE YOUR KNIVES! As a famous chef (we think it was John Ash) reminded us recently, don't use the sharp blade of your knife to scrape prepped vegetables off the chopping board, which will dull the blade and may even damage it. Use the other edge of the knife or a pastry scraper.

To make the vinaigrette: In a small bowl, whisk together the vinegar, mustard, garlic, cumin, 1 teaspoon salt, and a few grinds of pepper. Add the olive oil in a slow, steady, thin stream, whisking as you go. This will form an emulsion and thicken the dressing. Stir in the parsley and mint.

To assemble the salad: Just before you're ready to serve the salad, pour the vinaigrette over the vegetables. Using a large metal spoon or your hands, toss until everything is evenly coated. Taste to see if the salad needs more of anything, particularly salt, and serve.

notes from our test kitchen

- Kirby cucumbers, the smaller pickling type, tend to have more crunch and fewer seeds than the larger standard varieties. They're not waxed, so you don't have to deal with that unpleasantly slick peel. English cucumbers, the seedless variety sold wrapped in plastic in supermarkets, work well here, too.
- Starting with whole cumin seeds will greatly improve the taste of the dressing. Toast them briefly in a dry skillet over medium-high heat until fragrant. Then grind to a fine powder in a spice or coffee grinder (or using a mortar and pestle) and add to the dressing.

green bean salad with cream

※

SOURCE *Guy Savoy: Simple French Recipes for the Home Cook* by Guy Savoy

COOK Guy Savoy

We fall in love with certain recipes every year and can't stop making them. This is one of those, a salad that requires only a 10-minute prep. The beans are cooked just to the point of crisp-tenderness, then chilled and combined with the simplest imaginable dressing — crème fraîche, lemon, and shallot, with some chives on top. Every time we see tender green beans beckoning to us at the market, we think, "What about that Guy Savoy recipe?"

As Savoy points out, the dressing is easier to make than a vinaigrette and can be used for lots of different salads, including potato salad. ❧

note from our test kitchen

We sometimes chop the chives and sprinkle them over the salad. Chives with snipped dill is also a good idea.

Salt

1¼ **pounds tender green beans or haricots verts, trimmed**

Juice of 1 lemon

Freshly ground black pepper

1 **shallot, minced**

½ **cup crème fraîche**

1 **small bunch fresh chives**

serves 4

Bring a large pot of salted water to a boil, add the beans, and cook for 6 to 8 minutes, or until tender but still slightly crisp. Drain and rinse under cold running water. Refrigerate until ready to serve.

Combine the lemon juice and salt and pepper to taste in a medium bowl. Stir well to dissolve the salt. Stir in the shallot and crème fraîche. Refrigerate the dressing until ready to serve.

Just before serving, combine the beans with the dressing. Arrange on individual serving plates and garnish with chives.

heirloom tomato and watermelon salad

SOURCE *New York* magazine   STORY BY Gillian Duffy
COOK Geoffrey Zakarian

Of all the watermelon-tomato combinations we've seen — and there are plenty — we like this one from Manhattan chef Geoffrey Zakarian best. It's a great jumble of tomatoes and watermelon cubes tossed with very little olive oil, salt and pepper, dill, and a big surprise: cracked coriander seeds. Because the salad is made with heirloom tomatoes — yellow, striped green, pink, whatever color you fancy — and both red and yellow watermelon, it's gorgeous as well. Even made with indifferent watermelon and low-wattage cherry tomatoes in the dead of winter, it's terrific.

The salad is perfect with grilled dishes or for a Fourth of July picnic or Labor Day barbecue. 🍃

tip

IT'S HARD TO IMPROVE on a great heirloom tomato at its peak of flavor, but Gabrielle Hamilton, the chef at Prune in Manhattan, has done just that. She drizzles melted butter on sliced ripe tomatoes just before serving.

6–8 **heirloom tomatoes, varying in size, at room temperature**

1 **small to medium yellow watermelon (cantaloupe size)**

1 **small to medium red watermelon (cantaloupe size)**

2 **tablespoons extra-virgin olive oil**

1 **teaspoon cracked coriander seeds (see note)**

Sea salt (preferably Maldon; see note, page 67) and cracked black pepper

1½ **teaspoons finely chopped fresh dill**

1½ **teaspoons finely chopped fresh flat-leaf parsley**

serves 6 to 8

Cut the tomatoes into chunks of varying sizes (1 to 1½ inches). Cut the watermelon flesh into cubes of varying sizes (1 to 1½ inches).

In a large bowl, combine the tomatoes, watermelon, oil, coriander, and salt and pepper to taste. Gently toss, taking care not to bruise the fruit. Sprinkle with the dill and parsley and serve immediately.

notes from our test kitchen

- Try sprinkling the tomatoes and watermelon with salt before they're mixed together. Let them stand for up to ½ hour to bring out the flavors.
- To crack the coriander seeds, you can either put them in a kitchen towel and smack them with a meat mallet or some other heavy object, or you can crush them using a small mortar and pestle.

carrot, parsley, and pine nut salad with fried goat cheese

———————————— ✳ ————————————

SOURCE Formaggiokitchen.com
COOK Ana Sortun

This bright salad delivers a lot of bang for the buck, in both taste and presentation. Created by Boston chef Ana Sortun, known for her bold Mediterranean dishes, it makes a lovely first course or light lunch—especially when summer's star vegetables are gone but you can still get good old carrots and parsley. Using yogurt as a base for the lemony-garlicky dressing gives the salad the right amount of tang and richness. Serve it on individual plates to really show it off, and be sure everyone is close by when you fry the goat cheese. You want to serve the salads immediately, so the luscious brown buttons of fried cheese melt onto the crunchy salads. ✎

2   2- to 3-ounce fresh goat cheese buttons (see notes)

1/3 cup all-purpose flour for dredging

1   egg, beaten with 1 tablespoon milk

2   garlic cloves, minced

1   teaspoon sugar

1   tablespoon fresh lemon juice

1   tablespoon good-quality white wine vinegar

1/2 cup plain whole-milk yogurt, preferably sheep's milk (see note)

1/4 cup extra-virgin olive oil

    Salt and freshly ground black pepper

2   cups peeled, shredded carrots (2 large or 3 medium)

1/4 cup finely chopped fresh parsley

1/4 cup pine nuts, toasted

3–4 tablespoons vegetable oil for frying

serves 4

Slice each goat cheese button in half crosswise so that you have four 3/4- to 1-inch-thick disks. Place the flour and egg mixture in separate small bowls. Lightly coat each piece of goat cheese with flour, shaking off any excess. Dip into the egg mixture and coat again with flour. Set aside on a plate.

In a medium bowl, combine the garlic, sugar, lemon juice, and vinegar. Let stand for 5 minutes. Whisk in the yogurt, olive oil, and salt and pepper to taste. Add the carrots, pars-

notes from our test kitchen

- For the goat cheese, you want something relatively fresh and mild so that it will have a bit of creaminess when fried. If you can't find small buttons (*crottin*), just get a log of chèvre, such as Montrachet, and cut it into four pieces (3/4- to 1-inch-thick disks). You'll need 4 to 6 ounces total.

- When coating the cheese, you can minimize the mess if you use one hand for the flour bowl and one hand for the egg wash.

- If your kitchen is warm, refrigerate the cheese before frying it.

- If you can't find sheep's-milk yogurt, use any good-quality whole-milk yogurt. Low-fat yogurt is too thin and won't work very well.

- The carrots can be shredded on a box grater, with a Mouli grater, or in the food processor, using the shredding disk.

- Flat-leaf parsley is nicest here.

ley, and pine nuts and toss to coat. Taste and season again. Divide the salad among four salad plates.

Heat a medium heavy or nonstick skillet over medium-high heat. Add enough vegetable oil to lightly coat the skillet. Fry the goat cheese, turning only once, until browned on both sides. The center of the cheese should be warm so that it will melt over the salad, but don't cook it so long that it loses its shape. Place a piece of goat cheese on top of each salad and serve immediately.

cherry tomato salad with olives

SOURCE *The Naked Chef Takes Off* by Jamie Oliver
COOK Jamie Oliver

We love everything about this rustic salad, which Oliver calls Squash and Smash. It's made in minutes with just a few ingredients, it tastes terrific, and it's a huge amount of fun to pummel defenseless little cherry tomatoes and olives.

It's such a minimal recipe, in fact, that brash British TV chef Jamie Oliver just tells you about it — doesn't actually write it up as a recipe. So this is our version, for which we ask his forgiveness, to make things a bit clearer. But you don't really need a recipe if you just remember to use 4 parts cherry tomatoes and 1 part olives, plus some vinegar, a little black pepper, and a few glugs of good olive oil. Add some basil and arugula, and you're done. If this sounds like pasta sauce, you're on: toss leftovers with hot spaghetti. 🍃

2 **pints cherry tomatoes**
1/3 **cup unpitted olives (any kind; see note)**
Red wine vinegar
Freshly ground black pepper
Extra-virgin olive oil
1 **handful of torn fresh basil leaves**
1 **handful of torn arugula leaves**

serves 6

In the serving bowl you plan to use, squash the cherry tomatoes with one hand while holding the other over them so they don't splatter all over everything. Put the olives on a cutting board and gently smash them with a rolling pin, a cup, or even your thumb. Remove the pits and add the olives to the salad bowl.

Drizzle in a little vinegar and grind some pepper on top. Add the oil and toss. Just before serving, "rip in," as Oliver says, the basil and arugula and toss well.

tip

SAN FRANCISCO–BASED cooking teacher Joanne Weir reminds us *never* to refrigerate tomatoes. Whether they are cherry tomatoes from the supermarket or heirloom varieties from the farmers' market, keep them away from the cold. Chilling destroys their flavors and turns them mealy. The ideal way to store tomatoes is out of direct light and at around 50 degrees.

notes from our test kitchen

- Oliver encourages using different-colored cherry tomatoes — yellow, green, striped, whatever you can find.
- You can use pitted olives, but you won't have the fun of squashing out the pits. And pitted olives have lost some of their flavor.

tomato, avocado, and roasted corn salad

❋

SOURCE *Food & Wine* STORY BY Jessie Carry Saunders

COOK Elizabeth Falkner

San Francisco pastry chef Elizabeth Falkner, who owns Citizen Cake, a bakery and restaurant, is an avid soccer player. Falkner likes to host postgame lunches for the other players and their kids, and she tosses together this memorable salad at the last minute. It has a definite Mexican accent, but it's also very versatile—great with grilled chicken, meat, or fish. Vegetarians can find enough sustenance here for an entire meal. All the work (which is minimal) can be done the day before.

Part of what makes the salad so good is roasting the corn, an easy step that delivers a huge amount of flavor.

This recipe serves a crowd, but it's easy to cut in half. ❧

5 **ears of corn, shucked**

$1/2$ **cup plus 2 tablespoons extra-virgin olive oil**
  Salt and freshly ground black pepper

$1/2$ **cup raw pumpkin seeds**

3 **tablespoons fresh lime juice**

2 **tablespoons sherry vinegar**

$1/4$ **teaspoon hot sauce**

1 **teaspoon sugar**

$1/8$ **teaspoon ground cinnamon**

$1 1/2$ **pounds arugula (4 bunches), large stems discarded and leaves torn into bite-size pieces**

3 **ripe avocados, cut into $1/2$-inch dice**

2 **large red tomatoes, cut into $1/2$-inch dice**

2 **large yellow tomatoes, cut into $1/2$-inch dice**

2 **medium cucumbers, peeled, seeded, and cut into $1/4$-inch dice**

3 **ounces queso fresco (see note, page 37) or ricotta salata, crumbled ($3/4$ cup)**

serves 12

Preheat the oven to 500 degrees.

On a rimmed baking sheet, drizzle the corn with 2 tablespoons of the olive oil. Season the ears with salt and pepper and roast, turning a few times, for about 25 minutes, or until the kernels are browned. Let cool. Cut the kernels from the cobs and transfer to a bowl.

Turn the oven down to 400 degrees. Spread the pumpkin seeds in a pie plate and bake, stirring occasionally, for about

ANOTHER GREAT USE for roasted corn kernels is to stir them into a lemony guacamole. The California Avocado Commission suggests adding ½ cup roasted corn kernels to a guacamole made with 2 mashed ripe avocados with ½ lemon (cut into very small dice, peel and all), 2 minced garlic cloves, 1 minced jalapeño pepper, and ½ teaspoon each ground cumin and salt.

4 minutes, or until lightly browned. Transfer to a plate to cool.

Put ½ cup of the corn kernels in a blender (see note). Add the lime juice, sherry vinegar, hot sauce, sugar, and cinnamon and puree. With the machine on, add the remaining ½ cup olive oil in a thin stream and blend until emulsified. Scrape the vinaigrette into a bowl and season with salt and pepper to taste.

In a large bowl, toss the remaining corn kernels with the arugula, avocados, red and yellow tomatoes, and cucumbers. Add the vinaigrette and toss well. Mound the salad on a large platter, scatter the pumpkin seeds and crumbled cheese on top, and serve.

notes from our test kitchen

- You can use cherry tomatoes instead of regular tomatoes.
- You can prepare the corn and vinaigrette 1 day ahead, but don't mix them together. The roasted pumpkin seeds will keep for several days in an airtight container at room temperature.
- This salad looks prettiest, we think, if you don't add the corn to the vinaigrette. Just toss all of it into the salad.
- This salad has no oniony element and doesn't need one. But if you'd like, you can toss in some chopped scallions or chives.

tomato salad with cumin

SOURCE *The Cuisines of Spain* by Teresa Barrenechea

COOK Teresa Barrenechea

You know you're about to be introduced to something delicious when a recipe begins with the direction to mash garlic and salt to a paste using a mortar and pestle. That's the basis for the dressing in this terrific tomato salad from the Spanish region of Murcia. One of the tomatoes is pounded into the vinaigrette along with cumin seeds and smoked paprika. It's a fantastic but extremely simple combination. Although this salad is best at the height of summer with perfectly ripe beefsteak tomatoes, it's also delicious in midwinter with hothouse Campari tomatoes. ❧

2   **garlic cloves, peeled**
1   **teaspoon salt**
5   **tomatoes, peeled (see note)**
2   **tablespoons red wine vinegar**
    Pinch of freshly ground black pepper
1   **teaspoon cumin seeds**
1/2 **teaspoon sweet pimentón (Spanish smoked paprika) or paprika (see note)**
6   **tablespoons extra-virgin olive oil**

serves 4

Using a mortar and pestle, mash the garlic with the salt until a paste forms. Coarsely chop 1 tomato and add it to the mortar. Pound the tomato together with the garlic paste until well blended. Add the vinegar, pepper, 1/2 teaspoon of the cumin seeds (see note), and the pimentón to the mortar and pound until smooth. Add the olive oil and stir with the pestle to mix well, forming a vinaigrette.

Cut the remaining 4 tomatoes crosswise into 1/2-inch-thick slices. Arrange them on a serving platter in a single layer, overlapping them as little as possible. Pour the vinaigrette over the tomatoes, sprinkle with the remaining 1/2 teaspoon cumin seeds, and serve.

notes from our test kitchen

- You don't have to peel the tomatoes, except for the one that gets pounded into the vinaigrette. To peel them, have ready a pot of boiling water. Make a small X in the base of the tomato with a sharp knife. Drop the tomato into the boiling water for half a minute and remove quickly. Starting at the X, pull the tomato skin up – it should peel right off.

- Pimentón is a staple in our kitchens (both the hot and the sweet), and we urge you to try it. It's available in some gourmet shops or by mail from the Spanish Table: spanishtable.com. To approximate the sweet pimentón, you can substitute 1 teaspoon regular paprika mixed with ½ teaspoon ground chipotle chiles for a similar smoky taste.

- We think the salad is even better if you slice the tomatoes first and sprinkle them with sea salt, preferably Maldon salt (see note, page 67), and let them sit for 20 minutes before adding the vinaigrette.

- The cumin seeds can get stuck in your teeth, so we like to crush them a bit in the mortar before we begin making the vinaigrette.

beet salad with horseradish and fried capers

SOURCE *New York Times Magazine*

COOK Amanda Hesser

This sensational salad gets its power from fried salt-packed capers. They fluff up in the hot olive oil like the tiny curled-up flower buds they are, producing a crunchy outer shell that's a salty complement to the fine balance of sweet beets, horseradish, and Dijon mustard. You can use regular bottled brined capers, but they won't open up in the same way and give the full explosion of flavor. The fried capers are also delicious with vegetables, fried seafood, and fish, as well as in a Caesar salad.

Don't be scared off by the word *fry*. This is shallow frying in a small saucepan with just a little oil, and it's a great trick to have up your sleeve. ❧

1½ **pounds small beets, trimmed and scrubbed**

5 **tablespoons olive oil, plus more for frying the capers**

2 **tablespoons salt-packed or brined capers**

1½ **tablespoons prepared horseradish, or more to taste**

1 **tablespoon Dijon mustard**

1 **tablespoon white wine vinegar**

1 **tablespoon sour cream**

Sea salt, if needed

1 **garlic clove, crushed**

serves 4

Preheat the oven to 350 degrees.

Place the beets on one half of a large piece of aluminum foil. Drizzle with 1 tablespoon of the oil. Fold the foil over the beets and seal the edges. Lay the package on a baking sheet and place it in the oven. Roast until the beets are tender, 45 to 60 minutes. (Test by poking a fork through the foil into a beet.) Remove from the oven. Be careful when opening the foil; steam will race out. Peel the beets while they're still warm, then cut into wedges and place in a bowl.

Soak the salt-packed capers in water for 10 minutes. Drain, rinse, and pat dry. (If you're using brined capers, just drain and pat dry.) Pour ½ inch oil into a small saucepan over medium-high heat. When the oil is hot enough to toast a

- Salted capers are available in Italian markets and many gourmet shops and supermarkets. They keep almost forever, so buy them when you see them.

- We love the touch of the crushed garlic clove on the platter; it really adds something. It reminds us of those 1950s salad recipes that instruct you to rub the wooden bowl with a garlic clove.

bread cube in 30 seconds, add the capers. Be careful; the oil may sputter. Fry until the capers fluff up and begin to brown on the edges, 30 to 60 seconds. Drain on paper towels.

Whisk together the horseradish, mustard, and vinegar in a small bowl. Whisk in the remaining 4 tablespoons oil, followed by the sour cream. Pour half of the dressing over the beets and mix. Taste, adding more dressing or a little salt, if needed. Rub a platter with the crushed garlic, discard the garlic, and spoon the beets onto the platter. Sprinkle with the fried capers and serve.

sicilian slow-roasted onion salad

SOURCE *Food & Wine*

COOK Paula Wolfert

This simple dish from the ancient city of Siracusa is an onion salad unlike any other. Instead of cooking the onions whole, as they do in Sicily, Mediterranean cooking guru Paula Wolfert cuts them into slices, paints the slices with olive oil, and slowly roasts them into caramelized deliciousness. Then they get a simple dressing — not too concentrated, because it's diluted with water — with tiny bits of fresh garlic and the occasional bite of crushed red pepper.

This salad is wonderful with grilled meat or fish and great on a buffet. ❧

2 **tablespoons olive oil**

3 **large onions (about 2 pounds)**

2 **tablespoons water**

1 **garlic clove, minced**

1 **tablespoon minced fresh flat-leaf parsley**

$\frac{1}{2}$ **teaspoon red or white wine vinegar**

$\frac{1}{2}$ **teaspoon salt**

$\frac{1}{4}$ **teaspoon freshly ground black pepper**

$\frac{1}{4}$ **teaspoon crushed red pepper flakes**

serves 4

Preheat the oven to 300 degrees. Brush a heavy baking sheet with some olive oil (see note).

Cut off and discard the ends of the onions. Leaving the outer skin intact, slice the onions crosswise $\frac{1}{2}$ inch thick. Lay the slices on the prepared baking sheet and brush them lightly with oil.

Bake the onions for 1 hour, or until just tender. Turn the slices and bake for 30 minutes more, or until deeply browned. Transfer to a large shallow serving dish and let cool to room temperature. Discard the onion skins and any dried-out rings.

In a small bowl, whisk together the 2 tablespoons oil, water, and remaining ingredients. Spoon the vinaigrette over the onions and serve.

tip

LEAVE IT TO Martha Stewart to come up with a romantic kitchen tip. When you're working with onions, you can avoid tears by lighting a votive candle and keeping it next to your chopping board. Amazingly, this really works, although you may feel a bit like Liberace in the kitchen.

notes from our test kitchen

- For easier cleanup, line the baking sheet with aluminum foil and brush the foil with oil before adding the onion slices.

- You can take the salad in another direction by skipping the dressing and just drizzling balsamic vinegar over the onion slices after you turn them, crumbling a little oregano or thyme on top, and adding salt and pepper to taste. When the onions are golden brown and soft, remove them from the oven. Discard the skins and any dried-out onion rings. Serve as a side dish, warm or at room temperature.

- If you make the onions and dressing a day ahead, refrigerate them separately and bring to room temperature before combining and serving.

fennel, red pepper, and mushroom salad

❋

SOURCE Martha-Rose-Shulman.com

COOK Martha Rose Shulman

This chopped salad with mostly Mediterranean flavors is made of everyday ingredients but manages to take off and fly because they're so perfectly balanced. Shulman served it at a cookbook fair in Austin, Texas, and had so many requests for the recipe, both from casual passersby and her fellow cookbook authors, that she posted it on her Web site.

It's great for a party or on a buffet because the ingredients hold up very well. It's also a hit during the holidays because its colors are festive and it's refreshing in a season of overindulgence. ❧

salad

2 pounds fennel bulbs, trimmed, quartered, and cut crosswise into very thin slices

2 large red bell peppers, cored, seeded, and cut into thin 2-inch slices

8 mushrooms, wiped clean and thinly sliced (about 4 ounces)

2 tablespoons minced fresh flat-leaf parsley

1 tablespoon minced fresh chives

2 ounces Parmesan cheese, shaved

dressing

1/4 cup fresh lemon juice

2 tablespoons sherry vinegar

1 garlic clove, very finely minced or pressed
Salt and freshly ground black pepper

1/2 cup olive oil

serves 6

Combine the salad ingredients in a large bowl.

Whisk together the dressing ingredients in a small bowl. Toss the dressing with the salad and serve.

87

wild rice and chickpea salad

SOURCE *The Pastry Queen* by Rebecca Rather and Alison Oresman
COOK Paula Disbrowe

People adore this big, hearty grain- and bean-filled salad. It's based on nutty, crunchy wild rice, but so many elements are at play here that you just have to take another bite and then another to taste all the wonderful flavors.

The room-temperature salad works virtually anywhere—at a picnic, at a dinner party, on a buffet table, at a potluck supper. We've yet to serve it without being asked for the recipe. ∾

1½ cups wild rice, preferably organic, rinsed
   Kosher salt
2½ tablespoons fresh lemon juice
2 tablespoons red wine vinegar
2 tablespoons Dijon mustard
1 tablespoon honey
1 tablespoon ground cumin
1 teaspoon curry powder
   Pinch of cayenne pepper
¼ cup extra-virgin olive oil
1 15-ounce can chickpeas (garbanzos), rinsed and drained
8 ounces smoked ham, diced (see note)
8 small scallions, white and light green parts, thinly sliced
¼ cup golden raisins
   Freshly ground black pepper
   Hot pepper sauce

serves 6

Fill a large saucepan three-quarters full of water and bring to a boil. Add the wild rice and 1 tablespoon salt and simmer over medium heat until the rice is tender but still firm to the bite, about 45 minutes. Drain and rinse under cold water.

Meanwhile, whisk together the lemon juice, vinegar, mustard, honey, cumin, curry powder, and cayenne in a large bowl (see note). Add the oil and whisk until combined.

notes from our test kitchen

- If you can't find wild rice, in a pinch you can use Uncle Ben's Long Grain & Wild Rice in a box, minus the seasoning packet.

- You can substitute dried cranberries for the golden raisins.

- The ham makes the salad a bit sturdier, but the dish is fine — and vegetarian — without it.

- Though convenient, the method of mixing the salad dressing directly in the bowl and then adding the other ingredients makes it difficult to adjust the amount of dressing if you need to. Instead, we recommend putting only about ½ cup mixed dressing in the bowl and adding more gradually after tossing the salad.

Add the chickpeas, ham, scallions, raisins, and wild rice and toss well. Season to taste with salt, pepper, and hot pepper sauce. Serve at room temperature. The salad can be refrigerated overnight. Let it come to room temperature and toss before serving.

sugar snap pea and prosciutto salad

SOURCE *Food & Wine*

COOK Joanne Weir

In less than 20 minutes, you can have an irresistible dish that also works well as a starter. The sweet crunch of snap peas is punched up by the salty prosciutto, then given a fresh zing with lemon zest and mint.

The salad won't wilt, but the snap peas will discolor slightly if they sit around in the dressing for a long time. The solution is to prepare the elements separately and combine them at the last minute. ೪

3/4 **pound sugar snap peas**

Salt

3 **tablespoons extra-virgin olive oil**

1½ **tablespoons fresh lemon juice**

3 **tablespoons finely chopped fresh mint**

1 **teaspoon finely grated lemon zest**

3 **ounces thinly sliced prosciutto, cut into thin strips**

Freshly ground black pepper

serves 4

Have ready a large bowl of ice water. Drop the peas into a medium saucepan of boiling salted water and boil until crisp-tender, about 1 minute. Drain the peas and plunge into the ice bath. Drain again. Pat the peas dry with a kitchen towel (see note).

In a medium bowl, whisk together the oil, lemon juice, mint, and lemon zest. Add the peas and prosciutto, season with salt and pepper to taste, and toss. Arrange the salad on a platter and serve.

note from our test kitchen

Once the peas have been patted dry, you may want to cut them in half on the diagonal so they'll be easier to eat.

corn bread salad with grilled sausage and spicy chipotle dressing

SOURCE *Let the Flames Begin* by Chris Schlesinger and John Willoughby

COOKS Elmer Sanchez and Amilcar Baraca

We find ourselves looking for excuses to make corn bread (and whisking it away from the table before someone innocently finishes it) just so we can have leftovers to make this salad.

Pretty much any corn bread will do, as long as it's firm enough to cut up into big croutons and toast. The dressing has earned the nickname "smoky lava," and it's about the spiciest we've ever tasted. You could certainly tame its firepower by using less chipotle, but where's the fun in that?

Serve as a starter course for a meal from the grill. ✎

dressing

- 1/2 **cup olive oil**
- 1/4 **cup fresh lime juice (about 2 limes)**
- 1/4 **cup chipotle chiles in adobo sauce, pureed**
- 1 **tablespoon ground cumin**
- **Kosher salt and freshly ground black pepper**

salad

- 2 **ripe tomatoes about the size of baseballs, cored and cut into large dice**
- 1 **ripe Hass avocado, cut into medium dice**
- 1/2 **red onion, cut into small dice**
- 1/3 **cup coarsely chopped fresh cilantro or flat-leaf parsley**
- 1 **pound fresh sausages (see note)**
- 2 **cups 3/4-inch cubes corn bread, toasted until golden brown (see note)**

serves 4

Build a fire in your grill and let it die down to medium. (You should be able to hold your hand about 5 inches above the grill rack for 4 or 5 seconds.)

To make the dressing: Meanwhile, in a large bowl, whisk together the olive oil, lime juice, chiles, cumin, and salt and pepper to taste.

tip

IF YOU LOVE the butteriness of avocados, you might want to try a trick we learned from the grill-meisters Schlesinger and Willoughby in *Let the Flames Begin.* Next time you set out to make guacamole, fire up the grill to medium. Cut ripe avocados in half and remove the pits, but leave the skins on. Rub the cut sides with olive oil and season generously with salt and pepper. Grill the avocados cut sides down until you see grill marks and the flesh is nicely softened, 3 to 4 minutes. Remove from the grill and as soon as the avocados are cool enough to handle, scoop the pulp into a bowl, mash it, and proceed with your favorite guacamole recipe. The guacamole will be even richer than usual, with a nice whiff of smokiness.

To make the salad: Add the tomatoes, avocado, onion, and cilantro or parsley to the dressing and toss gently to combine. Set aside.

Put the sausages on the grill and cook well, 5 to 8 minutes per side. To check for doneness, cut into one and peek to be sure it's cooked through, with no trace of pink inside. When the sausages are done, slice them neatly on the diagonal so they keep their shape.

Add the toasted corn bread to the salad and toss gently. Divide the salad among four plates, fan the sausage slices over the top, and serve.

notes from our test kitchen

- Choose whatever kind of sausage you favor, even chicken sausage, if you like. Avoid any super-spicy sausage, since the dressing carries enough Btu's on its own.
- To toast the corn bread, spread out the cubes on a baking sheet and bake at 325 to 350 degrees for about 10 minutes, turning once or twice.
- If you can't get outdoors to fire up the charcoal grill, you can certainly broil or pan-fry the sausages.

Main Dishes

Main Dishes

southwestern black bean burgers 98

pasta with asparagus lemon sauce 99

tagliatelle with crème fraîche and arugula 102

spaghetti with slow-roasted cherry tomatoes, basil, and
 parmesan cheese 105

rigatoni alla toto 107

cremini mushrooms with chive pasta 108

spaghettini with tuna sauce 110

tex-mex macaroni and cheese with green chiles 112

onion, bacon, and ricotta tart 114

spanish-style shrimp cooked in olive oil 117

shrimp and grits 118

crab cakes with scallions and jalapeños 121

sear-roasted salmon fillets with lemon ginger butter 124

mussels with smoky bacon, lime, and cilantro 126

stir-fried chicken with lime and coconut 129

garlicky baked chicken 130

chicken thighs baked with lemon, sage, rosemary, and thyme 133

zuni roast chicken with bread salad 136

southwestern black bean burgers

SOURCE *Good Housekeeping*

COOK Susan Westmoreland

This everyday recipe, modestly wedged into a section of *Good Housekeeping* magazine favorites, looked simple — downright plain. But there was just something about it . . .

It turned out the something was mayonnaise, a wonderful binding ingredient that adds a little richness and pulls the beans together into moist burgers. Another surprise is that the black burgers topped with vivid red salsa are gorgeous — we like them nude as much as we do tucked into pita breads. ❧

1 **15- to 19-ounce can black beans, rinsed and drained**

2 **tablespoons mayonnaise**

¼ **cup packed fresh cilantro leaves, chopped**

1 **tablespoon unseasoned fresh bread crumbs**

½ **teaspoon hot red pepper sauce, or more to taste**

½ **teaspoon ground cumin**

Salt and freshly ground black pepper

1 **cup loosely packed sliced lettuce**

4 **mini (4-inch) whole wheat pita breads, warmed**

½ **cup salsa, mild or hot (your choice)**

serves 4

In a large bowl, using a potato masher or fork, mash the beans with the mayonnaise until almost smooth; leave some lumps for texture. Stir in the cilantro, bread crumbs, hot pepper sauce, cumin, and salt and pepper to taste, mixing well.

With lightly floured hands, shape the bean mixture into four 3-inch burgers. Lightly spray both sides of each with non-stick cooking spray.

Heat a wide skillet over medium heat until hot. Add the burgers and cook until lightly browned on the bottom, about 3 minutes. Turn and cook for 3 minutes longer, or until heated through.

Divide the lettuce among the pitas, add a burger to each, top with salsa, and serve.

pasta with asparagus lemon sauce

SOURCE *Red, White and Greens* by Faith Willinger

COOK Faith Willinger

Here just five easy pieces come together magically to deliver a dish that's
much more than the sum of its parts.
You'll make this meal-in-a-bowl long
after your local asparagus season has
come and gone — though it's also the
perfect way to welcome the new crop.

Faith Willinger lives in Italy and
knows her pasta. She uses penne for
this dish, but *Gourmet*'s executive food
editor, Zanne Stewart, tried it with
mafalde — a sort of skinny lasagna
noodle — and liked it very much. ☙

1 **pound asparagus, tough ends trimmed**
  Salt
1 **teaspoon finely grated lemon zest**
1/4 **cup extra-virgin olive oil**
1 **pound penne, mafalde, or other pasta**
1/2 **cup freshly grated Parmigiano-Reggiano cheese**
  Freshly ground black pepper

serves 4

Cut the asparagus into 1-inch pieces, reserving the tips separately. Bring 5 to 6 quarts water to a boil, add 2 tablespoons
salt, and cook the asparagus stems until very tender, 6 to 8
minutes. Transfer with a slotted spoon to a colander, reserving the cooking water in the pot, and rinse under cold water.
Drain the asparagus well and transfer to a food processor or
blender.

Cook the asparagus tips in the same boiling water until just
tender, 3 to 5 minutes. Transfer with a slotted spoon to the
colander, reserving the boiling water in the pot, and rinse
under cold water. Drain the tips well.

Puree the asparagus stems with the lemon zest, oil, and 1/2
cup of the asparagus cooking water. Transfer to a large
saucepan.

Cook the pasta in the boiling asparagus cooking water until
it still offers considerable resistance to the tooth, about
three fourths of the recommended cooking time on the

best served in warm pasta bowls, and here's a neat tip from Carla Cimarosti, a *Fine Cooking* reader. When you drain pasta, put the serving bowl (or bowls) in the sink under the colander and fill with the hot pasta cooking water. The hot water will warm the bowl(s) while you finish the sauce. If you need to reserve some cooking water for the sauce, just measure it out before draining the pasta into the sink. There will be more than enough hot water for heating the bowls and finishing the sauce.

package. Reserve 2 cups of the cooking water and drain the pasta.

Add the pasta, asparagus tips, and $1/2$ cup of the reserved water to the asparagus sauce and cook over high heat, stirring, for 3 to 5 minutes, or until the pasta is almost al dente and the sauce coats the pasta. Add more cooking water, $1/4$ cup at a time, until the sauce coats the pasta but is a little loose (the cheese will thicken it slightly).

Stir in the cheese and salt and pepper to taste. Cook, stirring, until the cheese is melted. Serve immediately.

tagliatelle with crème fraîche and arugula

SOURCE *Italian Easy* by Rose Gray and Ruth Rogers
COOKS Rose Gray and Ruth Rogers

In the time it would take to extol the virtues of this remarkable recipe, you could nearly have dinner on the table. Aside from a little zesting (zip-zip with a Microplane zester) and squeezing a couple of lemons, there's really nothing to it. Stir together the lemon and crème fraîche, chop the arugula, cook the pasta, toss the whole thing together, top with cheese, and presto—a spectacular meal. The tart lemon balances the rich cream, the arugula adds freshness, and the resulting pasta is about as sexy and sublime as you could want dinner to be. This also makes an elegant first course for a multi-course dinner.

This streamlined recipe comes from the dynamic duo behind London's phenomenally successful River Café. Known for cooking with imagination and panache, Rose Gray and Ruth Rogers set out to show us that first-rate food doesn't have to be an ordeal to prepare. You'll hear no argument from us! ❧

Salt

2 lemons

5 ounces arugula leaves

5 ounces Parmesan cheese

1 cup crème fraîche

Freshly ground black pepper

1 pound fresh egg tagliatelle (see note)

serves about 4 (see note)

Bring a large pot of salted water to a boil.

Finely grate the lemon zest and squeeze the juice from both lemons. Coarsely chop the arugula. Grate the Parmesan.

Put the crème fraîche in a medium bowl, stir in the lemon juice and zest, and season with salt and pepper to taste.

Cook the tagliatelle in the boiling water until al dente. Drain and return to the pot. Pour the crème fraîche sauce over it and add the arugula and half the Parmesan. Toss to combine.

Serve immediately, dusting each serving with the remaining Parmesan.

notes from our test kitchen

- If you're serving this as a main course, expect 1 pound of fresh pasta to serve 4. As a starter course, it will serve 6.

- Tagliatelle are long, flat egg noodles. Imagine fettuccine, but a bit wider. Fresh tagliatelle can be hard to find. You have several options. You can make your own pasta or find another fresh pasta shape that you like — keeping in mind that wide, flat noodles are best for creamy sauces. Since traditional Italian dried pastas do not usually contain eggs (the Cipriani brand is an exception), you won't get the same silky texture using dried, but the dish will still be quite good. We sometimes make this recipe with one of those big bags of wide egg noodles and love the way it comes out.

spaghetti with slow-roasted cherry tomatoes, basil, and parmesan cheese

SOURCE *The Tomato Festival Cookbook* by Lawrence Davis-Hollander

COOK Jody Adams

Jody Adams, the award-winning chef-owner of Rialto restaurant in Cambridge, Massachusetts, and the author of *In the Hands of a Chef,* is best known for her forceful interpretations of traditional Mediterranean dishes. When we heard that this was one of her favorite meals to cook at home, we took note. Now that we've made it countless times ourselves, we can see why.

In the summer months, when local cherry tomatoes are at their peak, there's no better way to do them justice than by slow-roasting them. This highlights their natural sweetness and caramelizes their fresh juices. In the off-season, when all we can find are the ordinary supermarket variety, this technique transforms them into a rich-tasting, sweet tomato "sauce." Spaghetti and red sauce never looked or tasted so good. ❧

1/4 cup extra-virgin olive oil, plus more (about 1/4 cup) for roasting

1 large white onion, cut into 1/2-inch dice

6 garlic cloves, smashed and peeled

18 fresh basil leaves, plus 1/4 cup cut into thin ribbons (see note)

1/8 teaspoon crushed red pepper flakes

48 ripe cherry or grape tomatoes, rinsed and patted dry (see note)

3 teaspoons kosher salt

2 teaspoons sugar

1 pound spaghetti

2 cups loosely packed arugula (see note)

1/2 cup finely grated Parmesan cheese for serving

serves 4

Preheat the oven to 250 degrees.

Heat the 1/4 cup oil in a large skillet over medium heat. Add the onion and garlic and cook, stirring occasionally, until tender, about 5 minutes. Remove from the heat. Add the whole basil leaves and red pepper flakes and stir well.

Toss the tomatoes with 1 teaspoon of the salt and the sugar and place in a roasting pan. The pan should be large enough to hold them in a single layer (see note). If they won't fit, use another roasting pan and more oil. Spoon the onion mixture over the tomatoes. Add enough oil to come halfway up the tomatoes. Roast until the tomatoes are tender but not falling

tip

ACCORDING TO Anne Willan in *The Good Cook,* thinly slicing is better than chopping for leaves such as basil, arugula, and lettuce, because it's less likely to bruise them. Begin by separating the leaves from the stems (or from the head in the case of lettuce). Wash and dry them thoroughly. Then stack the leaves neatly and roll up the pile tightly — imagine rolling up a big fat cigar. Using a large chef's knife, slice across the roll to make fine or coarse strips. This technique creates what French chefs refer to as a *chiffonade.*

apart, about 3 hours. Stir once, gently, during the roasting. You can roast the tomatoes up to 6 hours ahead.

Bring a large pot of water with the remaining 2 teaspoons salt to a boil. Add the spaghetti and stir constantly until the water returns to a boil. Cook until the pasta is al dente, about 7 minutes.

Meanwhile, heat the tomatoes and onion in a large saucepan over low heat. When the pasta is done, drain and transfer to the saucepan with the tomatoes. Add the arugula. Toss well. Add the basil ribbons and toss again.

Serve immediately in warm shallow bowls with Parmesan sprinkled over the top.

notes from our test kitchen

- It's best to wait to cut the basil into thin ribbons until just before you're ready to add it to the sauce. Otherwise, it will darken (see tip).
- If you haven't bought a jar of crushed red pepper flakes in a while, add an extra pinch — the heat mellows over time.
- Since cherry and grape tomatoes vary quite a bit in size, the better way to measure is by volume: figure 2 heaping pints of tomatoes.
- If you can't find any good-tasting arugula, substitute baby spinach.
- Ideally, the roasting pan should accommodate the tomatoes in a relatively snug single layer. If they are spread too far apart, you'll need to add too much oil to come halfway up the sides of the tomatoes.

rigatoni alla toto

SOURCE *Rome, at Home* by Suzanne Dunaway
COOK Suzanne Dunaway

This is one of those miraculous recipes that appears somewhat plain on the page (nothing new about onion, sausage, basil, and cream), but one taste can absolutely make you swoon. We've yet to serve it when someone didn't plead for the recipe. It's one of those beautifully adaptable dishes that are quick enough for a weeknight yet elegant enough for your best company. Make it when you're craving something soothing and satisfying that won't tax you. While the creamy sauce simmers, you can have the salad made, the table set, and the wine uncorked.

By the way, it's not named after Dorothy's dog. Toto is an affordable trattoria in the center of Rome that turns out unassuming and delicious meals like this meaty pasta. 🐾

note from our test kitchen

Grind whole fennel seeds by crushing them with a mortar and pestle, or chop them on a cutting board with a large knife.

3 tablespoons extra-virgin olive oil

1 small onion, finely chopped

1 pound sweet Italian sausages, with or without fennel, casings removed

1 cup dry white wine

A few fresh basil leaves

Pinch of ground fennel seeds, if using plain sausage (see note)

1½ cups heavy cream

Salt

1 pound rigatoni

½ cup freshly grated Parmigiano-Reggiano cheese for serving

serves 4

Heat the oil in a large skillet over medium heat. Add the onion and cook until translucent, 3 to 4 minutes. Add the sausage and brown on all sides. Add the wine and cook for 1 minute. Add the basil, ground fennel (if using), and cream and simmer over low heat for about 20 minutes, or until the sausage is cooked through.

Meanwhile, bring a large pot of salted water to a boil. Cook the rigatoni in the boiling water until al dente. Drain well and toss with the sauce. Serve immediately with the Parmigiano-Reggiano sprinkled on top.

cremini mushrooms with chive pasta

SOURCE *High Heat* by Waldy Malouf and Melissa Clark
COOK Waldy Malouf

This pasta from Manhattan restaurateur Waldy Malouf is such a minimalist recipe that we nearly missed it. That would have been a huge mistake, because now it's one of our all-time favorites. At once earthy and fresh, it's easy to make, easy to serve, and easy to love. If you're going to be grilling something else, you can grill the mushrooms, or you can just roast them in the oven. The sauce is in-stant—a lot of chives blended with olive oil, salt, and pepper, and that's it.

More things to love about it: You can serve it as a light main course or as a memorable side. You can serve it hot or at room temperature. It can sit on a buffet for a couple of hours with no loss of flavor, unlike almost any other pasta we can think of. Oh, and it's vegetarian, too. 🌰

Coarse sea salt or kosher salt

1 pound cremini mushrooms, wiped clean and stem ends trimmed

½ cup plus 2 tablespoons extra-virgin olive oil

Freshly ground black pepper

1 cup roughly snipped fresh chives (2–3 bunches; see note)

1 pound spaghettini or angel hair pasta

Freshly grated pecorino Romano cheese for serving

serves 4 or more (see note)

Light the grill or preheat the oven to 500 degrees.

Bring a large pot of salted water to a boil for the pasta. Toss the mushrooms in a bowl with 2 tablespoons of the olive oil and generous pinches of salt and pepper.

To cook on the grill: Place the mushrooms in a grill basket. Grill, turning once, until tender and browned, about 8 min-utes. When cool enough to handle, cut the mushrooms into quarters.

To cook in the oven: Spread the mushrooms in a single layer on a rimmed baking sheet. Roast, turning once, until tender and browned, about 10 minutes. When cool enough to han-dle, cut the mushrooms into quarters.

In a food processor or blender, combine the remaining ½ cup olive oil, the chives, and generous pinches of salt and pepper. Process until pureed.

notes from our test kitchen

- This pasta is so simple and pure that it pays to use really good ingredients: imported pasta, estate-bottled olive oil, and a good pecorino Romano, such as Fulvi.

- You can substitute scallions for the chives if you must, but the flavor won't be as delicate.

- Obviously, the number of servings this makes depends on whether you serve it as a main course or side dish. For a main, expect to serve 3 or 4; for a side, closer to 6.

Cook the pasta until al dente. Drain, reserving 2 tablespoons of the cooking water if you plan to serve the pasta hot. In a large serving bowl, toss the pasta with the mushrooms and chive oil. If serving immediately, toss with 1 to 2 tablespoons of the reserved cooking water. Otherwise, let the pasta cool to room temperature. Serve with the cheese on the side.

spaghettini with tuna sauce

SOURCE *Boston Globe Magazine*   STORY BY Sheryl Julian and Julie Riven
COOK Daniele Baliani after his aunt Adriana

When a first-class chef like Daniele Baliani—who has worked in the kitchens of Daniel Boulud and Fauchon, among other prestigious places—treasures a hand-me-down recipe from his family, you know it's going to be good. Although we've seen several spaghettinis with tuna sauce, when we did a mini cook-off, this one was the clear winner. It's just a little spicy, with bursts of surprising flavor. In winter, you can use little cherry tomatoes (don't bother peeling them).

Except for some fresh tomatoes and parsley, everything here is more or less a staple, so you can make this dish on the spur of the moment. It's served at room temperature, and the balance of flavors is truly remarkable. No cheese, please. ❧

1	**tablespoon salt**
¼	**cup olive oil**
2	**tablespoons pine nuts**
2	**garlic cloves, finely chopped**
3–4	**anchovy fillets, preferably white (see note)**
1	**teaspoon capers, coarsely chopped**
1	**teaspoon crushed red pepper flakes**
1	**28-ounce can whole peeled tomatoes, crushed in a bowl, with their juice**
4	**vine-ripened tomatoes, cored, peeled, and finely chopped**
1	**6- to 8-ounce can Italian tuna in olive oil, partially drained**
¼	**cup golden raisins**
1	**pound spaghettini**
¼	**cup chopped fresh parsley**
	Freshly ground black pepper

serves 4 to 6

Bring a large pot of water to a boil and add the salt.

Meanwhile, in a large flameproof casserole, heat the oil over medium heat. Cook the pine nuts, stirring frequently, for 2 minutes, or until light golden brown. Add the garlic, anchovies, capers, and red pepper flakes. Cook, stirring often, for 2 minutes, breaking up the anchovies as you stir. Add the canned and fresh tomatoes and bring to a boil, stirring occasionally. Reduce the heat to low and simmer, stirring occasionally, for 30 minutes, or until the sauce thickens.

notes from our test kitchen

- White anchovies are lightly cured and marinated in white wine vinegar. Unlike the flat, brown, heavily salted anchovies that we're used to, white anchovies remain plump and tender and have a delicate flavor. Until recently, you had to be a chef to find these sweet-tasting fillets, but more and more you can find them in the refrigerator case at specialty food markets. And of course you can use ordinary anchovies — look for the ones packed in extra-virgin olive oil and in small jars, which are likely to be of higher quality than the tinned ones.

- Good canned tomatoes, either Italian tomatoes from the San Marzano region or Muir Glen organic tomatoes, are crucial, as is a good artisanal pasta, such as Latini.

- Don't substitute water-packed tuna. Two good brands of Italian tuna are Progresso and Genoa.

Stir the tuna and raisins into the sauce. Break up the tuna into small pieces as you stir. Return the sauce to a simmer, then remove from the heat and set aside.

Meanwhile, add the spaghettini to the boiling water and return to a full boil, stirring. Cook for 6 minutes, or until not quite cooked through.

Drain the pasta in a colander and immediately transfer to the sauce. Add the parsley and pepper to taste. Toss well to coat the spaghettini. Let cool and serve at room temperature.

tex-mex macaroni and cheese with green chiles

❊

SOURCE *Fine Cooking*

COOK Robert Del Grande

Leave it to a Texan to elevate homey macaroni and cheese to a blockbuster dish with a serious kick. Robert Del Grande, the executive chef and partner at Café Annie and Café Express in Houston, explains that comfort food in Texas means cheese and chiles. It also means corn tortillas. So his version of macaroni and cheese combines roasted poblanos, toasted white corn tortillas, fresh cilantro, and, of course, elbow macaroni. And to provide the right amount of creaminess, the casserole is bound together with a savory custard of eggs and half-and-half.

Del Grande warns us that poblanos can vary in heat: smaller, darker ones can sometimes be spicier. If your nose stings when you handle the chiles, or if the raw chiles taste wildly spicy when you touch them to your tongue, use fewer. ❧

About 1 tablespoon softened butter for the baking dish

1 **pound poblano chiles (4–6 chiles)**

   Olive oil for rubbing

6 **white corn tortillas**

1 **cup fresh cilantro leaves**

2 **cups half-and-half**

3 **large eggs**

   Kosher salt and freshly ground black pepper

8 **ounces elbow macaroni**

8 **ounces Monterey Jack cheese, grated**

8 **ounces sharp cheddar cheese, grated**

serves 4 to 6

Put a large pot of water on to boil. Butter a shallow 2- to 3-quart baking dish. Preheat the broiler.

Rub the poblanos lightly with olive oil and arrange them on a baking sheet lined with foil. Broil the peppers as close to the element as possible, turning as needed, until the skins are blackened all over. Transfer to a bowl, cover with plastic wrap, and let cool to room temperature.

Turn off the broiler and preheat the oven to 350 degrees.

Remove and discard the charred poblano skins, along with the stems and seeds. Chop the chiles coarsely and put them in a food processor. In a hot, dry skillet over medium-high heat, lightly toast the tortillas until they're just softened and give off a toasted-corn aroma, 30 to 60 seconds per side (don't let them become crisp). Coarsely chop the tortillas and add them to the chiles in the food processor. Add the cilantro leaves and pulse until finely chopped but not pureed.

In a large bowl, whisk together the half-and-half, eggs, and salt and pepper to taste until well combined. Stir in the chopped chile mixture.

When the water boils, salt it generously and cook the macaroni until al dente. Drain well, shaking to eliminate any excess water. Add the pasta to the egg mixture along with two thirds of the grated cheeses. Stir to combine. Pour the mixture into the buttered dish. Scatter the remaining cheeses evenly over the macaroni. (If baking in a 2-quart dish, set it on a baking sheet to catch any drips.)

Bake until browned and bubbling, about 40 minutes. If you want to brown the center more, flash it briefly under the broiler. Let sit for 10 minutes before serving.

onion, bacon, and ricotta tart

***

SOURCE *Sunday Suppers at Lucques* by Suzanne Goin and Teri Gelber

COOK Suzanne Goin

This opulent tart is Los Angeles chef Suzanne Goin's interpretation of an Alsatian specialty, *Flammeküche*. We can't imagine anything better—flaky pastry topped first with a creamy layer of ricotta and crème fraîche, then a nicely gooey bit of melted cheese, and finally a mixture of smoky bacon and thyme-scented onions.

Accompanied by the herb salad, the tart makes a fine light supper. We also serve it as a starter—cut into small squares and passed with cocktails, or cut into larger pieces as a sit-down first course. Either way, it's perfect for entertaining because you can assemble it in the morning, cover and refrigerate it, and then bake it just before you're ready to serve. ☙

tip

SUZANNE GOIN recommends looking in the freezer section of the grocery store for a good, all-butter brand of puff pastry. She advises making sure the pastry is partially defrosted before you attempt to unroll or unfold the sheets. Puff pastry bakes best when very cold or frozen, so in between the steps of assembling the tart, return the pastry to the freezer for 5 to 10 minutes. This will ensure a good crust with flaky, delicate layers.

1 sheet frozen all-butter puff pastry ($9^{1}/_{2}$ x $9^{1}/_{2}$ inches or 8 x 12 inches)

2 extra-large egg yolks (see note)

8 ounces slab bacon, preferably apple wood smoked (see note)

2 tablespoons extra-virgin olive oil

2 cups sliced young onions, red and white if possible, plus $^{1}/_{2}$ cup diagonally sliced young onion tops or scallions (see note)

1 tablespoon fresh thyme leaves

Kosher salt

$^{1}/_{2}$ cup whole-milk ricotta, drained if wet

$^{1}/_{4}$ cup crème fraîche

Freshly ground black pepper

$^{1}/_{3}$ pound Cantal, Gruyère, or Comté cheese, thinly sliced

Herb Salad (recipe follows)

serves 6

Preheat the oven to 400 degrees.

Defrost the puff pastry slightly, then unroll or unfold it onto a parchment-lined baking sheet. Use a paring knife to score a $^{1}/_{4}$-inch border around the edge of the pastry. Make an egg wash by whisking 1 of the egg yolks with $^{1}/_{2}$ teaspoon water and brush the egg wash along the border (see note). You will not need all of the egg wash. Return the puff pastry to the freezer until you're ready to use it.

Cut the bacon into $^{3}/_{8}$-inch-thick slices. Stack the slices in two piles, then cut the bacon crosswise into $^{3}/_{8}$-inch even-sided rectangles, or lardons.

notes from our test kitchen

- Since we tend to stock large (not extra-large) eggs in our fridges, that's what we used here—with success.

- If your market doesn't carry slab bacon, just buy the best, thickest-cut bacon you can find and cut the slices crosswise into ⅜-inch pieces. Cheap bacon will make the tart greasy.

- We've made this tart using thinly sliced red onions, sweet onions, and even regular old cooking onions, and each time we've loved the results. For the young onion tops, just use scallions (or green onions, as they're known in the west).

- If you're looking for shortcuts, skip the first egg yolk and the egg wash. There's so much topping on this tart that you barely notice the sheen. Don't, however, skip scoring the edge with a paring knife. This helps the pastry rise. You can also skip the food processor. Instead, briskly whisk the ricotta, egg yolk, and olive oil together.

Heat a large sauté pan over high heat for 2 minutes. Add 1 tablespoon of the olive oil and heat for 1 minute more. Add the bacon and sauté over medium-high heat for 4 to 5 minutes, until slightly crisp but still tender. Reduce the heat to low and toss in the young onions, thyme, and ½ teaspoon salt. Stir together for 1 to 2 minutes, or until the onions are just wilted. Toss in the onion tops and transfer to a baking sheet or platter to cool.

Place the ricotta, remaining egg yolk, and remaining 1 tablespoon olive oil in a food processor. Puree until smooth, then transfer to a medium bowl. Gently fold in the crème fraîche and season with ⅛ teaspoon salt and a pinch of pepper.

Spread the ricotta mixture on the puff pastry within the scored border. Lay the sliced cheese over the ricotta and arrange the bacon-onion mixture on top. The tart can be prepared up to this point, covered, and refrigerated for up to 8 hours.

Bake the tart, rotating the baking sheet once, for 20 to 25 minutes, or until the cheese is bubbling and the crust is golden brown. Lift up the edge of the tart and peek underneath to make sure the crust is cooked through. (If you underbake the tart, it will be soggy.)

Meanwhile, make the herb salad.

Let the tart cool for a few minutes, then serve it from a cutting board, along with the salad. To serve individual portions, cut the tart into 6 pieces and garnish each with a little salad.

If you can't find a variety of fresh herbs,
use a mix of sharp-tasting salad greens.

herb salad

✳

1/2 **cup fresh flat-leaf parsley leaves**

1/4 **cup fresh tarragon leaves**

1/4 **cup fresh chervil leaves**

1/4 **cup 1/2-inch snipped fresh chives**

Kosher salt and freshly ground black pepper

Super-good extra-virgin olive oil for drizzling

1/2 **lemon**

Toss the herbs in a small bowl with salt and pepper to taste,
a drizzle of olive oil, and a squeeze of lemon juice.

spanish-style shrimp cooked in olive oil

SOURCE *New York Times*

COOK Mark Bittman

High-profile cook Mark Bittman is famous for his omnibus *How to Cook Everything*, for his "Minimalist" column in the *New York Times* (the source of this recipe), and for bringing the genius of chef Jean-Georges Vongerichten to home cooks via the cookbooks that Bittman writes. But possibly he should be best known as the creator of this wonderful recipe.

The shrimp are cooked in olive oil, with meltingly soft garlic and—the secret ingredients—cumin and paprika, the same spices that perfume North African *charmoula*.

It's essential to serve lots of bread with the dish, since the cooking liquid might just be the best part. Bittman recommends using Pacific or Gulf white shrimp. Black tiger shrimp aren't as tasty, but you can use them if you can't find anything else. ❧

tip

FOR TASTIER SHRIMP, give them a little salt rub, says Greek cook Eva Poulos in the *Washington Post*. Just peel and devein the shrimp, rinse, and gently rub with sea salt for a few seconds. Place the shrimp in a colander and rinse well. Don't worry—they won't taste salty.

¹⁄₃ **cup extra-virgin olive oil**

3–4 **large garlic cloves, cut into thin slivers**

1 **teaspoon ground cumin, or to taste**

1 **teaspoon paprika, or to taste**

2 **pounds shrimp (15–20 per pound; see note)**

Salt and freshly ground black pepper

¹⁄₄ **cup chopped fresh parsley**

serves 6

Combine the oil and garlic in a 10- to 12-inch skillet. Turn the heat to medium and cook until the garlic begins to sizzle. Add the cumin and paprika and stir. Raise the heat to medium-high and add the shrimp. Season with salt and pepper to taste.

Cook, stirring occasionally, until the shrimp are all just pink; do not evaporate the liquid. Turn off the heat, add the parsley, and serve.

notes from our test kitchen

- For guests, consider peeling the shrimp first. You won't lose much flavor, and unless you're serving a messy casual feast, peeling the shrimp is the kind thing to do.

- Two pounds of shrimp won't fit in one skillet, so you'll need two skillets unless you're cutting the recipe in half.

- To get a little crust on peeled shrimp, run the skillets (make sure they're ovenproof) under the broiler on the rack closest to the heat —just long enough to crisp the shrimp a bit on each side.

- For a scampi version, leave out the cumin and paprika and add lemon juice to taste at the last minute.

shrimp and grits

SOURCE *Bill Neal's Southern Cooking* by Bill Neal

COOK Bill Neal

Oh, my, here it is: the best shrimp and grits thing we know—and it's right off the back of a bag of grits. Both the grits and the cook—the late Bill Neal—have a pedigree. The grits are ground to the specifications of Crook's Corner, an institution in Chapel Hill where the legendary Neal perfected the classic southern dishes that made him famous.

For many Southerners, this Low-country breakfast classic would be nominated for their last meal; for others, it would probably be up there in the top ten choices of what to have for dinner. ✎

grits

- 4 cups water
- 1 cup grits
- 1/2 teaspoon salt
- 2 tablespoons butter
- 1 cup grated sharp cheddar cheese (4 ounces)
- 1/2 cup freshly grated Parmesan cheese (2 ounces)
  Freshly ground white pepper, cayenne pepper, and nutmeg (preferably freshly grated)

shrimp

- 6 slices bacon, cut into small pieces
  Peanut oil for frying
- 1 pound shrimp, peeled, deveined if desired, rinsed, and patted dry
- 2 cups wiped clean and sliced mushrooms
- 1 cup sliced scallions
- 1 large garlic clove, crushed
- 4 teaspoons fresh lemon juice
  Hot red pepper sauce to taste
  Salt and freshly ground black pepper
- 1/2 cup chopped fresh parsley

serves 4

To make the grits: Bring the water to a boil in a large heavy saucepan. Slowly stir in the grits, reduce the heat, and cook, stirring frequently, for about 20 minutes, or until they are thick and tender. Stir in the salt, butter, and cheeses. Add a

note from our test kitchen

Fresh stone-ground grits are the best—they have more taste and character. But stone-ground grits that have been sitting in a fancy food shop for two years (and you won't know—packages aren't dated) will not only taste stale but probably harbor weevils. If in doubt, order the Crook's Grits from A Southern Season: southernseason.com or (800) 253-3663. Store your grits in the freezer, where they'll keep for a long time.

pinch each of the white pepper, cayenne, and nutmeg, or to taste.

To make the shrimp: Meanwhile, in a large skillet, cook the bacon until browned at the edges. Remove with a slotted spoon, drain on paper towels, and set aside.

Add enough peanut oil to the bacon fat in the skillet to make a thin layer of fat. Heat over medium-high heat until the fat is quite hot. Add the shrimp and stir, then add the mushrooms and stir well. Cook until the shrimp start to color, then add the scallions, bacon, and garlic. Season with the lemon juice, hot pepper sauce, and salt and pepper to taste. Sprinkle with the parsley.

Divide the grits among four warm plates. Spoon the shrimp over the grits and serve immediately.

crab cakes with scallions and jalapeños

❋

SOURCE *New York Times Magazine*

COOK Jason Epstein

The original title for this recipe was Jason's Best Ever — a claim that usually sends us running in the other direction, but these crab cakes sounded so good that we had to give them a try. And it's true — these *are* the best we've ever tasted (and we've tasted a lot). We've even converted die-hard fans of Old Bay–seasoned crab cakes with this recipe.

They are extravagant in every way (starting with the high price of the crab), and they're incredibly rich with butter and cream. The piquant jalapeños and delicate scallions are terrific together — even better because they're gently sautéed in (what else?) butter. But the truly brilliant thing here is using the bread crumbs only on the outside of the crab cakes — none inside to muffle the flavors and gum up the crab.

You need to refrigerate the crab cakes for 2 hours before cooking, so be sure to allow time for that. ❧

12 **tablespoons (1½ sticks) unsalted butter, plus 1–2 tablespoons for sautéing the crab cakes, or more if needed**

1 **cup finely chopped scallions, including some of the firm greens**

½ **cup finely chopped jalapeño peppers (see note and tip)**

¾ **cup heavy cream**

2 **teaspoons dry mustard**

Cayenne pepper

2 **pounds jumbo lump crabmeat, drained well, patted dry, and picked over for cartilage and shell bits**

2 **large eggs**

2 **cups fresh white bread crumbs**

1–2 **tablespoons vegetable oil, or more if needed**

serves 6

In a large skillet, melt the 1½ sticks butter over medium-high heat. Sauté the scallions and jalapeños for about 2 minutes, or until bright green. Add the cream and bring to a boil. Reduce the heat to medium and cook, stirring, for 3 to 4 minutes, or until thickened. Remove from the heat and stir in the mustard and a pinch of cayenne. Let cool for 5 minutes.

In a large bowl, gently stir together the crabmeat and scallion mixture. Form uniform cakes by placing spoonfuls of the crab mixture on a baking sheet (see note). Immediately place in the refrigerator for about 2 hours to firm up.

When ready to serve, beat the eggs in a shallow bowl and place the bread crumbs in a separate shallow bowl. In a large skillet, heat the remaining 1 to 2 tablespoons butter and the vegetable oil over medium heat (you want enough fat to generously coat the skillet). Working with half the crab cakes at a time (keep the rest in the refrigerator), dip each cake into the beaten eggs and then coat with the bread crumbs. Sauté the crab cakes until browned, 2 to 3 minutes per side, turning only once, or they will break. Repeat with the remaining crab cakes, adding more butter and oil if needed. Drain on paper towels and serve immediately.

notes from our test kitchen

- It's best to remove the seeds from the jalapeños before chopping.
- A little salt may brighten the flavors. Cook a bit of the crab mixture before forming the cakes to see if it needs salt.
- When spooning the mixture onto the baking sheet to shape the crab cakes, avoid making the cakes too fat. Use the spoon or your fingers to shape them, keeping in mind that they will cook more evenly if they have a flatter, patty shape.
- Your guests may want some lemon wedges to squeeze over the crab cakes, but taste them without first. Or consider a spritz of lime instead.
- Miniature crab cakes are great cocktail party fare. The cooking time is just slightly less for little crab cakes.

sear-roasted salmon fillets with lemon ginger butter

SOURCE *Fine Cooking's Quick and Delicious Recipes*

COOK Isabelle Alexandre

When this recipe appeared in *Fine Cooking* in the 1990s, we immediately added it to our repertoire. So we were thrilled — and not the least bit astonished — to see it reappear years later as part of the magazine's 101 favorite quick recipes. Sear-roasting is one of those great restaurant tricks that works well at home. You quickly brown the fish on one side in a skillet on the stove and then slide it into the oven to finish cooking. The initial searing produces a delicate crust on the outside, and the enveloping blast of high heat from the oven cooks the fish through without drying it out or creating a heavy crust. The fish comes out perfectly done — crisp and golden on the outside, moist on the inside.

The accompanying compound butter melts onto the warm fish, making an instant lemon ginger sauce. We sometimes play around with this formula, substituting orange for the lemon, shallots for the ginger, and fresh thyme for the chives. Feel free to create your own salmon-friendly combinations. ❧

6 tablespoons (³⁄₄ stick) unsalted butter, softened

2 tablespoons fresh lemon juice, warmed slightly (see note)

2 tablespoons peeled, minced fresh ginger

2 tablespoons snipped fresh chives

Olive oil for searing

4 salmon fillets (5 ounces each), skinned if you like, patted dry

Kosher salt and freshly ground black pepper

serves 4

In a small bowl, stir together the butter, lemon juice, ginger, and chives until well blended. Set aside at room temperature.

Preheat the oven to 500 degrees.

Set a large ovenproof skillet over medium-high heat and add just enough oil to make a light film. Sprinkle the salmon lightly with salt and pepper. When the oil is very hot, add the salmon, skin side up, and cook until nicely browned, about 1 minute. Flip the fish over and immediately put the skillet in the oven. Roast for 2 minutes for medium-rare, 4 minutes for medium–well done. Check for doneness with the tip of a knife.

To serve, remove the pan from the oven, transfer the fish to serving plates, and top with a dab of lemon ginger butter.

notes from our
test kitchen

- Warming the lemon juice before adding it to the butter makes it easier to mix in, but don't get the liquid boiling hot, or it will melt the butter. A quick blast in the microwave is all you need.

- We like to let the salmon fillets sit at room temperature for 15 to 20 minutes before cooking. They seem to sear better when not ice-cold. Just be sure to pat them dry immediately before searing. Moisture will interfere with the browning.

- Any leftover lemon ginger butter can be wrapped in plastic and kept for days in the refrigerator or for weeks in the freezer.

tip

ANOTHER GREAT WAY to cook salmon is the low-heat way. James O'Shea, co-owner of the West Street Grill in Litchfield, Connecticut, sets the oven to 250 degrees and has his salmon fillet at room temperature. He places it skin side down on a foil-lined baking sheet, brushes the flesh side lightly with olive oil, and adds a thatch of minced chives plus some salt and white pepper. Then he cooks the salmon for exactly 17 minutes. This method delivers moist, delicate salmon with no fishy cooking odor. When you slide the salmon off the foil, the skin stays behind.

If you slow-cook salmon without the chives on top, when it's done, it may have patches of white albumin (the protein that's in egg whites) on top. Just wipe it away with a paper towel before serving.

O'Shea also has a clever trick to make farm-raised salmon taste more like its wild cousins. He wraps it in dried kelp (available in natural food stores) — which is a bit like wrapping it in newspaper — and leaves it overnight in the refrigerator under a small weight, such as a full carton of eggs. The briny flavor of the sea goes right into the fish. He then discards the kelp and lets the salmon come to room temperature before cooking it.

mussels with smoky bacon, lime, and cilantro

SOURCE *Food & Wine*

COOK Michael Romano

Our testing notes for this recipe start with one word: *Killer!* Perhaps it's the combination of smoked bacon and jalapeño. Or maybe it's the little bit of ketchup, or the butter, lime juice, and cilantro swirled into the sauce at the end.

If your only experience with mussels has been the standard version steamed in white wine with shallots, you owe it to yourself to try this bold version from Michael Romano, the chef and co-owner at Union Square Cafe in New York City. It will be a revelation. And don't forgo the crusty bread, because you really will want to mop up every bit of juice. ❧

4 ounces thick-sliced lean smoked bacon, cut into $1/2$-inch pieces (see note)

2 large shallots, thinly sliced

1 large jalapeño pepper, thinly sliced into rings, seeds removed (see tip)

Salt and freshly ground black pepper

8 ounces plum tomatoes, coarsely chopped (see note)

$1/2$ cup dry white wine

2 tablespoons ketchup

$3^{1}/2$ pounds medium mussels, scrubbed and debearded

2 tablespoons fresh lime juice

$1/4$ cup chopped fresh cilantro

2 tablespoons unsalted butter

Crusty bread for serving

serves 4

Cook the bacon in a large enameled cast-iron Dutch oven over medium heat until crisp, about 8 minutes. Pour off all but 2 tablespoons of the fat. Add the shallots and jalapeño and season with salt and pepper to taste. Cook, stirring occasionally, until softened but not browned, about 4 minutes. Add the tomatoes and cook for 3 minutes. Add the wine and ketchup and simmer until reduced by half, about 4 minutes.

Increase the heat to high and add the mussels. Cover and cook, shaking the pan a few times, until the mussels

tip

IN *LEMONGRASS AND LIME,* London-based chef Mark Read explains how to remove the seeds from a skinny chile without cutting into it, so you can cut it into thin rings. Cut off the top and the tail, then rub the chile between your palms. The seeds will fall out, and any remaining seeds can be removed easily from the rings.

open, about 5 minutes. Discard any mussels that don't open.

With a slotted spoon, transfer the mussels to four large shallow serving bowls. Remove the Dutch oven from the heat and stir in the lime juice, cilantro, and butter. Ladle the sauce over the mussels and serve at once with the bread.

notes from our test kitchen

- Look for a thick-cut smoked bacon with a good bit of lean. It will make a difference. This recipe was developed using smoked bacon from Niman Ranch, a top-quality producer of natural, hormone-free pork products: nimanranch.com or (866) 808-0340.

- If fresh tomatoes are out of season, substitute one 14-ounce can whole peeled tomatoes, drained.

- For the freshest mussels, don't debeard until immediately before you plan to cook them. To do so, grab the thin wiry threads (or beards) that extend from the shell and yank or cut them off with a small knife. Some farm-raised mussels will have only the thinnest beards, which take no force at all to remove.

- If you don't have a large enameled cast-iron Dutch oven, use a stainless steel or other nonreactive pot with a tight cover.

stir-fried chicken with lime and coconut

※

SOURCE *How to Cook* by Delia Smith

COOK Delia Smith

The cheery British cook Delia Smith has become a TV household presence in America, where fans of her reliably delicious food are legion. Her books are full of wonders such as "toad in the hole" and "bubble and squeak," but we passed those by in favor of this startlingly uncomplicated work-night supper that we return to again and again. Smith manages to capture the haunting flavors of Southeast Asian cuisine in a format so simple it amazes us every time.

Although the quantities are calibrated for two diners, you can easily double the recipe—just use two pans. ☙

2 **boneless, skinless chicken breast halves, preferably free-range**

Grated zest and juice of 1 large lime

2 **teaspoons olive oil**

1 **hot green chile, seeded and finely chopped**

2/3 **cup canned unsweetened coconut milk, well stirred**

2 **teaspoons fish sauce (nam pla)**

4 **scallions, cut into 1-inch shreds (including the greens)**

6 **tablespoons chopped fresh cilantro**

Cooked jasmine rice for serving

serves 2

Cut the chicken into bite-size pieces. In a medium bowl, combine the chicken and lime zest and juice. Stir well and let marinate for 1 hour.

In a wok or large skillet, heat the oil over high heat. Add the chicken and stir-fry for 3 to 4 minutes, or until golden. Add the chile and stir-fry for 1 minute more. Add the coconut milk, fish sauce, half the scallions, and 3 tablespoons of the cilantro. Cook for 1 to 2 minutes more. Serve with the rice, sprinkling the remaining scallions and 3 tablespoons cilantro over the top.

garlicky baked chicken

SOURCE *Sara Moulton Cooks at Home* by Sara Moulton

COOK Sara Moulton after Jean Anderson

When we first discovered this super-simple, incredibly fragrant crunchy chicken recipe back in 2000, we had no idea it had a long pedigree. It debuted in the *Ladies' Home Journal* in 1959, when cookbook author Jean Anderson was among the staff recipe developers. Over the years Anderson tweaked it in several published versions and shared the recipe with Sara Moulton (of TVFN and *Gourmet* magazine fame). Moulton made her own changes, more than once (see note). The *Best American* version, found on New York food critic Arthur Schwartz's Web site, is Sara's original (more garlic, more cheese, less butter), which was wildly popular on TVFN. This is a minimalist version; at times the recipe has included herbs (fresh parsley, plus thyme or sage) and chopped pecans—all good. It just goes to show that a great recipe always works, however much you play with the elements. ❧

8 **tablespoons (1 stick) butter**

4 **garlic cloves, chopped**

2 **cups fresh bread crumbs, from about 6 slices of day-old firm-textured white bread**

1 **teaspoon kosher salt**

1/2 **teaspoon freshly ground black pepper**

1 **cup freshly grated Parmesan cheese**

8 **chicken thighs or 4 bone-in single chicken breast halves with skin (cut in half if very large)**

serves 4

Preheat the oven to 350 degrees.

In a small saucepan, melt the butter with the garlic and pour it into a shallow bowl.

In a pie plate or shallow bowl, mix the bread crumbs with the salt, pepper, and cheese.

Dip the chicken pieces one at a time into the garlic butter, coating them well on all sides. Then dip them into the bread crumb mixture, patting the crumbs on so the coating is thick.

Place the chicken pieces skin side up in a shallow baking pan and pat on any remaining bread crumb mixture. Drizzle any remaining garlic butter over the chicken.

Bake the chicken for 50 minutes to 1 hour, or until crisp and golden brown. Serve hot or at room temperature.

tip

FOR THE CRISPEST chicken, bake the bird on a rack in a roasting pan. The quality of chicken you use will make a difference, too. Regular supermarket chicken will give off a fair amount of water, which may make the bottoms of the pieces soggy. For best results, look for organic, free-range chicken from a reliable supplier.

notes from our test kitchen

- For Sara Moulton's latest version of the chicken, cut up a 3½-pound chicken into 8 to 10 pieces. Use 1½ sticks (12 tablespoons) of butter, 3 garlic cloves, and ½ cup grated Parmesan cheese; other ingredients remain the same.

- Although it's not our favorite cut, you can use skinless, boneless chicken breasts here, too – check for doneness after 40 minutes in the oven.

- You don't need us to tell you how to speed things along by melting the butter and garlic together in the microwave and grinding pieces of bread into crumbs in the food processor.

chicken thighs baked
with lemon, sage, rosemary, and thyme

SOURCE *Fine Cooking*

COOK Bill Devin

Bill Devin was a California transplant to Tarragona, Spain, where he spent his time finding great ingredients and local products for export to other countries. Sadly, Bill passed away much too early, but we are thankful that he left behind this great recipe — his take on the excellent Catalan rotisserie chicken, which is stuffed with lemon wedges and herbs and turned on a spit. The trick Devin came up with eliminates the need for a real rotisserie. Instead, you roast chicken thighs on little thrones of lemon slices and herbs, and the meat becomes fully infused with citrus-herb flavor. *Allioli* — the classic Spanish garlicky sauce — rubbed under the skin before cooking does two things: it separates the skin from the meat so the skin gets super-crisp (the high oven temperature helps, too), and it adds a wallop of garlic flavor. ☙

allioli

2 large garlic cloves

Kosher or sea salt

3–4 tablespoons extra-virgin olive oil

chicken

12 chicken thighs, trimmed of fat, rinsed, and patted dry (see note)

2 large lemons, each cut into six $\frac{1}{4}$-inch-thick rounds

1 bunch fresh rosemary, snipped into twelve 2-inch pieces

1 bunch fresh thyme, snipped into twelve 2-inch pieces

12 fresh sage leaves

Salt and freshly ground black pepper

serves 6

To make the allioli: Using a mortar and pestle (or a small mixing bowl and the back of a spoon), mash the garlic with a large pinch of salt to create a coarse paste. (Or mince the garlic very finely on a cutting board.) Add the oil very slowly in drops while pounding and grinding the paste until the *allioli* is thick, creamy, and emulsified.

To make the chicken: Put the chicken in a large bowl. Rub the *allioli* all over, including under the skin. Cover and refrigerate for at least 2 hours or overnight.

notes from our test kitchen

- These are skin-on, bone-in chicken thighs. Boneless and/or skinless just won't do.
- Be sure to really smash the garlic to a paste when making the *allioli;* otherwise it won't emulsify. A mortar and pestle is definitely the best option.
- It may look as if you don't have enough *allioli,* but trust us, it's potent and goes a long way.

Preheat the oven to 425 degrees and set a rack in the middle level.

Arrange the lemon slices in a single layer in a large shallow roasting pan or a 9-x-13-inch baking dish. Top each slice with a piece of rosemary, a piece of thyme, and a sage leaf. Place the chicken thighs skin side up on top; sprinkle generously with salt and pepper. Bake until the skin is golden and the juices run clear, 45 to 60 minutes.

Sometimes the lemon slices and chicken produce a lot of juices, in which case you can make a delicious pan sauce. Transfer the chicken (keeping the herbs and lemon slices underneath) to a plate and cover loosely with aluminum foil. Tilt the pan to pool the juices in one corner. Spoon off the fat that rises to the top. Set the pan over medium heat (if the pan isn't flameproof, pour the juices into a small skillet) and scrape up any stuck-on bits. Let the juices boil and reduce so they thicken to a sauce. To maintain the bird's crisp skin, drizzle the sauce around, not on, the chicken. Serve the chicken pieces sitting on their beds of lemon and herbs.

zuni roast chicken with bread salad

zuni roast chicken with bread salad

❋

SOURCE *The Zuni Café Cookbook* by Judy Rodgers

COOK Judy Rodgers

Among the cognoscenti in the food world, there are two acknowledged great roast chickens: Marcella Hazan's chicken stuffed with lemons and this succulent presalted, preseasoned chicken from Judy Rodgers's Zuni Cafe in San Francisco.

Chef Rodgers cooks her bird in the restaurant's brick oven, but the recipe also works in a home oven. At the restaurant, the chicken is cut up and nestled in a bread salad made with currants and pine nuts that's just about perfect. But even if you don't make the bread salad, this is a sensational way to roast a chicken. As a bonus, you can season the bird up to 2 days ahead and then roast it just before serving. In fact, you should start at least the day before for the best flavor. ❧

1 $2^3/_4$- to 3-pound chicken

4 thumbnail-size thyme, marjoram, rosemary, or sage sprigs

4 small garlic cloves, slightly crushed and peeled

$2^1/_2$ teaspoons salt

Freshly ground black pepper

Bread Salad (recipe follows)

serves 4

Pat the chicken dry inside and out. Slide your fingers between the skin and meat of each of the breasts and the thighs and tuck an herb sprig and a garlic clove into each pocket. Sprinkle the chicken all over with the salt and pepper, sprinkling a little of the salt just inside the cavity on the backbone. Refrigerate the chicken (uncovered for a really crisp skin) for at least 1 day or up to 2 days.

About 2 hours before you plan to serve the chicken, remove it from the refrigerator to let it come to room temperature and start preparing the bread salad.

Preheat the oven to 500 degrees and set a rack in the lower-middle level.

Place a shallow roasting pan (or an ovenproof skillet with a shallow, flared edge) that is just large enough to hold the chicken on a stovetop burner and heat until hot. Meanwhile, pat the back of the chicken dry with paper towels. When the skillet is very hot, place the bird in the skillet, breast side up; it will sizzle. Place the skillet with the bird in the oven and roast until it begins to brown, about 25 minutes. If it

MOST AMERICAN poultry recipes begin like this one: "Rinse the chicken [or duck or turkey]." But a growing number of experts, including the food science guru Harold McGee, believe that rinsing spreads bacteria all over the place, whereas cooking destroys it. Journalist Kim Severson, writing in the *New York Times,* reported that Linda Harris, a microbiologist at the University of California at Davis, and other microbiologists have been trying to get American cooks to stop rinsing poultry since the 1990s. Jacques Pépin agrees, maintaining that rinsing washes away some of the flavor. For the best skin and flavor, McGee says, the bird should be patted dry and then air-dried, uncovered, in the fridge, ideally for a couple of days. The flavor argument is usually the one that convinces us, and we don't mind skipping an unnecessary step.

hasn't browned in that time, raise the oven rack; if it's starting to char, lower the rack.

After the chicken has been in the oven for 35 minutes, turn it over and roast, breast side down, for another 15 minutes. Then flip it back over to finish roasting, breast side up, for about 10 minutes longer.

Once you've flipped the chicken the second time, bake the bread salad. (It will take about 15 minutes.)

After 1 hour altogether, the chicken should be done. Check it by piercing the thickest part of the inside of one thigh. If the juices run clear, it's done. Remove the chicken from the oven and make a little slash in the skin between the thighs and breasts. Tilt the bird to drain the juices into the skillet. Transfer the chicken to a cutting board and let rest in a warm place for 10 minutes. Skim the fat from the juices in the skillet and moisten the bread salad with the juices.

Cut the chicken into serving pieces and nestle them in the bread salad. Serve immediately.

notes from our test kitchen

- Use a modest-size chicken (don't go over 3 pounds), not the whoppers you usually see in the supermarket.
- In a pinch, you can use a cast-iron skillet to cook the chicken.

bread salad

✳

Judy Rodgers recommends tasting the bread mixture at several stages, thoughtfully, to get the flavor exactly right. ☙

1 teaspoon red wine vinegar

1 tablespoon warm water

1 tablespoon dried currants

8 ounces day-old loaf of chewy, rustic Italian bread

$^{1}/_{2}$–$^{3}/_{4}$ cup olive oil

2 tablespoons champagne vinegar, or more to taste

Salt and freshly ground black pepper

4 scallions, trimmed and cut into slivers

3 garlic cloves, cut into slivers

1 tablespoon pine nuts

Several handfuls of arugula for serving

serves 4

Mix the red wine vinegar with the water in a small bowl. Stir in the currants and let plump for 10 minutes. Drain.

Meanwhile, carve most of the crust off the bread, leaving just a little for texture. Cut the loaf into 2 large chunks and paint them roughly with a little of the olive oil, using a pastry brush. Toast the bread lightly in a toaster oven or under the broiler just to crisp the surface. Tear the toasted chunks into irregular bite-size pieces — you should have about 4 cups. Place them in a large bowl.

Combine $^{1}/_{2}$ cup of the olive oil and the champagne vinegar and season with salt and pepper. Sprinkle over the bread pieces and toss well. Add the drained currants and toss.

Cook the scallions and garlic in a trickle of olive oil in a small sauté pan to soften them. Meanwhile, toast the pine nuts just to warm them in a small dry pan, taking care not to burn them. Then combine the scallions and garlic and the pine nuts with the prepared bread. Taste. If it's too bland, add more champagne vinegar or salt and pepper. If it's tasty but dry, add a few drops of warm water. If it seems lean, add more olive oil.

Place the bread salad in a 1-quart baking dish and loosely tent the top with aluminum foil.

After the chicken has roasted for 50 minutes, put the bread salad in the oven and bake for 15 minutes.

Remove the bread salad from the oven and transfer it to a warm deep platter. Toss with a spoonful or two of the clear roasting juices from the chicken and the arugula. Taste again and season with salt, olive oil, and/or champagne vinegar before serving with the chicken.

chicken fricassee
with lemon, saffron, and green olives

SOURCE *Atlanta Journal-Constitution*
COOK Reagan Walker

This gem surfaced as one of the *Atlanta Journal-Constitution*'s top ten recipes from 2001, and we find ourselves going back to it every year. Reagan Walker went to France to take some cooking classes at Julia Child's old cottage in Provence, and out of the dozens of recipes she returned with, this affordable dish is her hands-down favorite, especially for a casual dinner party. The aromas from the kitchen will greet your guests at the door — always a good way to start an evening.

The combination of lemon, saffron, tomatoes, and green olives creates a wonderful sunny, tangy flavor — especially welcome in the dark winter months. Although cream is added to finish the sauce, it doesn't have the heaviness associated with many cream sauces. In fact, this sauce is actually rather thin, so you'll want to serve bread to sop it up, or even consider serving the fricassee in shallow bowls if you want more sauce. ❧

1 3½-pound chicken, cut into 8 pieces
   Coarse salt and freshly ground black pepper
¼ cup olive oil
2 medium carrots, peeled and diced
1 large onion, diced
1 celery rib, diced
3 garlic cloves, chopped
¼ cup dry white wine
½ cup chicken broth
2 large tomatoes, peeled, seeded, and chopped
2 ounces cracked and pitted green olives (about ¼ cup)
1 tablespoon freshly crushed coriander seeds
1–2 large pinches of saffron
   Juice of 1 lemon
¾ cup heavy cream
1 preserved lemon, quartered and sliced (see note)
1 bunch fresh cilantro, thick stems discarded and leaves chopped, for garnish

serves 4

Season the chicken pieces with salt and pepper. In a large sauté pan, heat the oil over medium-high heat. Add the chicken and brown on all sides, turning with tongs, for about 10 minutes. Add the carrots, onion, celery, and garlic and sauté until the vegetables are limp but not browned.

WHAT TO DO with the rest of the wine? Since conventional wisdom says it deteriorates almost immediately, you should either turn it into vinegar, as a thrifty French person would; preserve it using a fancy gizmo from the wine store; or just dump it down the drain. But when Karen MacNeil-Fife did an exhaustive experiment for *Sunset* magazine — using three different wines and every possible preservation method — she made an amazing discovery. No preserving system worked better than just recorking the bottle, and in some cases the opened wine actually tasted better than its freshly uncorked self, even several days later.

Add the wine and bring to a boil. Add the chicken broth, tomatoes, olives, coriander seeds, and saffron and return to a boil.

Cover the pan with parchment paper and then with a lid, reduce the heat to medium-low, and simmer for about 45 minutes, or until the chicken is tender.

Transfer the chicken to a serving platter and keep warm. Increase the heat to medium-high, add the lemon juice, and scrape the bottom of the pan to loosen the browned vegetables. Add the cream and preserved lemon slices and boil until the liquid is reduced by half or until slightly thickened. Strain, if desired (though the bits taste great), and season with salt and pepper to taste. Pour the sauce over the chicken and scatter the cilantro over the top. Serve immediately.

notes from our test kitchen

- To double this recipe and serve 8, you'll need two large sauté pans.
- The nice part of cutting up a whole chicken is that you get a mix of white and dark meat. If you'd rather not cut up a chicken, use chicken pieces, preferably a mix of breasts and thighs. You'll need about 2½ pounds of chicken pieces.
- Preserved lemons can be found in markets that specialize in Middle Eastern foods or in gourmet specialty stores. Alternatively, you can substitute 1 small lemon, unpeeled and very thinly sliced, and add the slices to the chicken along with the tomatoes and olives.

the amazing five-hour roast duck

SOURCE The Vinegar Factory newsletter
COOK Mindy Heiferling

This is one of those breakthrough recipes everyone needs to know. You can now disregard received wisdom about how to roast a duck and produce a gorgeous one with very little effort. Bonus: you won't be appearing at the dinner table as a grease-stained wench. Your duck slow-roasts all afternoon, releasing its fat into the roasting pan, while the flesh stays moist and succulent under a crisp, mahogany brown skin.

Don't forget to save the duck fat, which is wonderful for cooking potatoes or livening up a winter soup with just a spoonful. ✎

tip

HOW DO YOU DEAL with a basting brush that's sticky with sauce and drippings? Wash it with dishwashing liquid and very hot water, rinse well, and shake dry. Place the brush in a cup with the bristles pointing down, cover the bristles with coarse salt, and keep the brush in the cup until the next time you need it. The salt will draw moisture out of the bristles and keep them fresh and dry between uses. (From "The Clever Cook," *Kansas City Star;* tip originally appeared in *365 Quick Tips* by the editors of *Cook's Illustrated.*)

1 **Pekin (Long Island) duck, wing tips cut off (not necessary, but more elegant)**
Salt and freshly ground black pepper
2 **tablespoons chopped garlic**
1 **small handful of thyme sprigs**

serves 4

Preheat the oven to 300 degrees and set a rack in the middle level.

Remove the giblets from the duck; save the giblets and wing tips for stock, if you like. Dry the duck well with paper towels. Remove any loose globs of yellow fat from the two cavities. Rub the large cavity with salt and pepper and the garlic and put the thyme in it. With a small sharp paring knife, make dozens of slits all over the duck, piercing the skin and fat but being careful not to pierce the flesh. The easiest way to do this is to insert the knife on the diagonal, not straight in.

Put the duck breast side up on a rack (a cake cooling rack is fine) set on a jelly-roll pan and put it in the oven. Every hour for 4 hours, take the pan out of the oven, pierce the duck all over with the knife, and turn it over. Each time, pour off the fat in the pan.

After 4 hours, increase the oven temperature to 350 degrees (see note). Sprinkle the duck with salt and pepper and cook for about 1 hour longer, or until the skin is

notes from our test kitchen

- You can serve the duck after it has cooked for 4 hours. It will be juicier than the 5-hour duck, but not as tender.
- Leftovers (probably not possible) are delicious, of course, in stir-fries and duck salads.

crisp and browned. Let rest for 20 minutes before serving.

Instead of carving the duck in the usual way, try sectioning it with heavy kitchen shears: cut it in half along the backbone and then cut each half into 2 pieces. Or use a cleaver and hack it into small pieces, bones and all, to serve Chinese style.

⇥ VARIATION ⇤

Mindy Heiferling suggests taking the duck in a couple of Asian directions. For a Chinese duck, put peeled, chopped fresh ginger, scallions, and garlic in the cavity and brush the duck during the last hour of cooking with a mixture of hoisin sauce, soy sauce, toasted sesame oil, and a little honey. For a Thai duck, put chopped fresh lemongrass, fresh cilantro, and garlic in the cavity and brush during the last hour with a mix of Thai curry paste, unsweetened coconut milk, and lime juice.

turkey sloppy joes

*

SOURCE *Hartford Courant*   STORY BY   Linda Giuca and Christopher Prosperi
COOK   Christopher Prosperi

Sloppy Joes are one of those diner dishes we have an occasional hankering for, but we've never found a recipe that's really good—until now. Connecticut chef Christopher Prosperi had a similar hankering for his old school-lunch favorite, but his updated palate led him toward a lighter meat—turkey—and a big glug of red wine, along with a little cumin and molasses. Genius!

This recipe is perfect for a winter day, a come-on-over dinner, or a special treat when you want something simple with some nostalgic charm. ❧

notes from our test kitchen

- You're unlikely to find a 1.3-pound package of ground turkey in the meat case, so just choose whatever's closest to that amount (1.3 pounds is just over 1¼ pounds).
- You can make the Sloppy Joe mixture a day or two ahead. It also freezes well, so you can be ready to serve this dish at a moment's notice.

1 tablespoon vegetable oil
2 cups finely diced onions
1.3 pounds ground turkey (see note)
1 teaspoon kosher salt
1 tablespoon ground cumin
1 cup dry red wine
1 28-ounce can crushed tomatoes
2 tablespoons Worcestershire sauce
1 tablespoon molasses
1 tablespoon red wine vinegar
6–8 kaiser rolls
2 cups shredded cheddar cheese

serves 6 to 8

Heat the oil in a medium saucepan over medium-high heat. Add the onions and cook until lightly caramelized, about 5 minutes. Add the ground turkey and salt and mix well. Cook for 5 to 7 minutes, or until the meat is thoroughly cooked. Mix in the cumin and cook for an additional 1 minute.

Add the red wine and reduce by three quarters. Pour in the crushed tomatoes and simmer for 15 minutes. Add the Worcestershire sauce, molasses, and vinegar and cook for 2 more minutes to blend the flavors.

To serve, toast the kaiser rolls, split them, and top with cheddar cheese. Spoon on the Sloppy Joe mixture and serve right away.

spice-rubbed turkey
with sage gravy and wild mushroom stuffing

SOURCE *Food & Wine*   STORY BY   Christopher Solomon

COOK   Tom Douglas

Seattle chef Tom Douglas cooks all the time at home for his family, so we were especially interested to see what he makes for Thanksgiving. We've made it for our Thanksgiving almost every year since — and had guests clamoring for the recipes.

There are several unusual elements here. First of all, Douglas makes, hands down, the best turkey gravy you'll ever taste. The secret is his rich turkey broth, made with a whopping 7 pounds of turkey parts well ahead of time. You end up with about 3 quarts of delicious broth, which flavors the stuffing as well.

The turkey itself is rubbed with sage butter and left naked in the fridge overnight so it will have a particularly crisp skin. The stuffing, which is cooked separately, is full of woodsy flavor, with its wild mushrooms, hazelnuts, dried cranberries, and echo of sage.

A number of these elements can be made ahead — the broth, the sage butter, and the dressing — which makes it possible to have a relatively stress-free Thanksgiving and still produce a stunning feast. You must start the turkey the day before roasting and serving. ❧

10 tablespoons (1¼ sticks) unsalted butter: 6 softened, 4 melted
¼ cup plus 2 tablespoons minced fresh sage
    Kosher salt and freshly ground black pepper
1½ teaspoons coriander seeds (see note)
1 15-pound turkey, cavity fat removed, neck and wing tips reserved for broth, and gizzard reserved for gravy
2 large shallots, each cut in half
½ orange, quartered
¾ cup plus 1 tablespoon all-purpose flour
2 quarts Turkey Broth (page 152)
    Wild Mushroom Stuffing (page 150)

serves 12

In a small bowl, mash the 6 tablespoons softened butter with ¼ cup of the sage and season with salt and pepper.

In a small skillet, toast the coriander seeds over medium heat until fragrant, about 1 minute. Let cool, then transfer to a spice grinder and grind to a powder. In a small bowl, mix the ground coriander with 1½ tablespoons salt and 1½ teaspoons pepper.   •

Starting from the cavity end of the turkey and using your fingers, carefully separate the skin from the breast meat. Gently rub the sage butter under the skin, evenly coating the breast. Sprinkle the turkey inside and out with the seasoned salt. Refrigerate the turkey, uncovered, overnight. Let come to room temperature before roasting (allow 3 hours).

WE'VE BEEN hearing from more and more chefs that the best turkeys are the smaller ones (anything around 12 pounds is considered small), so we were happy to find an article by Judith Weinraub of the *Washington Post* that explained why. Apparently, like many American food trends, the Thanksgiving bird seems to get bigger each year. Up until the late 1940s, the average Thanksgiving turkey weighed in at 12 to 15 pounds. Now the average turkey is close to 28 pounds.

The problem with these big birds (aside from the logistics of hauling them, finding space to store them, and manhandling them in the kitchen) is that they are almost impossible to cook evenly. The bigger the turkey, the longer it cooks, and the more it will dry out. Plus bigger birds are older than smaller ones and tend to be tougher.

If you're serving a larger crowd, you're better off with 2 (or even 3) smaller turkeys than with 1 gigantic bird. Smaller turkeys cook more evenly, stay juicier, and taste better.

Preheat the oven to 350 degrees.

Put the shallots and orange pieces in the cavity of the turkey and tie the legs together. Set the turkey and gizzard on a rack in a roasting pan. Brush the 4 tablespoons melted butter over the turkey and roast for about $2\frac{1}{2}$ hours, basting every 30 minutes. Halfway through roasting, rotate the turkey for even cooking. Cover the breast loosely with aluminum foil during the last hour of roasting. The bird is done when an instant-read thermometer inserted in the inner thigh registers 165 degrees. Transfer the turkey to a carving board and let rest for at least 30 minutes.

Cut the gizzard into $\frac{1}{4}$-inch dice. Pour the pan juices into a measuring cup. Spoon off $\frac{1}{2}$ cup plus 3 tablespoons of the fat, add it to the roasting pan, and set the pan on two burners over medium heat. Stir the flour into the fat until blended, then gradually whisk in the turkey broth, scraping up the browned bits on the bottom of the pan. Reduce the heat to low and simmer until no floury taste remains, about 20 minutes. Add the reserved pan juices, gizzard, and remaining 2 tablespoons sage. Season with salt and pepper to taste.

Carve the turkey, arrange it on a platter, and serve with the gravy and stuffing.

notes from our test kitchen

- If you don't have a spice grinder, you can use ground coriander instead of grinding the seeds yourself.
- Decorate the turkey platter with sage sprigs and fresh cranberries or grapes, if you wish.

what we've learned about roasting a turkey

You can scrap our old reliable turkey recipes and join the institutions—*Gourmet,* the *New York Times,* Safeway supermarkets, and *Sunset* magazine—who cooked their way to the perfect turkey in 2005. It's hot-roasted, and it cooks in just 2 hours. The technique is revolutionary, and not only that, it's the best way to do it.

It's also the easiest. You don't need to baste or stuff your turkey. You don't need to brine it, put butter under the skin, or even rinse it all over (which just spreads bacteria). Get a nice small turkey—12 pounds is ideal, but up to 16 is okay (though obviously that will take more time). Set a rack in the lower-middle level of the oven. If there's room, the pan should go in lengthwise so that the legs are at the back of the oven, which is hotter.

Preheat the oven to 450 degrees.

Sprinkle the turkey inside and out with salt and pepper and place on a rack in a roasting pan. Roast for 1 hour, then turn the pan around. If the turkey breast seems to be browning too quickly, cover the bird loosely with aluminum foil. After 1¾ hours, check the temperature with an instant-read thermometer stuck between the inner thigh and the breast (but not touching any bone). When it reads 165 to 170 degrees, remove the bird from the oven, tipping it so the juices in the cavity run into the roasting pan. Let the bird sit on a serving platter, covered loosely with foil, for 30 minutes to finish cooking (it will be 180 degrees).

Meanwhile, make the gravy with the pan juices (see page 148) and brush up on your carving skills. Instead of whacking away at the big bird, cut straight down along the high ridge of the breastbone and straight across at the base of the breast. Remove the entire breast and carve it into perfect slices.

Susan Westmoreland, food director of *Good Housekeeping,* points out on the magazine's Web site that pink meat doesn't mean you should return the turkey to the oven. Nitrates in turkey feed or oven gases reacting with the meat can produce a pink color. Be guided by temperature, not color.

wild mushroom stuffing

*

The stuffing can be made a day ahead and refrigerated overnight. ❧

1	2-pound loaf of peasant bread, crust removed and bread cut into 1½-inch cubes
⅓	cup extra-virgin olive oil
	Salt and freshly ground black pepper
½	cup dried porcini mushrooms (about 1 ounce)
1	cup boiling water
1½	cups hazelnuts (about 6 ounces)
16	tablespoons (2 sticks) unsalted butter
1	medium onion, chopped
2	celery ribs, finely chopped
2	large shallots, minced
2	pounds mixed wild mushrooms, wiped clean, stem ends trimmed, and mushrooms finely chopped
3	cups Turkey Broth (recipe follows)
1	cup dried cranberries (about 4 ounces)
¼	cup chopped fresh parsley
1	tablespoon chopped fresh thyme
2	teaspoons chopped fresh sage

serves 12

Preheat the oven to 375 degrees. Butter two large baking dishes.

On two large rimmed baking sheets, toss the bread cubes with the oil and season with salt and pepper to taste. Bake for about 20 minutes, or until golden. Set aside to cool. Reduce the oven temperature to 350 degrees.

In a small heatproof bowl, soak the dried porcini in the boiling water until softened, about 20 minutes. Rub the porcini to remove any grit, then remove them from the liquid and coarsely chop. Slowly pour the soaking liquid into a small saucepan, leaving behind any grit. Boil the liquid over high heat until reduced to ¼ cup, about 5 minutes. Remove from the heat and set aside.

Spread the hazelnuts on a rimmed baking sheet and toast for about 12 minutes, or until richly browned. Transfer to a kitchen towel and let cool completely. Rub the hazelnuts in the towel to remove their skins. Coarsely chop and set aside.

In a large skillet, melt 4 tablespoons (½ stick) of the butter over medium-low heat. Add the onion and celery and cook until softened, about 10 minutes. Scrape the onion-celery mixture into a very large bowl. In the same skillet, melt the remaining 12 tablespoons (1½ sticks) butter over medium-high heat. Add the shallots and cook, stirring, until softened, about 3 minutes. Add the fresh mushrooms and the porcini and their reduced soaking liquid. Season with salt and pepper. Cook over high heat until the liquid evaporates, about 15 minutes. Add the mushrooms to the onion mixture, along with the toasted bread cubes, turkey broth, hazelnuts, dried cranberries, parsley, thyme, and sage. Toss well and season with salt and pepper to taste. The stuffing can be made ahead, covered, and refrigerated for 1 day.

Spread the stuffing in the prepared baking dishes and cover with aluminum foil. Bake for about 30 minutes, or until heated through. Uncover and bake until crusty, about 25 minutes more. If the stuffing is made a day ahead and refrigerated, it will take slightly longer to bake.

turkey broth

✳

7 **pounds turkey parts, such as wings, thighs, and drumsticks**

14 **cups water**

Reserved turkey neck and wing tips (optional)

1 **large onion, thickly sliced**

1 **large carrot, thickly sliced**

1 **large celery rib, thickly sliced**

2 **garlic cloves, sliced**

1 **teaspoon kosher salt**

Freshly ground black pepper

makes about 3 quarts

Preheat the oven to 400 degrees.

In a large roasting pan, roast the turkey parts, turning occasionally, for about 1 hour, or until well browned. Transfer to a large pot.

Set the roasting pan over two burners. Add 3 cups of the water and bring to a boil, scraping up the browned bits from the bottom of the pan. Transfer the liquid to the pot. Add the neck and wing tips, if using, to the pot, along with the onion, carrot, celery, garlic, salt, several pinches of pepper, and remaining 11 cups water. Bring to a boil, reduce the heat to medium-low, partially cover, and simmer for about $2^1/2$ hours. Strain the broth and skim off the fat before using.

spicy sirloin steak with cilantro relish

* * *

SOURCE *Bills Open Kitchen* by Bill Granger
COOK Bill Granger

Bill Granger, an exuberant chef, restaurateur, and food personality from Sydney, Australia, is applauded far and wide for his contagious passion for friendly, unpretentious food. What we appreciate most about Granger is the way his recipes produce the utmost flavor for minimal effort—and this spicy steak is no exception. The simple soy-based marinade adds a sweet-salty nuance to the sirloin, and the cilantro relish perks up the whole thing. Make this in the summer when you want to fire up the grill, or do it indoors in the winter to brighten up a dreary evening. 🖎

1/3 **cup Shaoxing rice wine or dry sherry**

1/4 **cup oyster sauce**

1/4 **cup light soy sauce (see note)**

 1 **tablespoon sesame oil**

 2 **tablespoons superfine sugar (see note)**

 4 **sirloin steaks (about 7 ounces each)**

Cilantro Relish (recipe follows)

About 8 ounces snow peas, trimmed (see note)

Steamed white rice for serving

serves 4

Combine the rice wine or sherry, oyster sauce, soy sauce, sesame oil, and sugar in a large bowl. Stir until the sugar is dissolved. Add the steaks, cover with plastic wrap, and refrigerate for 2 hours. Let the steaks come to room temperature for 30 minutes.

Meanwhile, prepare the cilantro relish.

Preheat a frying pan, grill pan, or outdoor grill until hot.

Sear the steaks for 2 minutes on each side for rare. Reduce the heat to medium and continue cooking for another 1 to 2 minutes per side for medium or 2 to 3 minutes for well-done.

Remove the steaks from the heat and let rest for 5 minutes in a warm place. Lightly blanch the snow peas in boiling water, then plunge them into cold water and drain well. Cut each steak into ½-inch-thick slices, top with the relish, and serve with the rice and snow peas. Pass any extra relish at the table.

notes from our test kitchen

- Regular soy sauce is fine.

- Superfine sugar is sold with the cocktail supplies and labeled as "bar sugar" (because it dissolves readily in drinks). If you can't find any, whisk regular sugar in the food processor until it's superfine. Ordinary granulated sugar will also do in both the marinade and the relish.

- The snow peas are mostly a garnish, but they add a welcome crunch and bit of color. You could certainly add another green vegetable in their place.

- These cooking times are for a very hot fire and relatively thin (about ¾-inch) steaks. If your fire isn't blazing hot or your steaks are thicker, the cooking time will be longer.

cilantro relish

※

As much as we love this colorful relish spooned over grilled steaks, we've also discovered that it does a fine job perking up grilled fish or shrimp. Don't expect leftovers. ❧

1 **cup chopped fresh cilantro, including tender stems**

¼ **cup vegetable oil**

2 **tablespoons fresh lime juice**

1 **large red chile, seeded and finely minced (see note)**

1 **tablespoon fish sauce (nam pla)**

1 **teaspoon superfine sugar**

Freshly ground black pepper

Place all the ingredients in a bowl and stir to combine. The relish is best served within 1 to 2 hours.

note from our test kitchen

For the chile, use a red jalapeño or serrano.

fillet of beef with roquefort sauce and mixed nuts

❋

SOURCE *The Cooking of Southwest France* by Paula Wolfert

COOK Paula Wolfert after André Daguin

This is the best beef fillet we've ever tasted. A regional French specialty, it's an excellent choice for an elegant dinner party. Although it's very simple to make, the flavors are complicated and exhilarating, just what you'd expect from a four-star French restaurant.

Paula Wolfert has figured out a great way to presear the fillet so it loses none of its crusty exterior and almost none of its precious juices. A final oven roasting brings it to the perfect temperature. ❧

notes from our test kitchen

- To serve 8 to 10, simply use 2 fillets and double the recipe.
- It may seem silly to whip a tiny amount of cream, but it's the consistency of the cream that thickens the sauce, as Wolfert notes. Put it in a small cup and use an immersion blender, if you have one.

1 center-cut beef tenderloin (about 2 pounds), trimmed of fat and sinew and tied at 1-inch intervals

Salt and freshly ground black pepper

2 tablespoons grapeseed or peanut oil, plus more for rubbing the meat

1 teaspoon rendered duck or goose fat or clarified butter (see tip, page 11)

1 tablespoon minced shallot

3 tablespoons dry Madeira or imported ruby port

1/2 cup demi-glace (store-bought is fine) or 1 1/2 cups unsalted meat broth reduced to 1/2 cup

1 1/2 ounces creamy Roquefort cheese

3 tablespoons unsalted butter, plus more if needed

2 tablespoons crème fraîche or whipped heavy cream

2 tablespoons pine nuts, lightly toasted

2 tablespoons walnut pieces, lightly toasted

2 tablespoons blanched sliced almonds, lightly toasted

1 tablespoon chopped fresh flat-leaf parsley

serves 4 or 5

Lightly sprinkle the meat with salt and pepper. Rub a little oil over the beef. Loosely cover with plastic wrap and refrigerate until 1 hour before cooking, preferably overnight (see tip). Pat the roast dry with paper towels.

THE 150 BEST AMERICAN RECIPES

156

tips

FRENCH CHEF André Guillot recommends lightly salting the meat the minute you bring it home. You won't need to salt it later, and you'll use half as much salt as you otherwise would. The lightly salted meat will tenderize and mature in flavor when stored in the fridge overnight. Coating it lightly with oil keeps it from drying out.

JUDGING THE QUALITY of a tenderloin can be difficult because the meat is often vacuum-sealed in heavy plastic. We were happy to find this useful tip in a flyer from Stew Leonard's, the giant supermarket chain in New York and Connecticut. Just squeeze the package and look for the softest tenderloin. If it's hard, you'll be buying more fat and less meat.

In a large heavy skillet, preferably enameled cast iron, heat the 2 tablespoons oil and the fat until very hot. Sear the meat over high heat, turning, until browned all over, about 4 minutes total. Transfer the meat to a wire rack placed over a platter and let rest for 20 minutes. Save any juices that collect on the platter to add to the sauce.

Throw out the cooking fat. Add the shallot and Madeira to the skillet and boil until reduced to a glaze. Add the demi-glace and bring to a boil. Reduce to a syrupy consistency and set aside.

Mash the Roquefort and butter to a smooth, creamy paste. Taste the mixture; if it's too salty, add another $1/2$ to 1 tablespoon butter. Cover and refrigerate.

About 30 minutes before serving, preheat the oven to 450 degrees.

Roast the fillet for 17 minutes for "blue," or very rare (120 degrees on an instant-read thermometer), 18 minutes for rare (125 degrees), or 19 minutes for medium-rare (135 degrees).

Meanwhile, gently reheat the syrupy sauce in the skillet. Divide the Roquefort butter into 4 or 5 chunks and swirl into the sauce one by one. Remove from the heat and fold the crème fraîche into the sauce.

Spoon the sauce onto a heated serving platter. Slice the meat and arrange overlapping slices on the platter. Combine all the toasted nuts and the parsley in a small bowl and scatter around the meat.

high-temperature rib roast of beef

SOURCE *The Best of Craig Claiborne* by Craig Claiborne
with Pierre Franey, edited by Joan Whitman
COOK Ann Seranne

This unique way of cooking a perfect roast beef has achieved cult status. No elaborate set of instructions, no annotated treatise on the art of roasting, and no high-tech thermometer gizmo has ever matched this simple formula. The recipe first appeared more than twenty years ago in an article Craig Claiborne wrote for the *New York Times* about Ann Seranne, a food professional whom he called "an innovative genius in the kitchen."

The roast will be in the hot oven (make sure your oven is well insulated; see note) for only 25 to 60 minutes, depending on its size. But start at least 5 hours before you want to serve it, which will allow time for the roast to reach room temperature and to finish cooking in the turned-off oven. It will have a crunchy brown exterior and will be perfectly cooked inside to that medium-rare state that most people prefer. Center slices will be rare.

The infallible formula has another bonus: once out of the oven, the roast

1 **2- to 4-rib roast of beef (4¹⁄₂–12 pounds), short ribs removed**

All-purpose flour for rubbing

Salt and freshly ground black pepper

¹⁄₂–1 **cup beef broth**

serves 4 to 8; each rib serves 2

Remove the meat from the refrigerator 2¹⁄₂ to 4 hours before cooking, the longer time for the largest roast.

Preheat the oven to 500 degrees.

Place the roast fat side up in a large shallow roasting pan. Sprinkle with a little flour, rubbing it into the fat lightly. Season with salt and pepper. Put the roast in the oven and bake according to the chart that follows, timing it exactly. When the cooking time is up, turn off the oven. Do not open the door at any time. Leave the roast in the oven until the oven is lukewarm, about 2 hours. If you need to use the oven to cook something else, remove the roast from the oven and tent it loosely with aluminum foil to keep it warm.

To make a thin pan gravy, remove the excess fat from the meat drippings, leaving any meat pieces in the pan. Stir in the beef broth. Bring to a boil, scraping the bottom of the pan to loosen the meat pieces. Simmer for 1 minute and season with salt and pepper to taste. Serve hot.

can wait at room temperature, and re-
tain its internal heat, for up to 4 hours
before serving. While it is resting com-
fortably, the oven is freed up for whatever else you want to make. We hope
one of those things will be Yorkshire
Pudding (recipe follows).

The crucial instruction is not to open
the oven door, not even for a peek, while
the roast is in there. Trust us: it is doing
beautifully undisturbed. ～

notes from our test kitchen

- Don't attempt this recipe if your oven isn't well insulated – that is,
  if it is extremely hot to the touch on the outside when it's in use.
  (Most commercial ovens are not well insulated, which is why
  restaurant kitchens are so hot.)

- The most delicious – and most expensive – roast will be dry-aged
  (not wet-aged), which has to be ordered from a quality butcher
  well ahead of time. It should be well marbled with fat. Some markets, such as Whole Foods Market, sell aged roasts that are bred
  and fed to be low fat, and those won't be as flavorful. This information isn't on the label, so ask if you're in doubt.

roasting chart

This works out to be about 15 minutes
per rib, or approximately 5 minutes
cooking time per pound of trimmed,
ready-to-cook roast.

If you prefer medium to well-done
beef, add 10 minutes to the maximum
cooking time for each size roast.

WEIGHT (without short ribs)	ROAST AT 500 DEGREES
4 1/2 – 5 pounds	25–30 minutes
6–8 pounds	30–40 minutes
8–9 pounds	40–45 minutes
9–11 pounds	45–55 minutes
11–12 pounds	55–60 minutes

notes from our test kitchen

- If your beef drippings are less than ½ cup, add bacon grease or melted butter to make up the difference.
- We add about ½ teaspoon salt to the flour mixture.
- The "pud" will puff up even more dramatically if you refrigerate the batter for 1 to 2 hours before baking.

yorkshire pudding

✳

1 **cup all-purpose flour**

1 **cup milk**

⅛ **teaspoon freshly grated nutmeg**

4 **large eggs**

½ **cup beef drippings from the roast (see note)**

serves 8

Preheat the oven to 425 degrees.

In a medium bowl, combine the flour, milk, and nutmeg (see note). In a small bowl, beat the eggs until frothy. Add to the milk and stir just until blended.

Pour the drippings into a flameproof 9-x-12-inch baking dish. Place on the stovetop over medium heat or put in the oven. When it is hot and almost smoking, add the batter. Smooth it with a rubber spatula. Bake for about 15 minutes, or until well puffed and golden brown. For even cooking, turn the baking dish as the cooking proceeds. Serve with the roast beef.

pomegranate-braised brisket
with onion confit

SOURCE *The Gefilte Variations* by Jayne Cohen

COOK Jayne Cohen

No question about it, American cooks have rediscovered braising — a development that we're more than a little pleased about. In this old-fashioned cooking method, a hunk of tough meat is transformed into sumptuousness through long, slow cooking. Although braising is a good technique for pot roasts, shoulder cuts, and shanks, the daddy of all braising cuts is brisket, the breast portion of beef.

Pomegranate juice brightens the deep flavors of this dish, and the vivid red juice results in an appealing amethyst-colored gravy. The crowning touch is the jammy onion confit that cooks on the stovetop while the brisket simmers in the oven.

Make the brisket a day or two ahead, and it will taste even better. ❧

3 tablespoons olive or vegetable oil

1 brisket (about 6 pounds), trimmed of excess fat, wiped with a damp paper towel, and patted dry

2 medium onions, coarsely chopped (about 2 cups)

2 leeks, white and pale green parts, washed well and coarsely chopped

6 garlic cloves, crushed

2 large carrots, peeled and coarsely chopped

1 celery rib with leaves, coarsely chopped

2 cups pomegranate juice (see note)

2 cups chicken broth

3 thyme sprigs or 2 teaspoons dried thyme

2 rosemary sprigs

2 bay leaves

Salt and freshly ground black pepper

Onion Confit (recipe follows)

serves 8 to 12

Heat the oil in a large heavy roasting pan or a wide 6-quart Dutch oven over medium-high heat, using two burners if necessary. Add the brisket and brown well on both sides, about 10 minutes. Transfer the brisket to a platter and set aside.

Preheat the oven to 325 degrees.

Pour off all but 1 tablespoon of the fat in the pan and add the onions, leeks, garlic, carrots, and celery. Cook over medium-

tip

TO BROWN or not to brown? Although many braising recipes begin with the direction to brown the meat, many cooks dispute the merits of this step. In an article on brisket, San Francisco food journalist Janet Fletcher quotes Marlene Sorosky Gray, author of several books on Jewish food, on the subject. Gray has experimented a lot with brisket and in the end eschews browning, saying, "If you overbrown it, it gets a crust and it's much harder to slice." Instead, just put the brisket and all the vegetables in the pan, pour in the juice and broth (use a bit less juice, since you won't be boiling it down), cover, and braise. Expect the braising to take 45 minutes to 1½ hours longer, since you're starting with cold meat.

notes from our test kitchen

- Unless you own an enormous Dutch oven, chances are you'll need to use a roasting pan to accommodate the brisket. Use aluminum foil to cover it tightly before sliding it into the oven.

- Most supermarkets sell pomegranate juice under the Pom Wonderful label, somewhere near the produce or specialty juices. Pomegranate molasses is *not* the same thing as pomegranate juice and cannot be substituted.

high heat, stirring occasionally, until the vegetables are softened, 5 to 7 minutes.

Add 1 cup of the pomegranate juice and bring the mixture to a boil, scraping up the browned bits from the bottom of the pan with a wooden spoon. Boil until the liquid is reduced by about half. Add the remaining 1 cup pomegranate juice, the broth, thyme, rosemary, and bay leaves and bring the mixture to a simmer. Season to taste with salt and pepper.

Lightly salt and pepper the brisket on both sides. Add it to the pan, fat side up, and add any juices that may have dripped from the meat onto the platter. Spoon the vegetable mixture over the meat. Cover the pan tightly and slide it into the oven to braise, basting every half hour, until the meat is very tender, 2½ to 3½ hours. If the liquid in the pot begins to bubble rapidly, reduce the oven temperature to 300 degrees — it should be a slow simmer.

Meanwhile, make the onion confit.

Transfer the brisket to a cutting board and cover loosely with aluminum foil. For the gravy, strain the braising liquid, discarding the thyme, rosemary sprigs, and bay leaves and reserving the vegetables. Skim and discard as much fat as possible from the surface of the liquid. Puree the vegetables and 1 cup of the degreased braising liquid in a food processor or blender. Transfer the pureed mixture and the remaining braising liquid to a skillet over high heat and reduce the gravy to the desired consistency. Taste for seasoning.

Cut the brisket into thin slices across the grain at a slight diagonal. Spread the onion confit on a serving platter and arrange the sliced brisket on top. Ladle over the hot gravy and serve.

, no-mess way to seed a pomegranate. The information comes from the California Pomegranate Web site (pomegranates.org):

1. Cut off the crown end with a sharp knife.

2. Lightly score the rind into quarters.

3. Immerse the fruit in a bowl of cold water for 5 minutes.

4. Holding the fruit under the water, break the sections apart. Separate the seeds from the membrane and let the seeds sink to the bottom of the bowl.

5. Skim off and discard the membrane and rind.

6. Pour the seeds into a colander to drain. Pat dry.

We heard Chef José Andrés on public radio offer another nifty trick for getting the seeds out of a pomegranate. Slice the fruit in half around its waist. Turn one half cut side down above a large bowl and whack the back repeatedly with a large spoon. The seeds will fall into the bowl. Repeat with the other half, then pick through the seeds to remove the pith. Andrés's way is a little messier than the underwater method, but smacking the fruit with a large spoon is surprisingly satisfying.

onion confit

❊

3   tablespoons olive oil

4   large onions (about 2$^1/_2$ pounds), very thinly sliced

Salt and freshly ground black pepper

$^1/_2$ cup dry red wine

$^1/_4$ cup chicken broth

$^1/_2$ cup pomegranate seeds (see tip)

Heat the oil in a 10- to 12-inch skillet over low heat. Add the onions, season lightly with salt and pepper, and toss to coat with the oil. Cook, tightly covered, over the lowest heat, stirring occasionally, until the onions are very soft and brown in color, about 1 hour. Season with salt and pepper to taste, and add the wine and broth. Increase the heat and boil, uncovered and stirring frequently, until all the liquid is evaporated and the onions are deeply colored, 4 to 8 minutes. Taste again for seasonings — the confit tends to take a bit of salt. Turn off the heat, cover, and keep warm. Stir in the pomegranate seeds just before serving.

note from our test kitchen

When shopping for a pomegranate, it should feel heavy — indicating that it's full of juice — and the skin should be thin, tough, and unbroken.

brisket à la carbonnade

SOURCE *Gourmet*

COOKS *Gourmet* staff

Carbonnade, the Belgian beef stew with beer, was a big hit in the 1960s. Back then, beef still tasted very beefy. Now meat with that deep, rich flavor is hard to come by, but brisket always delivers. So we were especially pleased to find this slow-cooked recipe, with the brisket nestled into a blanket of beery onions with the inspired touches of balsamic vinegar and a porcini bouillon cube.

Make the carbonnade a day or two ahead, and it will taste even better. If you can find the thick end of the brisket (aka the nose, thick cut, or point), so much the better. That end has a little more fat, so the meat will be more succulent. But the more commonly available thin flat brisket is good here, too. ❧

1 **3¹/₂- to 4-pound brisket, trimmed of excess fat**
   Salt and freshly ground black pepper
2 **tablespoons olive oil**
2 **pounds onions, halved lengthwise and thinly sliced lengthwise (about 6 cups)**
1 **Turkish bay leaf or ¹/₂ California bay leaf**
1 **12-ounce bottle beer (not dark)**
1 **tablespoon balsamic vinegar**
1 **dried porcini bouillon cube (less than ¹/₂ ounce) or 1 beef bouillon cube, crumbled**

serves 8

Preheat the oven to 350 degrees and set a rack in the middle level.

Pat the brisket dry and sprinkle with ³/₄ teaspoon salt and ¹/₂ teaspoon pepper. Heat the oil in a 6- to 8-quart, wide, heavy ovenproof pot over medium-high heat until hot but not smoking. Brown the meat well on all sides, about 10 minutes total. Transfer to a platter.

Add the onions and bay leaf to the fat in the pot and cook over medium heat, stirring occasionally, until the onions are golden, 10 to 12 minutes. Remove from the heat and transfer half the onions to a bowl. Set the brisket over the onions in the pot, then top with the remaining onions. Add the beer, vinegar, and bouillon cube. The liquid should come halfway up the side of the meat; if it doesn't, add water. Bring to a boil.

note from our test kitchen

To make the brisket up to 2 days ahead, which we advise, finish cooking it and let the meat cool in the sauce. Cover the meat with waxed paper, then the lid, and refrigerate.

To serve, remove any solid fat on the surface of the meat, slice the meat across the grain, and arrange the slices in a shallow baking pan. Spoon the sauce over the meat and reheat, covered, in a 325-degree oven for 45 minutes.

Cover the pot and braise in the oven until the meat is fork-tender, 3 to 3½ hours. Let the meat cool in the sauce, uncovered, for 30 minutes.

Transfer the brisket to a cutting board. Skim off any fat from the sauce, remove the bay leaf, and season with salt and pepper to taste. Slice across the grain and serve with the sauce.

braised beef short ribs chinese style

SOURCE *Come for Dinner* by Leslie Revsin

COOK Leslie Revsin

Beef short ribs have become a real darling of chefs and serious home cooks in recent years, and there's no mystery as to why. When tucked into a braising pot with a few aromatic ingredients and left to simmer quietly for hours, the meaty ribs emerge lusciously tender. Few dishes deliver such big flavor with so little fuss.

This version, one of the best we've tried, comes from the late Leslie Revsin, a superbly talented chef and food writer. The classic Chinese flavor combination of sherry, soy sauce, ginger, scallions, and star anise gives the ribs an intensely aromatic, slightly sweet character. In addition to penetrating the meat, the soy-based braising liquid bestows the ribs with a rich, caramelized appearance. Just one look at them, and you know they'll be good.

Like many slow-cooked dishes, these short ribs benefit from being made ahead and left to sit overnight in the braising liquid (see note). Serve with mashed potatoes, with some of the braising liquid spooned over the top. ❧

- ½ cup soy sauce
- ½ cup fino sherry, dry white wine, or dry vermouth
- 2 tablespoons packed light brown sugar
- 1⅓ cups drained and coarsely chopped canned plum tomatoes
- ⅔ cup water
- 4 star anise
- 6–6½ pounds beef short ribs on the bone, cut into 3-inch lengths
- Salt and freshly ground black pepper
- 1½ tablespoons vegetable oil, plus more if needed
- 6 garlic cloves, crushed and peeled
- 6 scallions, cut into 2-inch pieces
- 1 1-inch piece fresh ginger about the diameter of a quarter, cut into 8 slices
- 2 tablespoons thinly sliced scallions, cut on the diagonal, for garnish (see variation)

serves 6

Preheat the oven to 325 degrees and set a rack in the middle level.

Stir the soy sauce, sherry (or wine or vermouth), brown sugar, and tomatoes together in a bowl. Stir in the water and star anise. Set aside.

Dry the ribs with paper towels and season very lightly with salt and generously with pepper. Heat the oil in a large heavy flameproof casserole over medium-high heat. (The casserole should be large enough to hold all the ribs in no

note from our test kitchen

Short ribs are easier to degrease if you make them ahead and refrigerate them overnight. When the ribs are done, discard the ginger and star anise. Transfer the ribs to a baking dish or other container that can accommodate them in one layer. Pour the braising liquid over the ribs and refrigerate for up to 5 days or freeze for up to 2 months. Skim off the fat, then reheat the ribs and sauce in a moderate oven.

more than two layers.) When the oil is hot, add the ribs in batches (do not crowd) and brown on all sides. Remove them as they're browned, adding more oil, if necessary.

When all the ribs are browned, pour off the fat and reduce the heat to low. Add the garlic, scallion pieces, and ginger, alternately tossing and pressing them against the pot for 1 minute to bring out their flavors. Return the ribs to the pot and pour the soy sauce mixture over them. Bring the liquid to a simmer and cover. Transfer the pot to the oven and braise the ribs, turning occasionally, until extremely tender when pierced with a fork, 2½ to 3 hours.

Transfer the ribs to a serving platter. Discard the ginger and star anise and pour the remaining sauce into a large heatproof glass measuring cup. Let stand for about 5 minutes, then spoon off and discard any fat that has risen to the surface. Reheat the sauce, season generously with pepper, and pour over the ribs. Garnish with the thinly sliced scallions and serve hot.

↜ VARIATION ↝

In a similar recipe in *Fine Cooking,* Leslie Revsin garnished the ribs with sautéed leeks instead of chopped scallions. When we tasted it, we realized what a good idea it was. Wash 3 medium leeks (white and light green parts) and cut into 2-inch-long julienne strips (2 to 2½ cups). Rinse the strips, drain, and dry well. Melt 1 tablespoon unsalted butter in a large skillet. Add the leeks and cook, stirring frequently, until they begin to brown, 3 to 5 minutes. Reduce the heat to medium-low and continue cooking, stirring frequently, until tender, 3 to 5 minutes. Season with salt and pepper to taste. When the ribs are ready, scatter the leeks over the top and serve.

roasted sausages and grapes

SOURCE *Cucina Simpatica* by Johanne Killeen and George Germon
COOK Johanne Killeen

It's astonishing what happens when you roast Italian sausages with grapes and a little balsamic vinegar. The rich, spicy sausages are set off by the sweet, slightly tannic grapes (we like red grapes best) in a dish that tastes perfectly balanced. We've yet to serve it without eliciting little groans of pleasure from those at the table. This is an American version of a traditional Tuscan harvest dish, and it's great no-fuss home food, ready in a matter of minutes.

Johanne Killeen and her husband, George Germon, serve the sausages with coarsely mashed new potatoes, enriched with a little butter and cream, at their legendary restaurant, Al Forno, in Providence. We wouldn't dream of doing it any other way. ❧

note from our test kitchen

It's worth a little extra trouble to seek out the best handmade sausages you can find for this very simple dish.

$1^1/_2$	**pounds hot Italian sausages**
$1^1/_2$	**pounds sweet Italian sausages**
3	**tablespoons unsalted butter**
6–7	**cups seedless red or green grapes ($2^1/_2$ pounds), stemmed**
$^1/_4$	**cup balsamic vinegar**
	Al Forno's Mashed Potatoes (recipe follows)

serves 6 to 8

Preheat the oven to 500 degrees.

In a large saucepan, cover the sausages with water and parboil for 8 minutes to rid them of excess fat.

Melt the butter in a large flameproof roasting pan. Add the grapes and toss to coat.

Using tongs, transfer the sausages to the roasting pan and push them down into the grapes (so that they don't brown too quickly). Roast, turning the sausages once, for 20 to 25 minutes, or until the grapes are soft and the sausages are browned. With a slotted spoon, transfer the sausages and grapes to a heated serving platter.

Place the roasting pan on the stovetop over medium-high heat. Add the vinegar, scraping up any browned bits on the bottom of the pan. Reduce the vinegar and juices until they are thick and syrupy. Pour the sauce over the sausages and grapes and serve immediately, accompanied by the mashed potatoes.

al forno's mashed potatoes

✳

2 pounds small red-skinned potatoes, quartered

¹/₂ cup heavy cream

**8 tablespoons (1 stick) unsalted butter, softened
   Salt**

serves 6

Place the potatoes in a large saucepan and add water to cover by 1 inch. Bring to a boil, reduce the heat to low, and simmer until the potatoes are soft, about 15 minutes.

Drain and return the potatoes to the saucepan. Over low heat, coarsely mash the potatoes with a potato masher or two large forks, gradually adding the cream and butter. Stir in 1 teaspoon salt, or to taste, and serve.

tuscan pork roast with herbed salt

❋

SOURCE *Food & Wine*

COOK Sally Schneider after Piero Ferrini

A Tuscan chef produced this sensationally good roast pork from what appears to be an ancient recipe. It's based on herbs—rosemary and sage, although you can also use thyme and oregano—and a little garlic and salt, but these are applied to the roast in an unusual way. The loin of pork is first liberated from its bones, which then form a rack on which to roast it. Next, a long-handled wooden spoon is used to bore a hole through the center of the roast, which is then filled with the herbed salt and stuffed at either end with a branch of rosemary. The whole roast is rubbed with more herbed salt, a thick coat of pancetta is added, and more rosemary branches go on top.

As the pork cooks, it's basted with white wine, caramelizing it and producing a delicious sauce to serve with the roast. This dish will happily sit on a buffet for hours. ❧

1 **7-pound pork loin roast, rack bones removed in one piece and reserved**

Tuscan Herbed Salt (recipe follows)

4 **sturdy rosemary branches, 10 inches long**

Coarse salt

4 **ounces thinly sliced meaty pancetta**

1 **teaspoon extra-virgin olive oil**

2 **cups dry white wine**

Freshly ground black pepper

serves 8 to 10

Pat the pork loin thoroughly dry with paper towels. Using a long-handled wooden spoon, pierce a hole lengthwise through the center of the roast. Using your fingers and the wooden spoon handle, stuff 3 tablespoons of the herbed salt into the hole. Insert a rosemary branch in each end of the hole. Mix the remaining 1 tablespoon herbed salt with 1½ teaspoons coarse salt and rub it all over the roast. Cover with the pancetta and top with the remaining 2 rosemary branches. Tie the roast at 1-inch intervals to give it a neat shape. Transfer to a platter, cover with plastic wrap, and refrigerate for at least 2 hours or up to 24 hours. Let come to room temperature before cooking, at least 1 hour.

Preheat the oven to 450 degrees.

Set the rack of rib bones in a large roasting pan. Unwrap the roast, pat it dry, and rub it with the olive oil. Place the roast on the rack and roast for 15 minutes. Remove the pan from the oven, turn the roast over (see note), and baste it with a few tablespoons of the wine.

note from our
test kitchen

If you have trouble turning the roast, don't
bother — it will be fine with no turning.

Return the roast to the oven, reduce the temperature to 350 degrees, and cook for about 1½ hours, turning the roast and basting it with wine every 20 minutes. Reserve ½ cup of the wine for the sauce. The roast is done when an instant-read thermometer inserted in the center reads 145 degrees.

Transfer the roast and rack to a platter and pour the pan juices into a glass measuring cup. Skim off as much fat as possible. Set the roasting pan over two burners at medium heat. When it starts to sizzle, add the reserved ½ cup wine and cook for 2 minutes, scraping up the drippings from the bottom of the pan.

Pour the pan juices into the juices in the measuring cup and let the fat rise to the surface. Skim off the fat again and season the sauce with salt and pepper to taste. Remove the strings and carve the roast into thin slices. Serve the pork with the warm pan sauce.

tuscan herbed salt

✻

This salt is delicious as a seasoning
for pork, veal, or vegetables such as
potatoes or green beans. ❧

1   **garlic clove**
1   **tablespoon sea salt**
30   **fresh sage leaves**
     Leaves from 2 rosemary sprigs

makes about ¼ cup

Chop the garlic with the salt. Chop the herbs together, then chop again with the salt. Use the salt right away or let it dry out and store for up to 1 month in an airtight container at room temperature.

sorting out the salts

Some people say that all salt tastes the same, but we beg to differ. And now that upscale supermarkets are stocking dozens of kinds, it's good to know your way around the offerings.

Salt comes either from the ocean—sea salt—or from mines. Either variety can have additives that don't appear on the label, but the highly refined cheap supermarket salt has the most, as well as the harshest flavor.

Chefs prefer kosher salt (mined), which has large crunchy crystals or big grains, and sea salt, which is chunky or flaky and has some briny flavors, as well as some minerals, such as magnesium and potassium. For everyday cooking, kosher salt is a great choice. It's easy to grab a pinch, and the salt has a pleasant, clean taste. Depending on the brand, it can be either very salty or not especially so (see the chart below).

Sea salt is also good for everyday cooking, and because it's usually saltier, you should use a bit less of it. Look for sea salt that isn't iodized (iodine affects flavor) and that doesn't have any additives. Sea salt is our choice for finishing a dish: adding that little bit of salt after cooking really makes the flavors sing. For baking, you need fine salt.

Save the expensive fleur de sel and Maldon salt for sprinkling on summer tomatoes or finishing other simple dishes.

One spoonful of salt can be twice as salty as another. Here's how the sodium contents of various salts stack up for one-quarter teaspoon. The difference has to do with weight: Diamond Crystal kosher salt is made up of hollow pyramid-shaped crystals, while Morton's grainy kosher salt is almost half again as heavy as Diamond Crystal. It should be noted that sodium content for sea salts varies a bit from year to year.

BRAND	SODIUM	BRAND	SODIUM
Diamond Crystal kosher salt	280 mg	Celtic Fine Gray Sea Salt (unrefined)	460 mg
Morton kosher salt	480 mg	Morton table salt	590 mg
La Baleine sea salt	580 mg	Maldon sea salt	580 mg
Master Kalas sea salt	420 mg		

slow-roasted chipotle pork

※

SOURCE *The New Cook's Tour of Sonoma* by Michele Anna Jordan
COOK Michele Anna Jordan

This dish is the Mexican equivalent of pulled pork, and it's just the sort of mindlessly easy but sensationally flavored recipe we're always looking for, with that soul food quality that's universally appealing.

As Michele Anna Jordan says, chipotle pepper and pork is one of the best flavor combinations on the planet. She uses chipotle powder for its rich, complex flavor, but if you can't find either the powder or the whole chipotles, make this dish using pureed canned chipotles in adobo sauce. ❧

2 **tablespoons kosher salt**

1 **tablespoon chipotle powder (see note)**

1 **pork shoulder roast (about 3½ pounds; see note)**

24 **small corn tortillas**

2 **limes, cut into wedges**

¼ **cup minced fresh cilantro**

serves 4 to 6

In a small bowl, mix together the kosher salt and chipotle powder and rub it into the pork, being sure to cover the entire surface of the meat with the mixture.

Put the pork in a clay roaster or other deep roasting pan with a lid, place the covered roaster in the oven, and turn the heat to 275 degrees. (If you are using a clay roaster, don't preheat the oven.) Cook until the pork falls apart when you press it with the back of a fork, 3½ to 4 hours. Remove the pork from the oven and let rest, covered, for 15 minutes.

Heat the tortillas on a medium-hot griddle (see tip), turning them frequently, until they are warmed through and soft. Wrap them in a tea towel and place them in a basket. Transfer the pork to a large serving platter and use two forks to pull it into chunks. Add the lime wedges to the platter, place the cilantro in a small serving bowl, and serve immediately, with the tortillas on the side.

To fill the tortillas: set one on top of another on a plate, spoon some of the pork on top, squeeze a little lime juice

tip

TO WARM the corn tortillas all at once and ahead of time, preheat the oven to 350 degrees. Very lightly dampen a clean kitchen towel. Check the tortillas to make sure none are stuck together. Wrap them in the towel, then in aluminum foil, sealing the edges tightly. Place them in the oven and set the timer for 7 minutes.

over the pork, sprinkle some cilantro on top, and fold in half.

notes from our test kitchen

- To make chipotle powder, see the tip on page 7. Jordan especially likes the (very expensive) chipotle powder sold by Tierra Vegetables: tierravegetables.com or (888) 784-3772.

- There are two types of pork shoulder roast — Boston butt and picnic ham. We think the Boston butt is the more succulent of the two (richer-tasting and more tender), but either will do. And you can make this with a boneless or bone-in roast. Just figure you'll need a little more if it's bone-in.

- We've come to think of this more as a method than a recipe, and we adapt it according to any size or shape pork shoulder. Bone-in or boneless, 3 pounds or 5, just use 1 part chipotle powder and 2 parts salt, then rub the pork with enough spiced salt to cover.

pork chile verde with posole

pork chile verde with posole

SOURCE *Boston Globe* STORY BY Sheryl Julian and Julie Riven

COOKS Mary Sue Milliken and Susan Feniger

Here's a great party dish from TV's *Two Hot Tamales*. Better than regular chili and more festive than soupy posole, it's also easy on the cook, because it's made a day ahead and served with just plain rice and warm tortillas (see pages 175 and 176 for heating directions). Leftovers are especially good with poached eggs for breakfast.

If you live in posole country, you know that the dried corn the dish is named for takes a lot of fussing to cook. Milliken and Feniger have wisely used canned hominy here. Tomatillos, the golf ball–size green "tomatoes" with a papery husk available in supermarkets all across the land, work as a sort of secret ingredient here, contributing a piquant accent to the pork. ☙

pork chile verde

1 pound tomatillos, husked and rinsed, or green tomatoes

2 pounds boneless pork, cut into 1½-inch pieces

1 teaspoon salt

½ teaspoon freshly ground black pepper

All-purpose flour for dusting

2 tablespoons canola oil

1 onion, chopped

2 Anaheim or poblano chiles, seeded and chopped

2 jalapeño peppers, seeded and chopped

2 green bell peppers, cored, seeded, and chopped

3 garlic cloves, chopped

1½ cups canned hominy (posole), drained

½ cup chopped fresh cilantro leaves

1 tablespoon dried oregano

2 teaspoons ground cumin

3 cups chicken broth or water

salsa

2 plum tomatoes, cored and diced

½ small red onion, chopped

1 jalapeño pepper, seeded and chopped

¼ red bell pepper, cored, seeded, and chopped

1 tablespoon chopped fresh cilantro leaves

1 tablespoon fresh lime juice

Salt and freshly ground black pepper

Hot sauce (optional)

serves 6

To make the chile verde: Preheat the broiler.

Set the tomatillos or green tomatoes on a rimmed baking sheet and slide them under the broiler. Cook, turning often, for 5 to 8 minutes, or until charred. Set aside to cool.

Chop the tomatillos or green tomatoes, reserving all the juice.

Sprinkle the pork with the salt and pepper. Dust it with flour.

In a large skillet, heat the oil over medium-high heat. Add the pork in batches and brown it on all sides. Remove the pork from the skillet and transfer to a soup pot.

Using the same skillet, turn the heat to medium and add the onion. Cook, stirring often, for about 10 minutes, or until soft. Add all the chiles and the bell peppers. Cook, stirring often, for 4 minutes. Add the garlic and cook for 1 minute more. Transfer to the soup pot.

Stir in the hominy, cilantro, oregano, cumin, broth or water, and tomatillos and their juice. Bring to a boil, lower the heat, and simmer, partially covered, for $1\frac{1}{2}$ hours, or until the pork is tender.

To make the salsa: Meanwhile, in a medium bowl, combine the tomatoes, onion, jalapeño, bell pepper, cilantro, and lime juice. Add the salt and pepper and hot sauce (if using) to taste. Set aside until ready to serve.

Serve the chile verde hot in deep bowls, with the salsa on the side.

monte's ham

SOURCE *Saveur Cooks Authentic American* by Dorothy Kalins and Colman Andrews

COOK Monte Williams

Just the directions for buying the ham alerted us that something was up in this recipe from *Saveur Cooks Authentic American:* "Buy the cheapest ham you can find," said Monte Williams, a Manhattan advertising executive who has used this ham as a party staple for years. He first had it at a glamorous New York party when he was a young arrival in town. Watching the other guests devour the glazed, glistening hunk o' pork, he begged his hostess for the recipe. "Buy the cheapest ham possible, glaze the hell out of it, and cook it for a long time" was her pithy, right-on response.

So don't waste money on a fine aged ham. Use, as we do, a plain old bone-in, prepackaged, even "water-added" supermarket ham. 🥄

note from our test kitchen

If using half a 15-pound bone-in ham (7 to 8 pounds), halve the glazing ingredients and cook for half the time.

1	**15-pound smoked bone-in ham**
1½	**cups orange marmalade**
1	**cup Dijon mustard**
1½	**cups firmly packed dark brown sugar**
1	**rounded tablespoon whole cloves**

serves 30 or more

Preheat the oven to 300 degrees and set a rack in the lower-middle level.

Cut off and discard the tough outer skin and excess fat from the ham. Put it in a large roasting pan and, with a long sharp knife, score it, making crosshatch incisions about ½ inch deep and 1 inch apart all over the ham.

Roast for 2 hours. Remove the ham from the oven and increase the heat to 350 degrees.

For the glaze, stir together the marmalade, mustard, and brown sugar in a medium bowl. Stud the ham with the cloves, inserting them at the points where the cuts intersect. Brush the entire surface of the ham generously with the glaze and return to the oven.

Cook for another 1½ hours, brushing with the glaze at least 3 times. Transfer to a cutting board or platter and let rest for about 30 minutes.

Carve the ham and serve warm or at room temperature.

north african slow-roasted lamb

SOURCE David Rosengarten's *Taste*, TVFN
COOK Abdel Rebbaj

Say "Mesh-*we*"—one of the most succulent dishes in the world. A North African specialty, *mechoui* is simply a lamb
shoulder that is cooked and cooked
until the meat is so tender it collapses
and falls off the bones. In its native land,
mechoui is sometimes the last and most
spectacular dish in a progression of
banquet foods. Perhaps because guests
are so relaxed by the time it arrives, they
eat the meltingly tender pieces of lamb
with their hands or cradled in some pita
bread.

North Africans often dine on the
floor, sitting on cushions in a circle
around communal platters of food, although when David Rosengarten fea-
tured *mechoui* on his Food Network TV
show, *Taste,* he did not suggest sinking
to the floor. He did, however, give a
recipe for a dish that demands far more
unattended time than activity, as the
meat cooks almost by itself for 4 hours.

A lamb shoulder, which is full of
bones, is also full of flavor. Compara-
tively inexpensive, it is not always as
easy to find as a leg of lamb. Order it
from the butcher a couple of days in advance, then invite some very good
friends over for a very special meal. ❧

1 **6- to 7-pound lamb shoulder, bones left in**
8 **tablespoons (1 stick) unsalted butter, softened**
    Coarse salt
    Ground cumin

serves 4 to 6

Preheat the oven to 375 degrees and set a rack in the lower-
middle level.

Trim any loose bits of meat and excess fat from the lamb,
leaving about a ¼-inch layer of fat. Put the lamb skin side
up in a roasting pan, cover with aluminum foil, and roast for
1½ hours.

Remove from the oven, uncover, and rub generously with
about 2 tablespoons of the butter. Replace the foil and return the lamb to the oven. Repeat the butter rub three more
times, once every 15 minutes.

After 3½ hours, remove the foil, raise the heat to 425 degrees, and cook for 10 minutes more, or until the skin side is
golden and crusty. Remove the lamb from the oven, place on
a large platter, and let rest for 5 minutes.

Sprinkle the lamb with coarse salt and cumin. Carve it, or
pull it apart into serving pieces, and serve with additional
coarse salt and cumin in small dishes on the side.

MAIN DISHES

181

kashmiri-style leg of lamb

※

SOURCE *Stonyfield Farm Yogurt Cookbook* by Meg Cadoux Hirshberg

COOK Cynthia R. Topliss

This classic, elegant Mogul lamb recipe is one you'll make again and again once you try it. The delicate, fragrant seasonings subtly penetrate the lamb, and the yogurt gives it a tender, unctuous quality that's distinctive. The work — which is so minimal it shouldn't really be called work — is done ahead, so all you have to do is roast the lamb on the day you serve it. ☙

1 **5-pound leg of lamb**

spice mixture

2 **tablespoons fresh lemon juice**
1 **tablespoon peeled, grated fresh ginger**
4 **garlic cloves, crushed in a press**
1 **teaspoon salt**
1 **teaspoon ground cumin**
1 **teaspoon ground turmeric**
1/2 **teaspoon freshly ground black pepper**
1/2 **teaspoon ground cinnamon**
1/2 **teaspoon ground cardamom**
1/2 **teaspoon pure chile powder (see tip, page 7)**
1/4 **teaspoon ground cloves**

yogurt mixture

1 **cup plain yogurt**
2 **tablespoons blanched slivered almonds**
2 **tablespoons chopped pistachios**
1 **tablespoon ground turmeric**

1 **tablespoon honey**

serves 6 to 8

Remove any excess fat from the lamb. Using the point of a sharp knife, make deep slits all over the leg. Place the lamb in a large nonreactive dish.

To make the spice mixture: In a small bowl, combine all the ingredients. Rub over the lamb, pressing it into the slits.

notes from our test kitchen

- You can use a boned leg of lamb, which will make it easier to serve.

- Greek yogurt, which is strained, is even better in this recipe than supermarket yogurt. Low-fat yogurt is not a good option.

- An easy way to marinate the lamb is in a large resealable plastic bag. Marinating for 2 or even 3 days will deliver an even more flavorful piece of meat. Just be sure to turn it every now and then to redistribute the marinade.

To make the yogurt mixture: In a food processor or blender, thoroughly blend the yogurt, nuts, and turmeric. Spread over the lamb. Drizzle the honey over the lamb, cover, and marinate for 1 day in the refrigerator, turning occasionally.

Preheat the oven to 450 degrees.

Transfer the lamb to a roasting pan, cover (aluminum foil is fine), and cook for 30 minutes. Reduce the oven temperature to 350 degrees and cook for $1\frac{3}{4}$ hours more, or until meltingly tender. Uncover and serve warm or at room temperature.

⊰ VARIATION ⊱

A lovely touch — from a similar recipe in Jennifer Brennan's *One-Dish Meals of Asia* — is to add 10 saffron threads to the yogurt mixture. Soak them for 10 minutes in 2 tablespoons warm water; strain before adding them.

Side Dishes

Side Dishes

oven-roasted asparagus with fried capers

SOURCE *Cooking 1-2-3* by Rozanne Gold

COOK Rozanne Gold

Ruth Reichl, the esteemed editor in chief of *Gourmet* magazine, thinks this dish is the best one that chef and cookbook author Rozanne Gold has ever created—which is saying something. Over and over, James Beard Award–winner Gold comes through with minimalist dishes that sing with perfect pitch. This time she roasts asparagus spears at very high heat, then tops them with a surprise: fried capers.

Because the spears are in the oven for such a short time, they emerge with their green still intact, touched with roasty highlights. The final flourish of fried capers is, as Gold points out, startling. ❧

tip

WHEN YOU GET your asparagus home, remove its corseting so it can breathe and store it loose in a plastic bag in the vegetable bin of the fridge.

2 **pounds medium-thick asparagus spears**
¼ **cup extra-virgin olive oil**
   Salt
¼ **cup large capers, drained**
   Freshly ground black pepper

serves 4

Preheat the oven to 500 degrees.

Remove the woody bottoms of the asparagus, then trim the stalks to equal length. Drizzle 2 tablespoons of the olive oil on a rimmed baking sheet. Place the asparagus on the sheet and roll them in the oil. Sprinkle lightly with salt. Roast for 8 minutes, shaking the pan several times during the roasting. Transfer to a warm platter.

Meanwhile, heat the remaining 2 tablespoons oil in a small skillet. Fry the capers over high heat for 1 minute. Top the asparagus with the capers and serve, passing the pepper mill at the table.

---

notes from our test kitchen

- This dish is delicious hot, warm, or at room temperature, so it's a good choice for a party or buffet table.
- You can turn this into a brunch or lunch dish by topping it with a gently fried or poached egg and serving Canadian bacon on the side.

roasted green beans with garlic

* * *

SOURCE *Food & Wine*

COOK Nancy Verde Barr

If you've never tasted a roasted green bean, you're in for a big treat. What is arguably the most boring vegetable of them all takes on a big new personality once it gets the hot-hot treatment. And don't shy away from the anchovies here. If they usually taste too fishy for you, just soak them in milk for about 20 minutes to tame them. This is one of those astound-your-guests recipes, and few will guess the secret ingredient. *Food & Wine* named this recipe from Nancy Verde Barr one of the best they published in the 1990s. ❧

1 **pound green beans, trimmed**

¼ **cup extra-virgin olive oil**

3 **garlic cloves, smashed**

3 **thyme sprigs, each cut in half**

Salt and freshly ground black pepper

3 **anchovy fillets, mashed**

Finely grated zest of 1 lemon

2–3 **teaspoons fresh lemon juice (to taste)**

serves 4

Preheat the oven to 450 degrees and set a rack in the upper level.

Toss the beans with the oil, garlic, and thyme in a large baking dish. Season with salt and pepper. Spread the beans out in a single layer and roast, tossing occasionally, until tender and lightly browned, about 15 minutes.

Discard the thyme sprigs and transfer the beans to a bowl. Add the anchovies, lemon zest, and lemon juice and toss well to coat. Serve warm or at room temperature.

* * *

braised green beans with tomato and fennel

SOURCE *Washington Post*

COOK Ed Bruske after Anna del Conte and Corby Kummer

No single member of the vegetable kingdom benefits more from slow cooking than green beans. Although we'll always appreciate the crisp-tender goodness of summer's freshest (and skinniest) specimens, nothing beats the pleasure of digging your fork into a helping of tender braised beans. Sure, they turn drab and limp, but oh, man, one taste can make you weak in the knees.

Cooks from Italy and the American South were never brainwashed by the French blanch-and-shock method and have always known that long-cooked vegetables are best. The inspiration for this recipe comes from Anna del Conte, the Italian food historian and cookbook author, and it has both Italian (the fennel and tomato) and southern (the bacon) accents. The only liquid is the tomato juice and whatever juice the beans give off, which become intensely flavorful as they slowly cook. And when we say slow, we mean it: the beans simmer gently for 3 full hours. ❧

2 **tablespoons bacon drippings or olive oil**
1 **medium yellow onion, thinly sliced**
1 **pound green beans, trimmed (see note)**
1 **14½-ounce can diced tomatoes, with their juice**
2 **thick slices bacon, diced, or 1 ham hock**
1 **teaspoon freshly ground fennel seeds (see note)**
   Salt
   Freshly ground black pepper

serves 6 to 8

Heat the bacon drippings or oil in a heavy pot or Dutch oven with a tight-fitting lid over medium heat. Add the onion and cook, stirring occasionally, until tender, about 5 minutes. Add the beans, tomatoes and juice, bacon or ham hock, fennel, ½ teaspoon salt, and pepper to taste and bring to a simmer.

Cover, reduce the heat to very low, and simmer gently until tender, about 3 hours, stirring and tasting the beans occasionally. Season with salt and pepper to taste. Serve warm.

tip

IN HIS *Washington Post* article, Ed Bruske summarized research that Corby Kummer, one of the country's most authoritative food writers, published in the *Atlantic Monthly*. Flavor compounds take a long time (hours even) to develop. Indeed, flavor can appreciate as color fades, since the two are governed by distinctly different compounds. In addition, green beans contain a fibrous substance, lignin (also found in wood, hemp, and linen), which can be hard to digest unless fully cooked.

notes from our test kitchen

- The best beans for braising are mature ones—long and thick—not the skinny haricots verts. Save those for a quick dip in boiling salted water.

- To grind fennel seeds, use a mortar and pestle, or chop the seeds with a large chef's knife. Since they cook for so long, it's okay to leave them coarsely ground. The preground stuff won't give you the same flavor.

- If you like a kick to your food, go ahead and add a generous amount of coarsely ground black pepper. It will play nicely with the other flavors.

- These beans are just as good made ahead. Gently reheat them before serving.

roasted broccoli florets with gremolata

* * *

SOURCE *Bon Appétit*

COOK Diane Rossen Worthington

What a great way to serve broccoli! First you roast it with a little olive oil until it's crisp-tender and just browned at the edges, then you splash it with fresh lemon juice. Most cooks would be happy at this point, but California cook Diane Worthington tops it all with a variation on gremolata, the traditional garnish for osso buco: lemon zest, shallot, and crunchy golden bread crumbs.

Better yet, this way of cooking broccoli is fast and easy. You can make the gremolata up to 4 hours before you serve the broccoli, and roasting the florets in the oven makes the entire prep a cakewalk. ❧

4 tablespoons olive oil

1 shallot, chopped

½ cup coarse fresh bread crumbs made from crustless French bread

2 teaspoons grated lemon zest

Salt and freshly ground black pepper

2 pounds broccoli, stems removed and tops cut into 2-inch-long florets

Juice of ½ lemon, or more to taste

serves 6

Heat 1 tablespoon of the oil in a heavy medium skillet over medium-high heat. Add the shallot and sauté until it begins to brown, about 2 minutes. Add the bread crumbs and toast, stirring frequently, until golden, about 3 minutes. Transfer the mixture to a small bowl. Mix in the lemon zest and season with salt and pepper. You can make the gremolata up to 4 hours ahead.

Preheat the oven to 425 degrees.

Toss the broccoli with the remaining 3 tablespoons oil in a large bowl. Sprinkle with salt and pepper and toss to coat. Spread the florets out on a large rimmed baking sheet. Roast until the stems are crisp-tender and lightly browned, about 20 minutes. Sprinkle with the lemon juice. Transfer to a serving bowl or platter, sprinkle with the gremolata, and serve.

tip

A GREAT FAVORITE of Susan Westmoreland, food director of *Good Housekeeping,* is Roasted Cauliflower Florets and Red Onions with Rosemary. Cut 2 heads cauliflower (about 2 pounds each) into 1-inch florets. Combine them in a large bowl with 2 medium red onions (each cut into 12 wedges), 4 garlic cloves (crushed), 1 tablespoon fresh rosemary leaves (chopped), ¾ teaspoon salt, ¼ teaspoon freshly ground black pepper, and 2 tablespoons olive oil. Transfer the vegetables to two baking sheets and roast in a 450-degree oven for about 40 minutes, or until tender and browned, stirring occasionally and rotating the pans between the upper and lower levels halfway through the roasting time. Transfer to a platter and sprinkle with ¼ cup chopped fresh parsley. Garnish with rosemary sprigs and serve.

roasted brussels sprouts
with walnuts and pecorino

SOURCE *New York* magazine   STORY BY Rob Patronite

COOK Andrew Feinberg

No more wrinkled noses when people hear you're serving Brussels sprouts — they'll be begging for more. Properly cooked Brussels sprouts are sweet, nutty, and full of good flavor. In this preparation, from Franny's restaurant in Brooklyn, they're also anointed with olive oil and given a good roasting. The walnuts and pecorino are perfect counterpoints. Look for fresh Brussels sprouts on their long stalks in the fall at farmers' markets. ꕥ

1/2 **cup walnuts**
24 **Brussels sprouts, each cut in half**
Extra-virgin olive oil
Salt and freshly ground black pepper
Squeeze of fresh lemon juice
Aged pecorino Toscano cheese for topping

serves 4

Preheat the oven to 350 degrees.

Toast the walnuts on a rimmed baking sheet for about 10 minutes, or until they smell toasty; set aside. Crumble them when they're cool enough to handle.

Turn the oven up to 450 degrees.

Toss the Brussels sprouts in a bowl with enough olive oil to coat each sprout, 2 to 3 tablespoons. Season with salt and pepper to taste.

Arrange the sprouts in a single layer on the baking sheet and roast for about 20 minutes, or until fork-tender and some of the leaves have become crunchy.

Let the sprouts cool on the baking sheet, then toss in a large bowl with the walnuts. Drizzle liberally with olive oil, add a squeeze of lemon juice, and season with salt and pepper. Shave some of the cheese on top and serve warm.

pan-roasted carrots

❋

SOURCE *New York Times*

COOK Tom Colicchio

Pan-roasting brings out the natural sweetness of carrots, and that's underscored here by the touch of honey at the end of the cooking time. When you bring them to the table, expect a chorus of oohs and aahs as the rosemary fragrance wafts up.

The recipe comes from Tom Colicchio, the Manhattan chef and restaurateur known for his exquisite but straightforward comfort food — high-class home cooking. ◕

notes from our test kitchen

- High rollers can spring for the very expensive fleur de sel, the flaky salt from France, which is indeed delicious. But sea salt will do just fine.

- You want skinny, in-season carrots for this dish. You can also use big old carrots, but first cut them crosswise into quarters and then cut each quarter in half lengthwise. They will need to cook quite a bit longer to become tender. Because they're less sweet, they may not brown much until you add the honey and butter. Just turn the heat up a bit at that point, and you'll get a nice caramelization.

- Cook the carrots in a single layer. They'll shrink, so don't worry if they're a little tight in the pan at first.

2 **tablespoons extra-virgin olive oil**

16 **long, thin carrots, peeled and trimmed**
   Fleur de sel and freshly ground black pepper

4 **rosemary sprigs**

4 **teaspoons honey**

1 **tablespoon butter**

serves 4

In a large sauté pan, heat the oil over low heat. Add the carrots and fleur de sel and pepper to taste. Cook, turning the carrots occasionally, until golden brown on all sides, 15 to 20 minutes.

Add the rosemary during the last 5 minutes of cooking. Just before serving, add the honey and butter and mix well. Serve hot.

⊰ VARIATION ⊱

In his first cookbook, *Think Like a Chef,* Tom Colicchio uses this same brilliant technique with great success for asparagus. The technique works best with thin (even pencil-thin) asparagus, but thicker spears can also take this treatment, though they'll need to cook longer. Follow the method for pan-roasting the carrots, substituting peanut oil for the olive oil and 2 pounds thin asparagus (trimmed) for the carrots. Eliminate the honey and use 1 teaspoon fresh thyme leaves in place of the rosemary. Expect the asparagus to cook in about 10 minutes, and don't be afraid to add more butter (we use about 3 tablespoons) if the pan seems to be drying out.

cauliflower with garlic and paprika

SOURCE *Savoring Spain and Portugal* by Joyce Goldstein

COOK Joyce Goldstein

If you think you don't like cauliflower, you owe it to yourself to try this recipe from the Murcia region of Spain. The cauliflower takes on a deep, rusty color from the paprika. And the nutty, garlicky sauce, with its crisp bread crumbs, is perfect. Although it's meant to be served hot, the cauliflower is just as good at room temperature. ❧

2   pounds cauliflower, cut into florets
2   teaspoons fresh lemon juice
1/3   cup olive oil
2–3   slices coarse country bread, crusts removed
1   tablespoon paprika (see note)
2   cups water
    Salt
3   garlic cloves, coarsely chopped
3   tablespoons chopped fresh flat-leaf parsley
2   tablespoons pine nuts, toasted (see note and tip)
    Freshly ground black pepper

serves 6

Fill a bowl with water and add the cauliflower florets and lemon juice. Set aside until needed.

In a large frying pan over medium heat, warm the olive oil. Add the bread slices and fry, turning once, until crisp and golden on both sides, 3 to 5 minutes total. Remove from the pan, break into pieces, and place in a blender or food processor.

Add the paprika to the oil remaining in the pan and reduce the heat to low. Cook for 1 to 2 minutes to release the paprika's fragrance. Add the water and bring to a boil. Drain the cauliflower and add to the pan. Season with a little salt and cook, uncovered, until the cauliflower is tender, 10 to 15 minutes.

tip

TO AVOID BURNING delicate nuts such as pine nuts, which happens easily when you're toasting them in the oven or on top of the stove, Denise Landis (in the *New York Times*) recommends toasting them in the microwave. Spread a small amount of nuts evenly in a single layer in a 10-inch glass pie plate and stir every 30 seconds. They'll be done in a few minutes.

Meanwhile, add the garlic, parsley, and pine nuts to the bread in the blender or food processor and pulse until well crushed. When the cauliflower is tender, add about ¼ cup of the cauliflower cooking water to the bread crumb mixture, pulse once, and then transfer the mixture to the frying pan. Stir to mix, then cook for 5 minutes over low heat to blend the flavors.

Season the cauliflower with salt and pepper to taste, transfer to a warm serving bowl, and serve.

notes from our test kitchen

- If at all possible, use real Spanish paprika.
- If you think pine nuts taste soapy and unpleasant, you may have been using Chinese pine nuts (the usual supermarket variety). These are not nearly as nice as European ones, which are more likely to be found at specialty markets.

pan-roasted cauliflower with capers

SOURCE *The Maccioni Family Cookbook* by Egi Maccioni with Peter Kaminsky

COOK Egi Maccioni

The Maccioni family is part of Manhattan restaurant royalty. Paterfamilias Sirio Maccioni famously created Le Cirque. The Maccioni sons also work in the family business, and Egi Maccioni, their mother, participates mostly behind the scenes, contributing her signature Tuscan recipes. She's a superb home cook, unswayed by the gourmet trends of the moment.

When Egi decided to write her own cookbook, she had a number of favorite dishes in mind, but not this one, which seemed much too simple to her. Then one night she made it for Sirio, who took a second helping and said, "Why don't you put this in your book?"

Thank you, Sirio. This is now our favorite way to fix cauliflower. Cooking the cauliflower whole keeps it from getting watery and overcooked in places, and it's also easier. Then there are the capers. Sweetly delicious as it is, cauliflower needs help, and capers are the ticket. ❧

1 head cauliflower

¼ cup olive oil

4 garlic cloves, minced

2 tablespoons capers, rinsed and drained
Salt and freshly ground black pepper

serves 4

Place the cauliflower in a large pot and cover with water. Bring to a boil, reduce the heat, and simmer until the base is tender, about 15 minutes (see note). Drain the cauliflower. When it's cool enough to handle, cut into bite-size chunks.

Heat the olive oil in a large skillet over medium-high heat. Add the garlic and cook for 1 minute. Add the cauliflower chunks and cook, stirring, for about 5 minutes, or until lightly browned. Remove from the heat. Stir in the capers and season with salt and pepper to taste. Serve warm.

notes from our test kitchen

- Remove any green leaves from the cauliflower before cooking.
- If you have a relatively small head of cauliflower, it may take less time to cook. Check the base: if it's tender, it's done, which may happen in 8 to 12 minutes.

chard with ginger

❈

SOURCE Cooking at the Gardener (Healdsburg, California), cooking class handout
COOK Niloufer Ichaporia King

This well-traveled dish was taught to Niloufer King, a San Francisco cook born in Bombay, by a chef from the Seychelles. The recipe works for virtually all greens, although some tougher ones, such as kale, need a quick parboil first.

The simple seasonings here are key: fresh ginger, chiles, and garlic, with a bit of salt and oil to pull it together. The leaves and stems of the greens are shredded and cooked in just the moisture clinging to them after being washed. The ginger adds a wonderful zingy touch, but you can take the greens in another direction by using just the garlic and a bit of chile. Adding the salt to the oil, says Niloufer, is an old Chinese trick that brings everything into focus.

One of the best things about this uncomplicated preparation is that it's served at room temperature. ❧

About 15 leaves Swiss chard or other greens

2 **tablespoons olive or peanut oil**

Salt

1 **1- to 2-inch piece fresh ginger, peeled, sliced, and shredded (optional)**

1–2 **red chiles, fresh or dried (to taste)**

2 **garlic cloves, chopped**

serves 4

Wash and shred the greens. Heat the oil in a wok or deep skillet over medium-high heat. Add the salt to taste, ginger, chiles, and garlic. When the ginger is sizzling, add the greens and stir them around. The greens will quickly cook down. If they seem resistant, cover them briefly. They're done when they are tender and wilted. Serve at room temperature.

notes from our test kitchen

- If you have fresh red chiles (green ones are good, too), slit them lengthwise up to the stem. Leave the dried ones whole, to be eaten by the intrepid.
- For a very mild garlic flavor, use the garlic whole or cut it in half lengthwise. Remove it from the pan just as it begins to color.
- For a crowd, cook the greens in batches.

double-corn polenta

SOURCE *Martha Stewart Living* (TV program)
COOKS Johanne Killeen and George Germon

Summer is written all over this sensational polenta, with its ripe tomatoes and fresh corn. We also like the idea of this hearty dish for winter, made with cherry tomatoes, which taste good all year long, and frozen corn kernels.

We'd be as delighted to see it for brunch as we would for an appetizer, a main course, or a side dish at dinnertime. It's very rich and creamy, which made us think "appetizer." But it would also be a good vegetarian main dish (figure 4 servings). And we think it is superb alongside juicy grilled steaks or lamb as well. The recipe serves 6 to 8 as a side, but it's flexible — you can also cut it in half for an intimate two-person supper. 🥄

2 ripe tomatoes (see note)
1/4 cup extra-virgin olive oil
Coarse salt
4 cups water
1 cup heavy cream
2 tablespoons unsalted butter
1 cup medium-grind cornmeal
1 1/2 cups cooked corn kernels (see note)
2/3 cup loosely packed mixed fresh herbs, such as parsley, thyme, chives, and basil, coarsely chopped
2/3 cup freshly grated Parmesan cheese
4 large fresh basil leaves for garnish

serves 6 to 8

Core and roughly chop the tomatoes. In a small bowl, toss them with the oil. Season with salt to taste and set aside.

In a medium heavy saucepan, combine the water and cream over medium-high heat. Bring to a boil. Add the butter and salt to taste and stir to melt the butter. Whisking constantly, add the cornmeal in a slow, steady stream. Continue to whisk until all of the lumps have disappeared. Reduce the heat to low and gently simmer, stirring constantly with a wooden spoon, until the polenta is thick and creamy, about 20 minutes.

Fold in the corn, herbs, and Parmesan. Spoon into a heated serving bowl and top with the tomatoes and any

tip

YEARS AGO we learned a breakthrough formula for cooking polenta from Mediterranean cook extraordinaire Paula Wolfert. She adapted the method from the directions on the back of a polenta package. There's no stirring, and the polenta comes out so velvety and creamy that it pours like molten lava. For 6 servings, combine 2 cups medium-coarse or coarse cornmeal, 6 to 12 cups water or chicken broth (less water or broth for very stiff polenta, more for very soft), 2 tablespoons butter or olive oil, and 2 teaspoons salt in a greased, heavy 12-inch ovenproof saucepan or Dutch oven. Stir with a fork or whisk until blended. The mixture will separate, but don't worry — it won't come together until later. Bake in a 350-degree oven, uncovered, for 1 hour and 20 minutes, or until the polenta is creamy and tender. Stir the polenta with a long-pronged fork, adjust the seasoning, and bake for 10 minutes more. Remove from the oven and let rest for 5 minutes before pouring onto a wooden pizza peel or into a buttered bowl. Stir in softened butter or grated cheese, if desired.

accumulated juice. Tear the basil leaves into small pieces and sprinkle over the tomatoes. Serve immediately.

notes from our test kitchen

- To substitute cherry tomatoes, you'll need a generous ½ pint.
- For 1½ cups of corn kernels, boil 3 or 4 ears of corn for 3 minutes. Cool and scrape off the kernels. Alternatively, use frozen corn kernels, cooked for about 3 minutes in boiling water and drained.
- When serving this as a main course, divide the polenta among four warm bowls and serve immediately.

nutty roasted cremini

SOURCE *Vegetables from Amaranth to Zucchini* by Elizabeth Schneider

COOK Elizabeth Schneider

We presented these mushrooms to a mushroom-loathing member of our immediate family, and to our surprise he pronounced them wonderful. Mushroom lovers will be even more entranced by this brilliant side dish. The mushrooms stay juicy and a little chewy but take on a wonderful roasty aroma from the spices, sherry, and hazelnuts.

Elizabeth Schneider suggests cooking the mushrooms in the hot oven after a roast has come out and is standing, waiting to be carved. That's a great idea for everything from chicken to roast beef. ❧

tip

TO TOAST the hazelnuts, which can be done ahead, preheat the oven to 450 degrees. Arrange the nuts on a baking sheet and mist with water. Roast for 10 to 15 minutes, or until fragrant and beginning to color. Let cool slightly. Schneider has a great trick for husking hazelnuts: she chops them in the food processor, using the plastic blade. After removing the husks, she returns the nuts to the processor and chops them with the metal blade. Any stubborn husks can be ignored.

1 tablespoon sherry

1 teaspoon Chinese five-spice powder, ground fennel seeds, or ground aniseeds

About ¹/₂ teaspoon kosher salt

1¹/₂ pounds small cremini mushrooms, wiped clean and stems discarded

2 tablespoons hazelnut oil

¹/₃ cup coarsely chopped toasted husked hazelnuts (see tip)

Freshly ground black pepper

serves 4 to 6

Preheat the oven to 450 degrees and set a rack in the upper-middle level.

In a large bowl, combine the sherry, five-spice powder (or fennel seeds or aniseeds), and salt, mixing well. Add the mushrooms and oil, tossing to coat as evenly as possible. Place the mushrooms in a single layer in a roasting pan.

Roast until cooked through and browned, 10 to 15 minutes. Toss the mushrooms with the hazelnuts and pepper to taste. Serve hot.

creamy anchos and onions

SOURCE *Food & Wine* STORY BY Molly Glentzer

COOK Robert Del Grande

Texas chef Robert Del Grande took *Food & Wine* magazine south of the border for a Thanksgiving issue one year and came up with some sizzling recipes. One of our favorites is this spin on traditional creamed onions, made with real cream, not gluey white sauce, and enlivened with sweet, earthy ancho chiles, as well as some fresh tarragon and a touch of lime.

These onions are as wonderful with roast pork, or with any grilled meat or poultry, as they are with turkey. Best of all, you can make the dish a day ahead and reheat it gently. If the cream has thickened too much, just add a few tablespoons of water.

If you haven't worked with whole dried chiles before, this recipe is a great introduction; it couldn't be simpler. ❧

tip

WE HEARD a Bounty paper towel commercial recently that advocated putting garlic cloves in the microwave for 15 seconds (wrapped in paper towels, of course) to facilitate peeling. This method works for us, although it slightly cooks the garlic. Be careful when you retrieve the cloves from the microwave; they're extremely hot.

5   medium dried ancho chiles, stemmed and seeded

1   tablespoon unsalted butter

1   pound small white onions, trimmed but with the root ends left intact, then cut in half lengthwise

4   garlic cloves, coarsely chopped

1   cup turkey or chicken broth or canned low-sodium chicken broth

2   cups heavy cream

1/4   cup fresh tarragon leaves

1   teaspoon salt

1   teaspoon fresh lime juice

serves 8

In a large cast-iron skillet, toast the anchos over medium heat, pressing down with a spatula, until fragrant and blistered, about 20 seconds per side. Transfer to a small plate and let cool, then cut the anchos into 1/2-inch pieces.

In a large skillet, melt the butter over medium heat. Add the onions and garlic, cover, and cook, stirring occasionally, until the onions are softened, about 5 minutes. Add the broth and simmer until reduced by half, 6 to 7 minutes. Add the anchos, cream, and tarragon and cook over medium-low heat until the onions and anchos are tender and the cream is thickened, about 10 minutes. Add the salt and lime juice, transfer to a serving bowl, and serve warm.

potato–green chile gratin

SOURCE *Gourmet* STORY BY Zanne Stewart

COOK Deborah Madison

The Santa Fe–based vegetarian cook Deborah Madison has always produced the most exquisite vegetable dishes imaginable, but this time she's really outdone herself. There are just a few in-gredients in this dish — chiles, potatoes, cream, a solitary clove of garlic — and yet it has a complex flavor that's memo-rable. There's never any left, no matter how few people are at the table.

You can make the gratin a day ahead, let it cool completely before re-frigerating, and simply reheat (covered, in a 350-degree oven) after it has come to room temperature. This flexibility makes it a great candidate for a potluck supper. 🍃

note from our test kitchen

To roast the chiles, place them on the rack of a broiler pan about 2 inches from the heat. Roast, turning often with tongs, until the skins are blackened, 5 to 8 minutes. Put the chiles in a bowl and cover with a plate. Let steam for about 15 minutes. Peel off the skins with your fingers or rub them off with paper towels. Don't try to rinse the skins off, or you'll lose a lot of fla-vor down the drain. Remove and discard the stems and seeds.

6 **fresh green Anaheim or poblano chiles, roasted and peeled (see note)**

2 **cups heavy cream or half-and-half**

1 **large garlic clove**

2½ **pounds russet potatoes (about 5 medium)**
    Salt

serves 6

Preheat the oven to 375 degrees and set a rack in the lower-middle level.

Discard the chile seeds (and the ribs if you'd like less heat) and finely chop the chiles. Set aside.

In a medium saucepan, bring the cream with the garlic just to a simmer, then remove from the heat. Set aside to steep.

Peel the potatoes and cut crosswise into ⅛-inch-thick slices using a mandoline or sharp knife.

Arrange one fourth of the potatoes evenly in the bottom of a well-buttered, 2-quart shallow baking dish, overlapping them slightly, and sprinkle with salt and one fourth of the chiles. Make 3 more layers in the same manner. Remove the garlic from the cream and pour the cream over the potatoes.

Cover the dish with aluminum foil and bake for 45 minutes. Remove the foil and bake until the gratin is golden brown on top and bubbling, about 30 minutes more. Let cool slightly before serving.

roasted potato crisps with fresh herbs

* * *

SOURCE *Boston Globe*

COOKS Sheryl Julian and Julie Riven

Olive oil

1 tablespoon chopped fresh chives

2 teaspoons chopped fresh rosemary

1 teaspoon chopped fresh oregano

4 russet potatoes, peeled and placed in a bowl
of cold water

Salt and freshly ground black pepper

serves 4

These crusty herb-infused potatoes are good alongside summer grilled dishes and wintry roasts. This is one of those insouciant recipes in which quantities aren't particularly important, and the seasonings can be changed to suit your whim. In summer make them with fresh herbs, if you have them. In winter they're excellent with dried rosemary and thyme and fresh chives—just cut the amounts in half for the dried herbs.

The only trick is to cut the potatoes into the thinnest possible slices. For that, you need a mandoline or Japanese vegetable slicer—or your own excellent knife skills. ✍

Preheat the oven to 425 degrees. Sprinkle the bottom of a jelly-roll pan or shallow roasting pan with oil and set aside.

Combine the herbs in a bowl. Slice the potatoes as thinly as possible with a mandoline or Japanese vegetable slicer.

Arrange the potatoes on the pan in haphazard layers, sprinkling the layers with olive oil, herbs, and salt and pepper to taste.

Roast the potatoes for 20 minutes, then turn them with a spatula. The neat layers will break up, but that's fine. Roast for 20 to 30 minutes more, turning several more times, until the potatoes are cooked through and crusty.

To remove the potatoes from the pan, lift them with the spatula—they will separate as you do so—and transfer to a serving platter or individual plates. Serve at once.

tip

IF YOU HAVE no fancy slicing machine and your knife skills are not well honed, you might want to invest in an old-fashioned American tool that's great for making coleslaw, slicing cucumbers, and slicing these potatoes. It's called Feemster's Famous Slicer, and it's available in many hardware stores and some kitchen stores for under $10.

⊰ VARIATION ⊱

The potatoes are also delicious scattered with herbes de Provence.

party potatoes

SOURCE *One Potato, Two Potato* by Roy Finamore with Molly Stevens
COOKS Roy Finamore and Molly Stevens

Probably the most frustrating part of preparing Thanksgiving dinner is the last-minute potato mashing and gravy making. If you have this recipe in your arsenal, you can knock off the mashed potatoes 2 days ahead and have them sitting pretty in the refrigerator, ready for a last-minute heating. But that's not the only time you need these potatoes; they're also great for a buffet or for any crowd.

These luxurious mashed potatoes have a couple of other virtues, too. They're light and fluffy because they're whipped with an electric mixer, and they're incredibly luscious because they have sour cream and butter, plus cream cheese to give them a little edge. ॰

3 **pounds russet potatoes, peeled and cut into chunks**

   Coarse salt

8 **tablespoons (1 stick) unsalted butter, softened, cut into 8 pieces**

1 **8-ounce package cream cheese, at room temperature**

1/2 **cup sour cream, at room temperature**

2/3 **cup milk, warmed, or as needed**

   Freshly ground black pepper

   Paprika for garnish

serves 10 to 12

Place the potatoes in a large saucepan and add cold water to cover by at least 1 inch. Add a good pinch of salt and bring to a boil. Reduce the heat to medium, partially cover, and cook until the potatoes are very tender, 12 to 15 minutes. Drain the potatoes and return them to the pan over medium heat. Cook, shaking the pan and stirring so the potatoes don't stick, for 1 to 2 minutes, or until the potatoes are floury and have formed a film on the bottom of the pan.

Remove from the heat and break up the potatoes with a handheld mixer on low speed. Gradually drop in 6 table-spoons of the butter and beat until it is absorbed. Refriger-ate the remaining 2 tablespoons butter. Gradually add the cream cheese and sour cream, beating well after each addi-tion. Beat in the milk a little at a time. You want the potatoes to be fluffy and light. If they seem to be getting too wet, don't add all the milk. Season with salt and pepper to taste. (If you

note from our test kitchen

If you'd like to do a little lily gilding, you could add ¼ cup chopped fresh chives to the potatoes.

don't have an electric mixer, use a hand masher to start and then use a wooden spoon to beat in the butter, cream cheese, sour cream, and milk. Beat the milk into the potatoes one third at a time, beating vigorously after each addition.)

Butter a 9-x-13-inch baking dish and spoon the potatoes into it. Smooth the top, then use a spatula or fork to swirl or score the surface to leave little peaks that will brown nicely during baking. Refrigerate, covered tightly with plastic wrap, for up to 2 days before baking.

Preheat the oven to 350 degrees.

Dust the top of the potatoes with paprika. Cut the remaining 2 tablespoons butter into small pieces and scatter them over the top. Bake until the potatoes are heated through and the top is lightly golden, about 1 hour. (Expect it to take only half the time if the potatoes haven't been refrigerated.) Serve hot.

mashed potatoes
with sage and white cheddar cheese

SOURCE *Bon Appétit*

COOK Jeanne Thiel Kelley

When the holidays arrive, we look high and low for make-ahead recipes that can serve a crowd and that everyone will love. We've learned from experience not to stray too far from the classics, but we can't resist those with a twist or some surprise element to make a truly memorable feast. Here's one such recipe.

Regular mashed potatoes get a boost from sage-infused browned butter and grated sharp cheddar cheese. By using white cheddar—not the bright orange stuff—the potatoes don't look different, but one taste will tell you that they are deliciously so. ❧

4 pounds russet potatoes, peeled and cut into 1½-inch cubes

Salt

4 tablespoons (½ stick) unsalted butter

2 tablespoons plus 1 teaspoon minced fresh sage

¾ cup whipping cream

¾ cup whole milk

2¼ cups coarsely grated sharp white cheddar cheese (about 9 ounces)

Freshly ground black pepper

serves 10

Butter an 8- to 10-cup baking dish. Cook the potatoes in a large pot of boiling salted water until tender, about 12 minutes.

Meanwhile, melt the butter in a medium saucepan over medium-high heat. Add 2 tablespoons of the sage and stir until the butter begins to brown, about 3 minutes. Add the cream and milk and bring to a simmer.

Drain the potatoes and return to the pot. Stir over medium heat until the excess moisture evaporates. Begin to mash the potatoes with a hand masher. Add the cream mixture and continue mashing until the potatoes are as lump-free as you like. Stir in 1¾ cups of the cheese. Season with salt and pepper to taste and transfer to the prepared dish. Sprinkle with the remaining ½ cup cheese and the remain-

notes from our test kitchen

- For best results, start the potatoes in cold water and bring them to a gentle boil over medium-high heat. Dropping them into already boiling water will cause them to cook unevenly.

- Don't rush when you're browning the butter and sage. If the butter is not really browned, it won't have the same depth of flavor.

- For entirely lump-free, fluffy potatoes, use a ricer to mash them after you've dried them over the heat and before adding the cream mixture.

- The potatoes will take less time to bake if they haven't been refrigerated, a bit more if they've been refrigerated overnight.

ing 1 teaspoon sage. The potatoes can be made up to 2 days ahead, covered with plastic wrap, and refrigerated.

Preheat the oven to 375 degrees.

Bake the potatoes, uncovered, until heated through and golden brown, about 45 minutes. Serve hot.

sweet potatoes with ginger and apple cider

SOURCE *Bon Appétit*

COOK Rozanne Gold

With her inspired approach to cooking, chef and cookbook author Rozanne Gold adds only two ingredients to pureed sweet potatoes (three, if you count the butter) and thus transforms a bland side dish into something altogether unforgettable. An entire quart of apple cider is reduced to a deeply concentrated apple syrup spiked with fresh ginger. After tasting these sweet-and-spicy potatoes at Thanksgiving, one guest called more than a week later to say that she couldn't stop thinking about them. ❧

notes from our test kitchen

- Instead of boiling the sweet potatoes, you can roast them at 400 degrees until quite tender, about 1 hour. They will have a slightly richer, more concentrated flavor.

- Avoid clear, filtered apple juice. You want cloudy, unfiltered fresh cider if you can find it. In the fall, most natural food stores carry it.

2½ **pounds sweet potatoes (about 3 medium)**
4 **cups apple cider**
¼ **cup peeled, minced fresh ginger**
2 **tablespoons butter**
Salt and freshly ground black pepper

serves 6

Place the potatoes in a large pot and add water to cover by 2 inches. Bring to a boil over high heat. Reduce the heat to medium-low and simmer until very tender, about 40 minutes. Drain and let cool. Peel the potatoes and cut them into large chunks. Transfer to a food processor.

Bring the cider to a boil in a medium heavy saucepan over high heat. Reduce the heat to medium-low and simmer until the cider is reduced to 1 cup, about 30 minutes. Transfer the cider, ginger, and butter to the food processor with the potatoes and process until very smooth. Season with salt and pepper and serve hot.

⊰ VARIATION ⊱

For a spicier version, try chef/restaurateur Bobby Flay's Whipped Chipotle Sweet Potatoes. Bake as many sweet potatoes as you need until very soft. When the potatoes are cool enough to handle, cut them in half and scoop the flesh into a bowl. With an electric mixer on medium speed, whip the potatoes along with a bit of minced chipotle chile in adobo sauce to taste (start with about ½ teaspoon per pound of potatoes), a few tablespoons softened butter, and salt to taste. Spread into a buttered baking dish and bake in a 350-degree oven until heated through.

zucchini with cilantro and cream

SOURCE *Bon Appétit*
COOK Helene Wagner-Popoff

This quick recipe is inspired by the subtle flavors of Corsican cooking, as well as by the products of the author's bountiful backyard garden on the island. It's hard to put your finger on why these familiar tastes are so sensational together.

Serve it as a side dish or use it as a sauce, spooned over roasted fish. ❧

2 tablespoons butter

2 large garlic cloves, minced

1³⁄₄ pounds zucchini, trimmed and cut into ¹⁄₃-inch-thick rounds

4 tablespoons chopped fresh cilantro

¹⁄₃ cup whipping cream

Salt and freshly ground black pepper

serves 4

Melt the butter in a large heavy skillet over medium heat. Add the garlic and sauté for 10 seconds. Add the zucchini and 2 tablespoons of the cilantro and sauté until the zucchini is crisp-tender, about 5 minutes. Add the cream and simmer until just slightly thickened, about 1 minute. Season with salt and pepper to taste, sprinkle with the remaining 2 tablespoons cilantro, and serve.

mushy zucchini

SOURCE *The Whole Beast* by Fergus Henderson
COOK Fergus Henderson

St. John, Fergus Henderson's London restaurant, has become a mecca for serious eaters from all over the world. What they love about Henderson's cooking is his astonishing ability to take the most common thing and transform it into something extraordinary. Very often the transformations involve bits of a pig that are usually dismissed by other cooks—tail, snout, trotters. But Henderson is equally inventive with something as ordinary, and even boring, as zucchini. When you eat this dish, you feel as if you're tasting zucchini for the first time —as if its true spirit has finally been released. Lovers of al dente vegetables, beware—your days are numbered. ❧

8 tablespoons (1 stick) unsalted butter

4 garlic cloves, minced

1 pound zucchini, trimmed and cut into rounds a little thicker than $1/3$ inch

Sea salt and freshly ground black pepper

serves 6

Melt the butter in a large skillet over low heat. Add the garlic and cook, making sure it doesn't brown or burn. Add the zucchini, season carefully with salt and pepper to taste, and toss to coat. Cover and continue the gentle cooking, stirring occasionally.

After 15 minutes, uncover. When some of the zucchini slices start to break, binding the whole together, check the seasoning and serve.

pumpkin and goat cheese gratin

SOURCE The Vinegar Factory newsletter
COOK Allan Schanbacher

Manhattan chef Allan Schanbacher's glorious gratin—a wonderful mate for pork or turkey—has become a staple of our fall and winter cooking repertoire. It's also circumvented some potential holiday crises, solving the inevitable "But what can the vegetarians eat?" Thanksgiving dilemma. We found his terrific recipe in the newsletter of the Vinegar Factory, a gourmet store in New York City. Schanbacher was the chef at Across the Street, a restaurant owned by—and across the street from—the Vinegar Factory, which is now called Eli's Vinegar Factory after its owner, Eli Zabar.

2 small sugar pumpkins or 2 large butternut squash

3 tablespoons extra-virgin olive oil

1 tablespoon firmly packed dark brown sugar

1 teaspoon ancho chile powder (see tip, page 7)

8 fresh sage leaves, cut into slivers
   Salt and freshly ground black pepper

10 ounces fresh goat cheese

serves 6

Preheat the oven to 450 degrees and set a rack in the middle level. Grease a baking sheet and butter an 8-inch square baking dish.

Cut pumpkins in half crosswise or squash in half lengthwise. Peel and seed the pumpkins or squash. Cut the flesh into 1-inch cubes. You should have 8 to 10 cups.

Place the cubes in a large bowl, drizzle with the oil, and toss until thoroughly coated. Mix the brown sugar, chile powder, and sage leaves in a small bowl and toss them with the squash cubes. Season generously with salt and pepper.

Arrange the squash cubes in a single layer on the baking sheet and roast, turning once, until tender and lightly browned, about 15 minutes. Remove from the oven and let cool on the baking sheet for about 10 minutes.

Transfer the squash to the baking dish; the cubes should be loosely packed. Crumble the goat cheese over the top. The gratin can be prepared several hours in advance up to this point; refrigerate if it's up to 1 day in advance. Let come to room temperature before baking.

Bake for 15 to 20 minutes, or until the squash is heated through and the cheese is lightly browned. Let rest for a few minutes and serve.

butternut squash rounds with sage

※

SOURCE *Everyday Greens* by Annie Somerville
COOK Annie Somerville

This simple dish from the famous San Francisco vegetarian restaurant Greens is unusual and gorgeous. The intensely orange squash rounds are especially beautiful served on a rustic platter, as Somerville suggests.

But they're not just another pretty face. The squash, brushed with a little garlic oil, caramelizes as it roasts, becoming savory and just a bit sweet. The sage pulls it all together into what seems to be the essence of fall. 🍃

tips

REAL SIMPLE offers this helpful advice for buying and storing butternut squash. Choose a squash that feels heavy for its size. Shiny or slightly green skin indicates an underripe squash. Look for dull cream- or caramel-colored skin. Do not refrigerate butternut squash, or it will become mealy. Store in a cool, dark place for up to 1 month.

AMY GOLDMAN, author of *The Compleat Squash,* cautions against buying winter squash that may have been harvested while immature. If you can pierce the skin with your thumbnail, the squash will improve a lot if you keep it in a cool place for 2 to 3 weeks.

2	**butternut squash with long necks**
1	**tablespoon garlic oil (see note)**
10–15	**fresh sage leaves (to taste), chopped**
	Salt and freshly ground black pepper

serves 6

Preheat the oven to 400 degrees.

Cut each squash at the base of the neck, reserving the bulbous part with the seeds for another dish. Remove the stem, peel the neck, and cut into ¾-inch-thick rounds. You should have about 12 slices.

Lay the squash slices on a baking sheet. Brush both sides with the garlic oil and sprinkle with the sage and a little salt and pepper. Roast for 15 minutes, then loosen the rounds with a spatula, but don't turn them — they will brown on the bottom. Cook for another 5 minutes, until the squash is tender and the color is vibrant. Serve warm.

---

notes from our test kitchen

- Keep an eye out in the fall for butternut squash with very long necks. Sometimes you'll find one that's nearly all neck, which is convenient for making the squash rounds. Since butternut squash keeps well, you can acquire yours weeks ahead of when you plan to cook it. Save the bulbous part of the squash for soup, which you can garnish with the toasted seeds.

- You can buy garlic oil, or you can make your own on the spot. Smack a garlic clove with the side of a chef's knife so it breaks open and let it sit in olive oil for 30 minutes. Remove the garlic and use the oil. Refrigerate any leftover oil, tightly covered, for 1 to 2 days.

arroz verde

SOURCE *Jim Peyton's New Cooking from Old Mexico* by Jim Peyton

COOK Jim Peyton

If you asked us what we wanted to eat tonight, this emerald green, aromatic rice might well be the answer. Fortunately, it goes so well with so many main dishes that there's never a problem fitting it into the menu, and, to be honest, it has sometimes been dinner all by itself.

In *Fine Cooking* magazine, Jim Peyton, a Mexican cookbook author and cooking teacher in San Antonio, writes that he is increasingly amazed by Mexico's world-class rice dishes, many with Spanish antecedents, "which come to light, one after another, like unexpected treasures at a rummage sale." ✍

tip

THIS RECIPE is best served just after it's made, but you can prepare it a day or two in advance, if necessary, and reheat it in the microwave. To reheat, spread out the cooked rice in a shallow bowl, cover with plastic wrap, vent, and heat on high until the rice is steaming.

1 cup tightly packed stemmed spinach leaves (about 1½ ounces)

½ cup tightly packed cilantro sprigs (about ½ ounce)

1¼ cups homemade chicken broth or canned low-sodium chicken broth

1¼ cups milk

1 teaspoon salt

3 tablespoons unsalted butter

1 tablespoon olive oil

1½ cups long-grain white rice

¼ cup minced onion

1 garlic clove, minced

serves 6 to 8

Place the spinach, cilantro, and broth in a blender and blend until the vegetables are pureed. Add the milk and salt and blend until well combined.

In a medium saucepan, heat the butter and olive oil over medium heat. When the butter is melted, add the rice and sauté, stirring frequently, until it just begins to brown, 3 to 4 minutes. Add the onion and garlic and cook for 1 minute more, stirring constantly. Add the spinach mixture, stir well, increase the heat to high, and bring to a boil. Cover, reduce the heat to low, and cook for 20 minutes. Stir the rice carefully to avoid crushing it, cover, and cook for 5 minutes more.

Remove from the heat and let the rice steam in the covered pot for 10 minutes. Serve hot.

persian rice with dill and pistachios

SOURCE *Gourmet* STORY BY Bruce Feiler

COOKS *Gourmet* staff

Although we'd heard lots of tales about the legendary Persian rice, cooked in a deep pot with butter on the bottom so it has a crunchy crust, we'd never actually tasted it before we found this recipe. Now it's inevitably the hit of our dinner parties.

The rice is layered in the pot with the dill and pistachios, then slowly steamed. When the rice is done, it's scooped out into a serving bowl, and the pot gets a quick dip in cold water to release the crust, the famous *tah-dig*. Magically, the crust comes off in one piece — more or less — and you can either break it up to perch on top of the rice or simply cover the serving platter with the whole crust, letting each diner break off a little piece along with the rice. Or you can serve it separately, as this recipe suggests. ❧

3 cups basmati rice (1¼ pounds)

4 quarts water

3 tablespoons salt

6 tablespoons (¾ stick) unsalted butter

⅔ cup chopped fresh dill

1 cup coarsely chopped natural pistachios (5 ounces)

serves 8 to 10

In a large bowl, rinse the rice in several changes of cold water until the water runs clear. Drain in a large strainer.

In a large heavy pot, bring the water and salt to a boil. Add the rice and cook for 5 minutes. Drain in a large strainer.

Wash the pot and return it to the stovetop. In the pot, melt the butter over medium-low heat. Spoon the rice over the butter, alternating with layers of dill and pistachios and mounding it loosely, ending with a layer of rice.

Using the handle of a wooden spoon, make 5 or 6 holes in the rice mound, going all the way down to the bottom of the pot. Cover the pot with a kitchen towel and a heavy lid. Tuck the edges of the towel over the top of the lid so they won't burn.

Cook, undisturbed, until the rice is tender and a crust has formed on the bottom of the pot, 30 to 35 minutes. Spoon the loose rice onto a platter. Dip the bottom of the pot into a

tip

LEFTOVER PERSIAN rice makes great rice cakes. Just mix the rice with beaten egg, add salt and pepper to taste, and fry the rice cakes in a little butter.

bowl of cold water for 30 seconds to loosen the crust. Remove the crust with a large spoon and serve it in a separate bowl or on top of the loose rice.

notes from our test kitchen

- *Gourmet*'s tasters found that the best pistachios come from Iran and Turkey. You want the uncolored, unsalted ones.
- You may think an enameled cast-iron pan, such as Le Creuset, would be perfect for this job, but be warned: the change in temperature may crack the enamel. Choose a heavy stainless steel pot instead.

sardinian bread and tomato casserole

source *Lidia's Italian-American Kitchen* by Lidia Bastianich

cook Lidia Bastianich

This marvelous dish is one of those Italian inventions made out of almost nothing: some stale bread, canned tomatoes, an onion, fresh oregano, and cheese. Since thrifty cooking is something of a lost art in American kitchens, you'll probably need to buy a fresh loaf of bread and let it get stale overnight to make this cross between bread pudding and lasagna. But do make it; this is soul food.

It's great with either meat or fish, or on its own as a light meal with a salad. Lidia Bastianich points out that it makes a fine brunch dish, topped with an egg fried in olive oil. That's the way we like it best. ❧

1   **28-ounce can Italian plum tomatoes, preferably San Marzano, with their juice**

Sea salt

1   **pound day-old loaf of dry, crusty Italian bread, cut into ¾-inch-thick slices (about 16)**

4   **tablespoons extra-virgin olive oil**

1   **large yellow onion, sliced (about 2 cups)**

¼   **cup chopped fresh oregano**

2   **cups freshly grated pecorino Romano cheese**

serves 6

Chop the tomatoes in a food processor, using on-and-off pulses. Don't overprocess, or you'll incorporate too much air and the tomatoes will turn pink. Stir in 1 teaspoon salt.

In a small saucepan, bring 2 cups salted water to a boil. Lower the bread slices one by one into the boiling water for a second or two, just long enough to wet them. Place them on a kitchen towel on the counter to drain. Press the moistened bread lightly to remove excess water.

In a large skillet, heat 3 tablespoons of the oil over medium heat. Add the onion and cook, stirring, until golden, about 8 minutes. Pour in the tomatoes and bring to a boil. Reduce the heat so the sauce is simmering and cook until slightly thickened, about 20 minutes. Stir in the oregano and cook for 5 minutes more.

Preheat the oven to 375 degrees. Oil an 11-inch oval baking dish (or an equivalent baking dish) with the remaining 1 tablespoon oil.

THE 150 BEST AMERICAN RECIPES

224

Spoon in enough of the tomato sauce to coat the bottom and arrange half of the bread slices over the sauce, tearing them and wedging them as necessary to make an even layer. Spoon half of the remaining tomato sauce over the bread and sprinkle 1 cup of the cheese over the sauce. Make another layer of the remaining bread slices, tomato sauce, and cheese. Bake until the casserole is heated through and the cheese is browned, about 25 minutes. Serve hot.

Breakfast and Brunch

Breakfast and Brunch

christmas morning melon wedges

christmas morning melon wedges

SOURCE *Caprial Cooks for Friends* by Caprial Pence
COOK Caprial Pence

For Oregon chef Caprial Pence, breakfast on Christmas is almost more important than the big-feast dinner. But she's also not a morning person, so anything that can be prepared the night before gets a thumbs-up. These marinated melon wedges are deliriously good—fragrant, lightly sweet, a bit exhilarating, with ginger and mint delicately added. They're just as good for dessert, especially refreshing after a holiday dinner. ❧

1 large, ripe seasonal melon, seeded, rind removed, and flesh cut into 12 wedges

½ cup sugar

1 cup Riesling or other sweet white wine

¼ cup orange liqueur, such as Grand Marnier or Cointreau

1 large slice fresh ginger

1 cinnamon stick

1 teaspoon frozen orange juice concentrate, thawed

Dash of pure vanilla extract

1 teaspoon chopped fresh mint, plus sprigs for garnish

serves 6

Place the melon in a high-sided baking dish. In a saucepan over high heat, combine all the remaining ingredients except the mint sprigs. Bring the mixture to a boil and cook until the sugar has dissolved, about 5 minutes. Let the syrup cool completely, then pour it over the melon. Cover and refrigerate for at least 1 hour or up to 24 hours.

To serve, place the melon on a platter, pour the strained marinade over the top, and garnish with the mint sprigs. Serve cold.

sesame orange granola

SOURCE *Back to the Table* by Art Smith

COOK Art Smith

We've noticed a mini resurgence in granola recipes recently, not to mention a
bit more panache. This one, from
Oprah's highly touted chef, Art Smith, is
our favorite. It isn't one of those rugged
granolas, although it will carry you from
breakfast right through lunchtime. It's
sophisticated, with tropical elements —
coconut, cashews, sesame seeds, and
orange zest — which give it a special
quality.

Smith suggests serving it over
yogurt with fresh fruit, which is great.
But it's also good enough to eat out of
hand, so it makes a fine healthy snack
for kids. The only question here is what
fruit to use. After making several
batches, the one we like best is dried
cranberries. 🍊

1 cup shredded sweetened coconut

1/2 cup vegetable oil

1/3 cup pure maple syrup

Grated zest of 2 large oranges

4 cups old-fashioned rolled oats

1 cup sliced almonds

1 cup coarsely chopped unsalted cashews

1/3 cup sesame seeds

2 teaspoons ground cinnamon

1/2 teaspoon freshly grated nutmeg

1/3 cup honey

1 cup chopped dried fruit, such as apples, dates, apricots, cranberries, or a combination

makes about 8 cups

Preheat the oven to 375 degrees and set racks in the middle and upper-middle levels.

Spread the coconut on a baking sheet. Bake on the middle rack, stirring often, until lightly toasted, about 10 minutes. Set the baking sheet on a wire rack to cool.

In a medium saucepan, combine the oil, maple syrup, and orange zest and bring to a boil over medium heat. Mean-while, place all the remaining ingredients except the dried fruit in the bowl of a stand mixer and mix on low speed with the paddle attachment until combined, about 1 minute. (Or mix well with your hands in a large bowl.) Add the syrup

notes from our test kitchen

- You can play with the oil element, using half nut oil, such as almond or hazelnut.
- We like the stronger-tasting, cheaper Grade B maple syrup here.
- Be careful when toasting the coconut – it overbrowns easily.
- Although it will fit on one baking sheet, the granola won't be crunchy unless you use two.

mixture and mix (or toss with two large spoons) until well coated. Spread in a ½-inch-thick layer on each of two large baking sheets.

Bake, stirring often and switching the positions of the baking sheets from top to bottom and front to back halfway through baking, until the granola is golden brown, about 15 minutes.

Remove from the oven and let cool. In a large bowl, mix together the granola, toasted coconut, and dried fruit. The granola can be stored at room temperature in an airtight container for up to 1 month.

cherry almond twist pastry

SOURCE *Dierbergs Everybody Cooks* newsletter
COOKS Staff of Dierbergs School of Cooking

This scrumptious breakfast treat, like an almond croissant studded with dried cherries, is one of those gorgeous creations that looks complicated but is really a cinch to put together. Going into the oven, it may look atrocious, and you may think you've done something wrong. But don't despair: once in the oven, everything smooths out and puffs up into a bakery-perfect swirl.

The pastry would be perfect for Christmas breakfast, but it's so simple to make that it's good on any weekend morning. If you don't have time to make it in the morning, you can put it together the night before, refrigerate it, and then glaze and bake it the next day. 🍂

2/3 **cup dried cherries (about 3 ounces; see note)**

1 **7- to 8-ounce package almond paste (not marzipan)**

4 **tablespoons (1/2 stick) butter, softened**

1 **17.3-ounce package frozen puff pastry, thawed (see note)**

1 **large egg, beaten with 1 teaspoon water**

1/4 **cup sliced almonds (optional; see note)**

serves 8 to 10

Preheat the oven to 400 degrees. Line a baking sheet with parchment paper.

In a small bowl, combine the dried cherries and just enough warm water to cover. Let stand for 3 to 5 minutes. Drain and set aside.

In a food processor, process the almond paste and butter until smooth. Add the cherries and pulse until evenly mixed — the cherries should still be in chunks.

On a lightly floured surface, gently roll out one of the pastry sheets to remove any creases. Place on the baking sheet. Using a sharp knife or pizza cutter, trim the corners of the pastry to form a circle about 11 inches in diameter. Spread the almond filling over the pastry, leaving a 1/2-inch border around the edge. Roll out the second sheet of pastry to remove any creases and place over the filling. Trim to fit the bottom layer and press to seal the edges.

Lightly press a 1 1/2-inch-wide biscuit cutter in the center of the pastry to mark a circle (without cutting through the

notes from our test kitchen

- In our opinion, tart cherries are the ones to use for this pastry, and we wouldn't dream of leaving out the almonds.

- Several taste tests were conducted in recent years on almond paste. The Baker's Dozen, a Bay Area collective, liked canned almond paste better than the plastic-wrapped rolls. *Gourmet* magazine preferred the Odense canned brand.

- Most supermarket puff pastry doesn't contain butter. The kind made with butter, such as the Dufour Pastry Kitchens brand, is tastier, but non-butter pastry is less finicky to work with.

- When you're sealing the edges of the bottom and top sheets of pastry, it helps to brush the outer perimeter of the first sheet with a little egg wash before topping it with the second sheet.

- If the pastry gets too warm and slouchy while you're working with it, slip it into the refrigerator for a bit to firm it up. This can be a problem with butter pastry.

- Check the center of the pastry when you think it's done—it should be golden. If it's not, the pastry will be undercooked. It may take as much as another 5 to 7 minutes to cook completely.

pastry). This will serve as your guideline for cutting the pastry. Next, cut 16 evenly spaced spokes radiating out from the center of the circle, cutting all the way to the edge. Keep the spokes attached to the center of the circle. You'll end up with 16 attached wedges, each about 1½ inches wide at the outside edge. Once all the spokes are cut, gently grasp the outside edge of a wedge and give it a double twist. Twist gently so as not to tear the wedge away from the center. Place the twisted wedge back down and proceed to twist the remaining wedges, forming a starburst pattern. (Don't worry if your twists are uneven. The pastry will smooth out miraculously as it bakes.) Brush the egg wash over the pastry. Sprinkle the almonds over the top, if desired.

Bake until the pastry is golden brown and puffed, about 20 minutes. Let cool slightly; the pastry is best served warm.

marion cunningham's buttermilk pancakes

SOURCE *Crust and Crumb* by Peter Reinhart

COOK Marion Cunningham

One of our many recipe quests over the years has been to find the perfect pancake. Although there have been many contenders, none beat this simple formula for featherweight, tender hotcakes with custardy insides and lacy exteriors.

Peter Reinhart, an author and baking instructor, included this version of Marion Cunningham's celebrated recipe in his bread book, *Crust and Crumb.* He says the formula does not lend itself to multiplying, although if you are very careful (don't overmix!), you can double the batch. To be absolutely safe, make one batch right after another—no problem, since the ingredients take about a minute to assemble. ❧

1   **cup unbleached all-purpose flour**
1/2   **teaspoon baking soda**
1/4   **teaspoon salt**
1   **large egg**
1   **cup buttermilk**
2   **tablespoons unsalted butter, melted**
1   **tablespoon butter or oil for the pan (see tip)**
    Butter and/or maple syrup, fruit syrup, fresh fruit, or preserves for serving

serves 2 to 4

Preheat the oven to 200 degrees if you plan to keep the pancakes warm. Have ready an electric or stovetop griddle or a large heavy skillet.

Sift the flour, baking soda, and salt together into a bowl. Crack the egg open and pour it into the center of the flour mixture. Pour the buttermilk over the egg.

With a fork or large whisk, stir the ingredients together just until a lumpy batter forms and all the flour is absorbed; do not overmix. Pour in the melted butter and quickly mix the batter just until the butter is dispersed.

Preheat an electric griddle, or heat a skillet on top of the stove until a drop of water bounces on the surface. Swirl or brush the griddle or skillet with 1 teaspoon of the butter or oil. Using a large spoon or a 1/4-cup metal measuring cup, pour the batter onto the griddle. Spread the batter slightly

tip

THE ONLY PANCAKE recipe we know to challenge the eminence of Marion Cunningham's is the one that New York chef Eric Ripert acquired on a working trip to Vermont. Ripert's host, George Davis, served pancakes one morning, and the famous chef deemed the recipe worthy of inclusion in his magnificent cookbook, *A Return to Cooking*. In our tests, Davis's pancakes are quite good, but what we love most is the way they are cooked – in bacon drippings – a method you can adapt to any pancake formula. The drippings give the exterior a light crunch and a lovely savory edge. You'll need about 1 tablespoon of drippings for each batch, which is a simple matter if you fry up some bacon before making the pancakes.

with the back of a spoon to form a circle about $1/4$ inch thick. You can make tiny to large pancakes — your choice.

When bubbles begin to appear on the tops of the pancakes, turn them over and continue cooking for about 1 minute. They should be browned on both sides but tender in the middle.

Serve the pancakes right off the griddle or keep them warm in the oven while you finish cooking the remaining pancakes, adding more butter as needed. Serve with plenty of butter and/or maple syrup, fruit syrup, fresh fruit, or preserves.

⇥ VARIATIONS ⇤

Because the batter has no sugar, the pancakes can be savory, too. Try smoked salmon and sour cream, or caviar. This batter also makes terrific waffles.

Sour cream, cottage cheese, and yogurt also are good accompaniments. Or drop bits of fresh fruit, such as blueberries, directly on top of the batter on the griddle before the pancakes are flipped.

pecan praline french toast

pecan praline french toast

SOURCE **Virtualcities.com,** *1st Traveler's Choice Internet Cookbook*

COOK **Stage Stop Ranch**

One of the specialties of Stage Stop Ranch, a charming resort in the Texas Hill Country, in a little town called Wimberley, is this rich, pecan-studded French toast. It's custardy inside, with a crisp brown-sugar topping that doesn't, according to the ranch, require syrup (although some at your table may beg to differ). Unlike ordinary French toast that necessitates standing over the stove like a short-order cook, this version is baked in the oven, which leaves you free to squeeze the orange juice, make another pot of coffee, or simply read the paper. The recipe makes enough for a crowd, but we love it so much that we've adapted it for fewer folks (see tip). No matter how big the batch, leftovers are rarely a problem. ෴

3/4 **cup (1 1/2 sticks) butter**
1 **cup packed light brown sugar**
1 **cup coarsely chopped pecans**
8 **large eggs**
1 1/2 **cups milk**
1 **teaspoon pure vanilla extract**
Several dashes of ground cinnamon
1 **loaf of French bread, cut into 1-inch-thick slices**

serves 6 to 8

Preheat the oven to 350 degrees.

In a 12-x-15-inch baking pan, melt the butter in the oven as it heats, being careful not to burn it. Stir in the brown sugar. Sprinkle with the pecans.

In a medium bowl, beat the eggs and stir in the milk, vanilla, and cinnamon. Dip the slices of bread into the egg mixture. Arrange the slices over the brown sugar mixture in the pan. Pour any remaining egg mixture over the bread.

Bake for 35 to 40 minutes, or until the toast is golden brown. Invert each slice onto a plate and serve.

tip

IF YOU'RE MAKING BREAKFAST for a smaller group, you can make the French toast in a 9-x-13-inch baking dish or a deep 12-inch ovenproof skillet and use these proportions. Use as many slices of bread as will fit in the pan. This is two thirds of the original recipe and will serve 4 to 6.

8	tablespoons (1 stick) butter
2/3	cup packed light brown sugar
2/3	cup coarsely chopped pecans
5	large eggs
1	cup milk
3/4	teaspoon pure vanilla extract
2	dashes of ground cinnamon

amazing overnight waffles

❈

SOURCE *Mollie Katzen's Sunlight Café* by Mollie Katzen
COOK Mollie Katzen

There's nothing like a batch of waffles to brighten a morning, especially if they're homemade. It's hard to say if these are superb because they're so easy or because they're so delicious. Now you have no more excuses not to make the real thing, since you mix the batter the night before and all you have to do in the morning is beat an egg, melt some butter, and stir. At the very most, there's 15 minutes of work here. Yeast gives the waffles a special subtle quality, and the overnight rise adds a mellow tang and a pleasingly chewy texture that sets them apart from the usual baking powder and baking soda kind.

They make a great birthday breakfast. Although you could certainly offer some fancy toppings, we're partial to the classic butter and maple syrup. ☙

tip

A GREAT WAY to keep waffles warm until you're ready to serve them comes from Pam Anderson, author of *The Perfect Recipe*. Heat the oven to 200 degrees. As the waffles are done, place them directly on the oven rack without stacking. This keeps the waffles warm and crisp, whereas stacking makes them soggy.

2 cups all-purpose flour
1 tablespoon sugar
1 teaspoon active dry yeast (about $1/2$ packet)
$1/2$ teaspoon salt
2 cups milk
1 large egg, lightly beaten
6 tablespoons ($3/4$ stick) unsalted butter, melted

makes 6 to 8 waffles

Combine the flour, sugar, yeast, and salt in a large bowl. Whisk in the milk until blended. Cover the bowl tightly with plastic wrap and let stand overnight at room temperature. (If it's warmer than 70 degrees, refrigerate the batter.)

The next morning, heat the waffle iron. Beat the egg and melted butter into the batter, which will be quite thin.

Spray the hot wafffle iron with nonstick cooking spray and rub on a little butter with a paper towel or a piece of bread. Add just enough batter to cover the cooking surface, about $1^{1}/3$ cups for a Belgian waffle, $2/3$ cup for a standard waffle.

Cook the waffles until crisp and browned but not too dark, 2 to 3 minutes each. Serve hot.

---

note from our test kitchen

Use all the batter and freeze any leftover waffles individually. Reheat them in a toaster oven.

baked eggs in maple toast cups

❋

SOURCE Dakinfarm.com

COOK Unknown

Dakin Farm is a family-run company in northern Vermont that produces a superb line of smoked hams and bacon. The company also makes loads of real maple syrup, which they use in curing their hams and sell by the pint and gallon. We found this recipe posted on their Web site and think it's a fine way to start the day. The little bit of syrup adds a sweet note to the toast cup, and the crumbled bacon inside is a happy surprise.

Depending on who you're feeding or what you have planned for the day, figure on 1 or 2 cups per person. ❧

tip

CRACKING AN EGG on the edge of a bowl drives the shell fragments into the egg. Alton Brown, in *I'm Just Here for the Food,* says the best way to crack an egg is with a flat blow on the counter. It may take a little practice to get the amount of force right, but you'll find that the shell breaks cleanly.

1½ tablespoons butter
1½ tablespoons pure maple syrup, plus more for serving (optional)
6 slices bread (see note)
3 slices bacon, cooked until crisp and broken into small pieces
6 large eggs

serves 3 or 6

Preheat the oven to 400 degrees. Butter six muffin cups.

In a small saucepan, melt the butter and add the syrup. (You can also do this in a microwave.)

Remove the crusts from the bread. Flatten each slice with a rolling pin. Brush both sides of each slice with the syrup mixture. Pat one slice into each muffin cup and sprinkle the bacon pieces in the cups. Break an egg into each cup and bake until the eggs are set; start checking after about 5 minutes. Lift the toast cups from the pan and serve immediately, drizzled with additional syrup, if desired.

notes from our test kitchen

- Use a tight-crumb, relatively thin-sliced white bread, such as Pepperidge Farm, for this recipe.
- Use regular-size muffin cups here—not minis or oversize cups. You can also bake these in individual buttered ramekins. The eggs will take longer to cook, closer to 16 minutes, because it takes longer for the heat to penetrate the ramekins.

eggs with crunchy bread crumbs

SOURCE *The Zuni Cafe Cookbook* by Judy Rodgers

COOK Judy Rodgers

Just when you think there's no new way to fry an egg, along comes this delightful recipe, in which the eggs are cooked right over crisp bread crumbs. Judy Rodgers particularly enjoys this rendition for dinner when she's alone, but the dish also appears on the lunch menu at her San Francisco restaurant, Zuni Cafe, accompanied by bacon or sausage and grilled vegetables or roasted mushrooms.

You'll need a very large pan or two pans to make this dish for four. This is a terrific breakfast for houseguests. ❧

3 **tablespoons packed bread crumbs (see tip)**
Salt
About 2 tablespoons extra-virgin olive oil
A few fresh thyme or marjoram leaves (optional)
2 **large eggs**
About 1 teaspoon red wine vinegar, balsamic vinegar, or sherry vinegar

serves 1

Place the bread crumbs in a small bowl and sprinkle with salt to taste. Add enough olive oil to just oversaturate them.

Place the crumbs in a 6- to 8-inch French steel omelet pan or nonstick skillet over medium heat. (If you like your eggs over easy, reserve some of the oiled crumbs to sprinkle over the eggs just before you flip them.) Let the crumbs warm through, then swirl the pan as they begin to dry out—they'll make a quiet, staticky sound. Stir once or twice.

The moment you see the crumbs begin to color, quickly add the remaining oil and the thyme or marjoram (if using), then crack the eggs directly onto the crumbs. Cook the eggs as you like them.

Slide the eggs onto a warm plate. Immediately add the vinegar to the pan, swirling it once. Pour the sizzling vinegar over the eggs and serve.

tip

BY BREAD CRUMBS, Rodgers doesn't mean the kind you buy in a plastic bag at the supermarket. She's talking about good, chewy peasant bread, such as ciabatta, that's slightly stale. You can grate the crumbs by hand or in the food processor. If you're making the eggs for more than four people, it's easier to prepare the crumbs ahead in the oven instead of in the skillet. Toast them in a 425-degree oven until they are the color of weak tea, then scatter them in the skillet and proceed with the olive oil and the eggs.

notes from our test kitchen

- The herbs are a very nice touch, if you have them available. Rodgers also suggests rosemary, but use it sparingly; we found it a little strong for this dish. You can add a subtle garlic flavor by rubbing the bread with a cut garlic clove before you grate the crumbs.

- The measures of oil and vinegar are approximate because this isn't an exacting recipe. Feel free to eyeball the amounts.

- Making this dish is a bit like making a stir-fry: have everything at hand, and you won't have any trouble. If you're searching for the vinegar or plucking the herbs at the last minute, things can get tricky.

smoked salmon hash

SOURCE *Oregonian*

COOK Philippe Boulot

When the food-obsessed members of the International Association of Culinary Professionals held their annual conference in Portland, Oregon, the buzz quickly went out: the dish to have was the smoked salmon hash at the Heathman Hotel. The buzz was accurate—this is one great brunch dish. Once you taste it, you'll want to have it again and again.

Topping the hash with poached eggs is a great idea, but you can also leave them out and serve the hash at any time of the day. ❧

2 **pounds potatoes (about 7 medium)**
 Salt
1 **pound hot-smoked or kippered salmon**
1 **small red onion, minced**
1 **tablespoon prepared horseradish**
1 **tablespoon whole-grain mustard**
¼ **cup capers, drained**
¼ **cup sour cream**
 Freshly ground black pepper
2 **tablespoons butter**
2 **tablespoons vegetable oil**

poached eggs (optional)

1 **tablespoon vinegar (any kind)**
 Salt
8 **large eggs**
 Sour cream, thinned with a little heavy cream

serves 4

Place the potatoes in a large pan and cover with water. Bring to a boil, add a big pinch of salt, and cook until tender, about 20 minutes. Let cool completely, then peel and dice.

Shred the salmon into a medium bowl. Add the onion, horseradish, mustard, capers, and the ¼ cup sour cream. Toss to combine and season with salt and pepper to taste. Set aside.

Melt the butter in a large heavy sauté pan and add the oil. Add the cubed potatoes to the hot fat and sauté until golden

note from our test kitchen

Hot-smoked salmon is a Northwest specialty. If you can't find it, use kippered salmon, which is available in many supermarkets. It's drier and chunkier than regular smoked salmon, which is cold-smoked and won't be right for this dish.

brown and crisp. Add the salmon mixture and toss to combine and heat through. Add more salt and pepper, if desired.

To make the poached eggs (optional): Meanwhile, fill a large skillet with water. Add the vinegar and some salt and bring to a soft rolling boil. Break the eggs into saucers. Carefully tilt the eggs, one at a time, into the bubbling water. Cook until the whites are set and the centers are just soft, 2 to 3 minutes.

Divide the hash among four plates. If you poached the eggs, remove them from the water with a slotted spoon and place them on top of the hash. Top with a little of the sour cream mixture and serve immediately.

green chile cheese puff

SOURCE *Gourmet*

COOK Elizabeth Knowlton-Turney

Imagine a crustless quiche that's divinely light and given an extra dimension by glorious green poblano chiles. You can make it in just a few minutes, as long as you roast and peel the poblanos ahead of time (up to 1 day ahead; see tip). Then you'll have the perfect breakfast, brunch, or late supper—or, as *Gourmet* suggests, the perfect Mother's Day feast. Add your favorite salsa, and you're done. ❧

tip

TO ROAST AND PEEL the poblanos, arrange them on an aluminum foil–lined baking sheet and broil until blistered and blackened, turning frequently. Wrap in the foil and set aside to steam for 10 minutes. Open the foil. When the poblanos are cool enough to handle, peel them; the skin should come off easily. Cover and refrigerate until ready to use.

$1/4$ **cup all-purpose flour**

$3/4$ **teaspoon salt**

$1/2$ **teaspoon baking powder**

6 **large eggs**

2 **tablespoons unsalted butter, melted**

1 **cup cottage cheese**

8 **ounces Monterey Jack cheese, grated (about 2 cups)**

4 **green poblano chiles (about $3/4$ pound), roasted and peeled (see tip), then cut into $1/2$-inch dice**

Fresh store-bought or homemade tomato salsa for serving

serves 6

Preheat the oven to 350 degrees and set a rack in the middle level. Oil a 9-inch glass pie plate.

In a small bowl, sift together the flour, salt, and baking powder.

In a large bowl, with an electric mixer, beat the eggs until doubled in volume, about 3 minutes. Add the butter, flour mixture, and cheeses and beat well. Stir in the chiles and pour the mixture into the pie plate.

Bake until the top is puffed and golden brown and a tester comes out clean, 30 to 35 minutes.

Serve the cheese puff immediately—it will fall slightly—with the salsa on the side.

glazed bacon

SOURCE Sfgate.com

COOK Jacqueline Higuera McMahan after James Beard

If you need to serve breakfast to a crowd or you're just looking for something new and interesting to do with bacon, this recipe is for you. It calls for thick-sliced meaty bacon — we'd make it double-smoked — and brown sugar. In the oven, the bacon loses almost all of its fat and turns crunchy and sweet. ❧

8 ounces thick-sliced meaty bacon
1 tablespoon brown sugar per slice of bacon, or to taste (see note)

serves 6

Preheat the oven to 350 degrees.

Lay out the bacon on a jelly-roll pan and bake for 10 minutes. Pour off the fat. Sprinkle 1 tablespoon brown sugar over each bacon slice. Return to the oven for 8 minutes. Turn the bacon over and bake for 2 to 3 minutes longer, or until crisp. Watch carefully; the bacon can easily overbrown and burn.

Remove the bacon from the oven and place on a plate. Let cool slightly before serving.

tip

TO GIVE THE glazed bacon a spicy kick, take a tip from Amy Mastrangelo in *Gourmet*. In a small bowl, mix the brown sugar with cayenne pepper and freshly ground black pepper — somewhere in the realm of ¼ heaping teaspoon of each, or more to taste — and then sprinkle it on the bacon as directed.

notes from our test kitchen

- You can use light or dark brown sugar, as you please (we prefer light). You may find that 2 teaspoons is plenty of sugar for each slice.
- Although it's only a little unwieldy to pour off the bacon grease, it's even easier if you cook the bacon on a rack in the pan and just lift out the rack to drain the grease.

rosemary and mustard breakfast sausages

SOURCE *Bon Appétit*

COOK Kristine Kidd

Although there's nothing wrong with breakfast sausage links, they are made immeasurably better when you slip them out of their casings; season the sausage meat with sautéed onion, fresh rosemary, and whole-grain mustard; and shape the mixture into patties. In no time at all, you've turned something ordinary into something quite special. Make these sausage patties the day before, and all you'll have to do in the morning is pop them in the oven while the coffee's brewing. Any late sleepers will be lured from their slumbers. ❧

tip

IN *BON APPETIT*, cookbook author Betty Rosbottom suggests an even easier way to gussy up plain old breakfast sausage links—using an apricot mustard glaze. The recipe works equally well with sweet or hot sausages. Start by melting ½ cup apricot preserves in a medium saucepan over medium heat. Whisk in ¼ cup sweet-hot mustard (Dijon is fine, too) and simmer for 30 seconds. Remove from the heat and add 2 teaspoons chopped fresh rosemary and salt and pepper to taste. Fry the sausages until browned and cooked through. Add them to the glaze, stir carefully over medium heat until the sausages are glazed, and serve.

1   **tablespoon olive oil**

1   **medium onion, finely chopped**

1   **teaspoon chopped fresh rosemary, plus sprigs for garnish**

1   **14-ounce package breakfast sausage links, casings removed**

2   **teaspoons whole-grain mustard**

    Freshly ground black pepper

makes 12 patties

Heat the oil in a small skillet over medium-high heat. Add the onion and chopped rosemary and sauté until the onion is golden, about 10 minutes. Transfer to a medium bowl. Add the sausage, mustard, and a generous amount of pepper. Mix gently. Form into twelve 2-inch-wide patties. Arrange the patties on a rimmed baking sheet. The patties can be made 1 day ahead and refrigerated.

Preheat the oven to 500 degrees and set a rack in the lowest level.

Bake the sausage patties until just cooked through, about 6 minutes. If the patties have not browned, broil for 2 minutes. Transfer to paper towels to drain, then arrange on a platter. Garnish with the rosemary sprigs and serve.

note from our test kitchen

Not all breakfast sausage is sold in 14-ounce packages. Buy as close to this amount as you can get. If you find breakfast sausage without casings, buying that will save you a step.

Breads

Breads

buttermilk scones

※

SOURCE *The Foster's Market Cookbook* by Sara Foster with Sarah Belk King

COOK Sara Foster

Foster's Markets, in Durham and Chapel Hill, North Carolina, are just the kind of jazzy take-out markets we all wish we had right around the corner — refrigerator cases jammed with gorgeous prepared foods and counters loaded with tempting baked goodies. When we learned that this scone recipe has remained the most requested one at the market for years, we took note. Made with buttermilk and more butter than we've ever seen in a batch of scones, these magnificent pastries are light and flaky, with great flavor and just the right amount of crunch around the edges. We've tried a lot of scone recipes over the years, and these earn highest honors. ❧

tip

IF YOU'VE ALREADY taken advantage of powdered buttermilk, you know that you sift it first, mix it into the dry ingredients, and then add plain water in place of buttermilk. A reader of *Fine Cooking* has a good tip: keep powdered buttermilk in the refrigerator to extend its shelf life.

4½ cups all-purpose flour (see note)

½ cup sugar

2 teaspoons baking powder

½ teaspoon baking soda

½ teaspoon salt

24 tablespoons (3 sticks) cold unsalted butter, cut into ¼-inch pieces

1¼ cups buttermilk, plus more if needed

1 large egg, beaten with 2 tablespoons milk

makes 12 scones

Preheat the oven to 400 degrees. Lightly grease two baking sheets.

Combine the flour, sugar, baking powder, baking soda, and salt in a large bowl. Add the butter and cut it into the flour using a pastry blender or two knives until the mixture resembles cornmeal. (Or use a food processor fitted with the metal blade to cut the butter into the flour mixture by pulsing 10 to 12 times. Transfer the mixture to a large bowl to continue.) Do not overwork the dough.

Add the buttermilk and mix until just combined and the dough begins to stick together. Add more buttermilk, 1 tablespoon at a time, if the dough seems too dry. It should just hang together but not be at all wet or sticky.

Turn the dough out onto a lightly floured surface and roll or pat it into two 6-inch rounds about 1½ inches thick. Cut each round in half, then cut each half into 3 pie-shaped

measuring cup might mean the difference between success and failure in baking. The Good House-keeping Institute tested every brand it could find and discovered that only two, Oxo and Michael Graves (sold at Target), were accurate.

If you're using several sets of measuring cups in making a single recipe, as we often do, the quantities could be off by as much as 2 tablespoons, says Good Housekeeping. That could present serious problems if you're making a cake or another unforgiving recipe requiring exact measurements. The solution: use only one set, so that at least your proportions are consistent, or use only the two recommended brands.

wedges and place them on the baking sheets. Brush the tops with the egg wash.

Bake until golden brown and firm to the touch, 30 to 35 minutes. Remove from the oven and serve immediately.

◄ VARIATION ►

For a more sophisticated scone, add ½ cup chopped crystallized ginger to the dry ingredients before adding the butter. Toss to coat and continue with the recipe. This impossible-to-resist version came from Chuck Williams of Williams-Sonoma years ago and remains as popular today as it was when he first introduced the idea. The best crystallized ginger is baby Australian ginger, available at Williams-Sonoma (Williams-sonoma.com or 877-812-6235), Trader Joe's, and many gourmet shops. It's exceptionally tender, but any crystallized ginger that's not dried out and hard is fine. Just be sure to chop it by hand; it will gum up your food processor.

notes from our test kitchen

- For best results, measure the flour carefully using the spoon-and-sweep method: spoon the flour into a dry measuring cup until it's piled above the rim, then level the measure by sweeping the back side of a knife across the top. Never pack or tamp down the flour.

- If you want to add a little something to the basic recipe, toss 1¼ cups toasted, chopped pecans into the dry ingredients before adding the buttermilk.

- We generally end up needing an additional 2 to 6 tablespoons buttermilk. Just go easy so you don't end up with a soggy dough.

corn bread with sage leaves and feta

※

SOURCE *The Herbal Kitchen* by Jerry Traunfeld
COOK Jerry Traunfeld

If we had to select the most gorgeous recipes in our collection, this corn bread would certainly top the list. The idea comes from Jerry Traunfeld, the Pacific Northwest chef who's earned a name for himself through his innovative use of herbs. Before mixing up the corn bread batter, you decorate the bottom of a pie plate with fresh sage leaves — arranging them in a daisy pattern. Then, after baking, you turn out a lovely golden loaf accented by a ring of leaves — picture-perfect. As with all of Traunfeld's creations, the sage is more than just window dressing — it gives the bread a woodsy, earthy flavor. The little bit of feta contributes a creamy, salty bite.

If you're not in the market for another corn bread recipe, we suggest that you at least try decorating your own version with sage leaves. We promise you'll be impressed. ❧

1	tablespoon unsalted butter, softened, for the pie plate
18–24	large sage leaves
3/4	cup stone-ground cornmeal
1	cup all-purpose flour
2	teaspoons baking powder
2	teaspoons sugar
1/2	teaspoon fine salt
2	large eggs
1	cup buttermilk
1/4	cup olive oil
4	ounces Greek feta cheese, crumbled (1 cup)

makes one 9-inch round loaf

Preheat the oven to 400 degrees. Smear the butter over the bottom and sides of a 9-inch glass pie plate.

Press the sage leaves into the butter in a circular daisy pattern, saving about 6 leaves for the sides of the pan — press them in horizontally (see note).

Stir the dry ingredients together with a whisk in a medium bowl (see note). Whisk together the eggs, buttermilk, and olive oil in another bowl. Stir the liquid into the dry ingredients until the lumps smooth out. Stir in the cheese.

Pour the batter into the pie plate and bake for about 25 minutes, or until the top is browned and springs back when you

tip

WE USE SOME recipes so often that we know them by heart. Southern cooking authority John Martin Taylor's skillet corn bread is just such a recipe: pure, sensationally good, and foolproof. In a medium bowl, whisk together 1 large egg and 2 cups buttermilk. Add 1¾ cups cornmeal (preferably stone-ground) and beat well; the batter will be thin. Put enough strained bacon grease (1½ to 2 teaspoons) into a 9- to 10-inch cast-iron skillet to coat the bottom and sides with a thin film, then set the skillet in a cold oven. Preheat the oven to 450 degrees. When it reaches the right temperature, the bacon grease will be just at the point of smoking. Add 1 scant teaspoon each baking powder, baking soda, and salt to the batter and beat well. Pour the batter all at once into the hot pan. Bake for 15 to 20 minutes, or until the top of the corn bread just begins to brown. Turn the loaf out onto a plate and serve hot with lots of the freshest butter you can get your hands on.

touch it in the center. Let cool for about 10 minutes in the pan. Loosen the sides with a paring knife and flip the corn bread out onto a plate or board, with the sage leaves on top. Serve warm.

notes from our test kitchen

- As much as we love the ring of sage leaves that tops this bread, we found the ones along the sides to be overkill. We skip them.
- We can't help adding ½ teaspoon baking soda along with the baking powder. The acidity of the buttermilk reacts with the soda and lightens the loaf ever so slightly.
- Use only good-quality feta — never the precrumbled stuff.

green onion buttermilk biscuits

SOURCE *Bon Appétit* STORY BY Thomas Connors
COOK Debbie Day's grandmother

If you live on the West Coast, you call them green onions; on the East Coast, they're scallions. They're delicious in biscuits, as we've seen in several recipes over the years. This one, the favorite of a Missouri family, wins our vote. It's a little sweet, which is a nice foil for the onions; it's made with butter and buttermilk (more thumbs-up from us); and it has a lovely golden glaze on top.

These biscuits are very good for breakfast or dinner — even Thanksgiving dinner. They're also versatile and easy to make. You can make them up to 6 hours ahead and reheat them; you can play with herbs (try adding some fresh dill); or you can substitute chives for the green onions/scallions.

The recipe makes a lot of biscuits but cuts in half perfectly. ❧

4 **cups all-purpose flour**
¼ **cup sugar**
2 **tablespoons baking powder**
2 **teaspoons salt**
¾ **cup (1½ sticks) cold unsalted butter, cut into small pieces**
1½ **cups cold buttermilk, plus more if needed**
¼ **cup finely chopped green onions (scallions)**
1 **large egg, beaten, for glazing**

makes about 28 biscuits

Preheat the oven to 425 degrees.

In a large bowl, whisk together the flour, sugar, baking powder, and salt. Add the butter and rub it in with your fingertips until the mixture resembles coarse meal. Add the buttermilk and green onions and stir until moist clumps form. Add more buttermilk, 1 tablespoon at a time, if the dough is dry.

Gather the dough together and divide it in half. Flatten each half to a ¾-inch thickness on a floured work surface. Using a 2-inch cookie cutter, cut out biscuits. Gather the excess dough, pat it out again, and cut out more biscuits.

Place the biscuits on ungreased baking sheets and brush with the beaten egg. Bake until cooked through and golden brown on top, about 16 minutes. Serve hot. You can make

tips

FOR GREAT buttermilk biscuits, *The Baker's Dozen Cookbook* recommends kneading the dough briefly (about 15 turns), which will give it more strength to rise. You also can make the dough to the point of adding the buttermilk up to 12 hours ahead. Cover the bowl tightly and refrigerate it until you're ready to add the buttermilk and bake the biscuits. These biscuits taste a lot fresher than reheated biscuits.

IF YOUR cookie cutter collection looks a little more tired each year, try this tip from Regan Daley, author of *In the Sweet Kitchen*. Choose only stainless steel cookie cutters and dry them thoroughly after each use. Keep them in an aerated container and dust them with a little cornstarch before storing to absorb any moisture and prevent rusting. Another trick is to store them with one or two silica gel packs or capsules — the sort that come in vitamin bottles. Just make sure the packets are intact and not leaking silica.

the biscuits up to 6 hours ahead. Let them stand on the baking sheets at room temperature and reheat in a 325-degree oven for 5 minutes just before serving.

notes from our test kitchen

- We like to double the green onions in this recipe so you can really taste the onion flavor.
- Try to handle the dough as lightly as possible for the airiest biscuits.

lemon thyme biscuits

SOURCE *Moosewood Restaurant New Classics* by the Moosewood Collective

COOK Kip Wilcox

These very fragrant biscuits celebrate that great combination of lemon zest and fresh thyme that lights up all faces at the table. They're homey and elegant at the same time, great with soups and stews or roast chicken.

You can mix the dough in the food processor, which saves a lot of time. The dough is also wonderfully forgiving and easy to work with. Even if you're a novice baker or you don't usually feel comfortable rolling things out, these biscuits will be a snap. ❧

note from our test kitchen

To grate lemon zest, the best tool is a Microplane zester. Use it upside down, as though you were playing the fruit like a violin, and the zest will collect neatly on the back.

4   **tablespoons (¹⁄₂ stick) cold butter, cut into small pieces**

1   **tablespoon grated lemon zest**

2   **cups unbleached all-purpose flour**

1   **tablespoon sugar**

2   **teaspoons baking powder**

¹⁄₂   **teaspoon baking soda**

¹⁄₂   **teaspoon salt**

2–3   **tablespoons chopped fresh thyme**

³⁄₄   **cup plus 2 tablespoons buttermilk, plus more for brushing**

serves 6

Preheat the oven to 425 degrees. Lightly oil a baking sheet.

Place the butter pieces and lemon zest in a medium bowl or food processor. Sift the flour, sugar, baking powder, baking soda, and salt over the butter and lemon zest. By hand or in the food processor, mix the butter with the flour mixture until evenly distributed. Add the thyme and mix well. Add the buttermilk and stir or pulse briefly. The dough will be soft and a little sticky.

On a lightly floured work surface, pat the dough into a 9-inch circle about ¹⁄₂ inch thick. Cut into 6 wedges. Place the wedges on the prepared baking sheet and brush the tops with a little buttermilk. Bake for 20 minutes, or until firm and golden brown. Serve immediately.

kona inn banana muffins

SOURCE *Learning to Cook with Marion Cunningham* by Marion Cunningham

COOK Marion Cunningham

When you look at this recipe, you might pass it by, because nothing seems particularly special — no cinnamon, no flavorings at all, in fact, just pure banana. Marion Cunningham explains that the secret to these divine Hawaiian muffins is using lots of bananas and beating them into submission for an especially tender, moist result. These muffins are great keepers, and they freeze well, too.

Thanks, Kona Inn! ❧

½ cup vegetable shortening

1¼ cups all-purpose flour, plus more for the pan

5 very ripe medium bananas

1 teaspoon baking soda

½ teaspoon salt

1 cup sugar

2 large eggs, lightly beaten

½ cup chopped walnuts

serves 12

Preheat the oven to 350 degrees and set a rack in the lower-middle level. Smear the cups of a muffin pan with a little shortening, sprinkle with a little flour, and shake the pan to distribute the flour. Turn the pan upside down over the wastebasket and shake out any excess flour.

Peel the bananas, place them in a large bowl, and beat them well with an electric mixer. The riper the bananas and the more you beat them, the more tender your muffins will be. Don't expect absolute smoothness; there will always be a few lumps. Set aside.

In a small bowl, combine the flour, baking soda, and salt. Add the sugar, shortening, eggs, and walnuts to the bananas and mix well. Add the dry ingredients to the banana mixture and stir just until the batter is thoroughly blended.

Pour the batter into a large measuring cup with a spout and fill the muffin cups about two-thirds full.

Bake for 15 minutes, then check the muffins for doneness. A toothpick inserted in the center of a muffin should come out clean. If not, bake for 5 minutes more and check again. When the toothpick comes out clean, remove the muffins from the oven and let cool in the pan for 5 minutes.

Run a knife around the edges of the muffins and transfer them to a platter. Serve warm.

⊰ VARIATION ⊱

You can turn these muffins into a cake using the same recipe. Butter and flour two 9-inch round cake pans and divide the batter between them. Bake for 25 minutes, or until a toothpick comes out clean. Cool the cakes in their pans for 10 minutes. Loosen the edges with a knife and turn each out onto a platter. To give the cakes a nice finish, place ⅓ cup confectioners' sugar in a strainer and sift it over the cakes. Serve with whipped cream.

cinnamon buns from heaven

cinnamon buns from heaven

❋

source *Oregonian*
cook Nicki Cross

Americans' love affair with tender, gooey, oversize cinnamon buns seems to know no bounds. Just walk through any major airport or mall, any time of day, and witness the lines at the Cinnabon counter. It seems that somewhere in the back of our minds, there's a vivid memory of an archetypal cinnamon bun that conveys comfort and sweetness. Nicki Cross had such a memory from her eastern Oregon childhood, and fortunately for us, she worked out this version, which gathers so many raves it's been reprinted four times in the *Oregonian*. These are the real thing — rich, sweet, and huge — and we've yet to find another version (store-bought or homemade) that measures up. You can also tone these down a little by making slightly smaller buns (18 instead of 12) and skipping the glaze (see note). ❧

dough

- 1 cup warm water (105–115 degrees)
- 2 envelopes active dry yeast
- 1 teaspoon plus 2/3 cup sugar
- 1 cup milk, heated to lukewarm
- 10 1/2 tablespoons (1 1/3 sticks) butter, softened
- 2 large eggs, lightly beaten
- 2 teaspoons salt
- 7–8 cups all-purpose flour, or more as needed

filling

- 16 tablespoons (2 sticks) butter, melted and cooled
- 1 3/4 cups sugar
- 3 tablespoons ground cinnamon
- 1 1/2 cups chopped walnuts (optional)
- 1 1/2 cups raisins (optional)

creamy glaze

- 10 1/2 tablespoons (1 1/3 sticks) butter, melted and cooled
- 4 cups confectioners' sugar
- 2 teaspoons pure vanilla extract
- 1/4–1/2 cup hot water

makes 12 to 18 buns

To make the dough: Combine the water, yeast, and 1 teaspoon of the sugar in a cup and stir. Set aside. In a large bowl, combine the milk, remaining 2/3 cup sugar, butter, eggs, and

tip

TO SAVE TIME in the morning, make the rolls a day ahead up to the final rise, then let them rise slowly overnight in the refrigerator. Let come to room temperature before baking.

notes from our test kitchen

- A simple dusting of confectioners' sugar is a great topping for the buns, which are already so over-the-top that the glaze is almost too much.
- You can play with the filling ingredients: try golden raisins or currants, use pecans instead of walnuts, or add some nutmeg or mace and a little grated lemon zest.

salt. Stir well and add the yeast mixture. Add 3½ cups of the flour and beat until smooth. Stir in enough of the remaining flour until the dough is slightly stiff — it will be sticky.

Turn out the dough onto a well-floured surface and knead for 5 to 10 minutes, adding just enough flour to keep the dough from sticking. Place in a well-buttered glass or plastic bowl. Cover and let rise in a warm place free from drafts until doubled in volume, 1 to 1½ hours. Punch down the dough and let rest for 5 minutes. Roll out on a lightly floured surface into a 15-x-20-inch rectangle.

To make the filling: Spread half of the melted butter on the dough. In a small bowl, combine 1½ cups of the sugar and the cinnamon. Sprinkle over the dough, then sprinkle with the walnuts and raisins, if using. Roll up like a jelly roll and pinch the edges together to seal. Cut the roll into 12 or 18 slices.

If making 12 buns, use the remaining melted butter to coat the bottoms of a 9-x-13-inch baking pan and an 8-inch square baking pan; if making 18 buns, use two 9-x-13-inch pans. Sprinkle the pans with the remaining ¼ cup sugar. Place the cinnamon bun slices close together in the pans. Cover and let rise in a warm place until doubled in volume, about 45 minutes.

Preheat the oven to 350 degrees.

Bake for 25 to 30 minutes, or until the buns are nicely browned. Let cool slightly before glazing.

To make the glaze: In a medium bowl, combine the melted butter, confectioners' sugar, and vanilla. Add the water 1 tablespoon at a time until you have a spreadable glaze. Spread the glaze over the buns and serve.

cranberry pecan bread

SOURCE *Food & Wine*

COOK Maggie Glezer

It used to be that to get decent bread, you had to make it yourself or travel to Europe. Now bakers and markets all over are catching on, and we admit that we hardly ever bother to make our own anymore. We certainly make an exception, however, for this marvelous bread from Maggie Glezer, award-winning author of *A Blessing of Bread*. This chewy, moist loaf, jam-packed with pecans and cranberries, gets its subtle sweetness from the whole wheat flour (see tip) and the cranberries — no added sugar. The deep flavor and superb texture come from the slow overnight rise. And as any bread aficionado will tell you, the slower the rise, the longer the bread lasts. This one keeps for several days and also freezes well.

Glezer recommends serving thin slices with cheese and wine — a ripe Camembert and Pouilly-Fumé, to be exact. It's also quite good toasted in the morning. ❧

3½ cups all-purpose flour, plus more for kneading

3½ cups white whole wheat flour, preferably King Arthur (see tip)

1 tablespoon instant dry yeast

3¼ cups warm water, plus 2 tablespoons if needed

4 teaspoons fine sea salt

1½ cups (7 ounces) dried cranberries

2 cups (7 ounces) pecan halves

Vegetable oil

makes two 2-pound loaves

In a large bowl, combine both flours and the yeast. Add the 3¼ cups water and stir until a soft dough forms. If the dough is too stiff, add the 2 tablespoons water. Let rest for 15 minutes.

Scrape the dough onto a lightly floured work surface. Knead and work the dough until smooth but still very sticky, about 5 minutes (see note). Flatten the dough and sprinkle it with the salt; knead until the salt is evenly incorporated, about 5 minutes. The dough will tighten slightly. Flatten the dough and scatter the cranberries and pecans on top. Fold the dough over the fruit and nuts and knead them in. Lightly oil the bowl, add the dough, and turn to coat. Cover and let stand until doubled in volume, about 2 hours.

Line two large baking sheets with parchment paper. Brush the paper with oil. Punch down the dough, then cut it into 2 pieces. Flatten each piece into a 10-inch oval. Fold the short ends in toward the center and pinch so they stay in place.

tip

A NEW TYPE of flour has arrived on the baking scene. White whole wheat flour is not a misprint or some newfangled highly processed ingredient. It's light-colored and mild-tasting, but nutritionally identical to traditional darker, heavier whole wheat flour. There are a few brands available, but Glezer recommends King Arthur: bakerscatalogue.com or (800) 827-6836.

Pat the dough into two 9-inch oval loaves and place seam side down on the baking sheets. Lightly brush 2 pieces of plastic wrap with oil and loosely cover the loaves. Refrigerate overnight.

Uncover the loaves and let stand at room temperature for about 2 hours, or until slightly risen. Using a sharp knife, make a $1/2$-inch-deep slash down the length of each loaf.

Preheat the oven to 400 degrees with racks in the lower- and upper-middle levels.

Bake, rotating the baking sheets halfway through, until the loaves are crusty, very well browned, and sound hollow when rapped, 35 to 40 minutes. Transfer the loaves to a wire rack and let cool before slicing.

notes from our test kitchen

- This is a rather sticky dough and takes a little finesse to handle. Resist the urge to add a lot of extra flour; add only enough so that you can handle the dough. To get the right texture in the end, the dough should remain soft and somewhat sticky.
- We've not had much luck kneading this dough in a stand mixer—it's too wet. Instead, we recommend putting on some relaxing music and approaching the kneading as an exercise in mindfulness. You'll be well rewarded.
- Because the loaves are free-form, expect them to be low profile.
- We sometimes slice any leftover bread and then freeze it so that we can pop a few slices directly into the toaster for a quick breakfast.

Desserts

Desserts

hot blackberries and cream

SOURCE *The Fearless Chef* by Andy Husbands and Joe Yonan
COOK Andy Husbands after his mother

We're always delighted when chefs return to their mothers' recipes. This unfussy dessert comes from a lauded Boston chef, Andy Husbands. Having grown up in the Pacific Northwest, where the berries grow plumper, juicier, and more prolifically than just about anywhere, Husbands remembers his mother folding together sour cream and fresh berries, dusting the top with brown sugar, and popping the dish under the broiler. As the berries release their juices into the cream, the sugar caramelizes into a crunchy, sweet topping. We're guessing the lime zest is a little flourish of the chef's. It's just right.

Husbands advises making this only in the summer, when blackberries are at their prime, but we confess that we've broken down and made it off-season and still loved the results. ❧

1 **cup sour cream, at room temperature**
1 **tablespoon sugar**
   Finely grated zest of 1 lime
1/2 **teaspoon ground cinnamon**
1 **pint blackberries, rinsed and well drained**
1/2 **cup lightly packed light or dark brown sugar**

serves 4

Preheat the broiler and place the broiler rack in the lowest possible position, so that it is at least 6 inches from the top element.

Combine the sour cream, sugar, lime zest, and cinnamon in a small bowl. Gently fold in the blackberries and transfer to a small gratin dish. Sprinkle the brown sugar on top.

Broil until the brown sugar melts and caramelizes, 1 to 3 minutes, turning the dish halfway through so that the top browns evenly but does not burn. Serve hot.

---

note from our test kitchen

For a variation, follow the same formula using fresh blueberries and lemon zest. You can also substitute crème fraîche for the sour cream if you want to be really swish.

ported rhubarb

❈

SOURCE *Washington Post*
COOK Anne Willan

1½ pounds rhubarb, cut into 2-inch pieces
¾–1 cup sugar, depending on the sourness of the rhubarb
¾ cup ruby port
Grated zest of 1 orange

Americans don't have a history of cooking with port, as the British do, but Anne Willan opened our eyes to its great possibilities. This baked dessert is just amazing: the rhubarb holds its shape instead of dissolving into damp strings, and the port and orange zest add a complexity that is almost unbelievable in such a simple dish. It's wonderful served over vanilla or strawberry ice cream, but it's also a tasty relish for turkey or ham — all this for less than 5 minutes of work.

The right port for this dish is ruby port, the youngest and sweetest of the ports. If your rhubarb isn't very sour, you'll need much less sugar, since the port itself is quite sweet. ❧

note from our test kitchen

The rhubarb will look prettier if you cut it at an angle.

serves 4 to 6

Preheat the oven to 350 degrees.

Arrange the rhubarb in a baking dish large enough to hold it in a single layer. Sprinkle with the sugar to taste. In a small bowl, combine the port and orange zest and drizzle over the rhubarb.

Bake until the rhubarb is just tender when pierced with a knife, 20 to 30 minutes. Serve chilled.

tips

IF YOU'RE LOOKING for a savory use for port, Anne Willan recommends a great homemade Stilton cheese spread. Crumble ½ pound Stilton into a bowl, then beat in 16 tablespoons (2 sticks) butter (softened) and ½ cup port. Not only is this more delicious than the Stilton spread sold in crocks, but it's a fraction of the price.

HERE'S AN ELEGANT no-cook dessert idea from Joyce Dodson Piotrowski, a catering manager in Virginia. Stem seedless red grapes and freeze them on a baking sheet for at least 1 hour or up to 2 days. Meanwhile, place martini glasses in the freezer to frost. To serve, place the frozen grapes in the glasses and drizzle a few tablespoons of ruby or tawny port over the grapes. Serve immediately. This makes a fine addition to an after-dinner cheese course.

pear crisp with dried sour cherries

SOURCE *The Last Course* by Claudia Fleming
COOK Claudia Fleming

Claudia Fleming, who made her name as the celebrated pastry chef at Manhattan's Gramercy Tavern, specializes in upgrading homey desserts into something extraordinary. This wonderful fall dessert has a lovely, golden brown, crisp topping over bubbling, burgundy-colored juices. It's fragrant with wine, fruit, and spices, and the combination of sour cherries and sweet pears gives it a sophisticated edge — not too sweet, not too tart. Whipped crème fraîche is just the thing for a topping.

Be sure to plan ahead for this dessert, because you need to soak the cherries for at least 8 hours. ❧

- 1 **cup dried sour cherries**
- **Water and/or fruity red wine, such as Zinfandel**
- 2¹⁄₂ **pounds ripe pears (about 8 medium), peeled, cored, and sliced (5 cups)**
- ¹⁄₂ **cup sugar**
- 1¹⁄₄ **cups all-purpose flour**
- ¹⁄₃ **cup plus 1 tablespoon coarsely ground toasted almonds**
- ¹⁄₄ **cup firmly packed dark brown sugar**
- ¹⁄₄ **teaspoon ground cinnamon**
- ¹⁄₈ **teaspoon ground nutmeg**
- 8 **tablespoons (1 stick) unsalted butter, melted and cooled to room temperature**

serves 8

The day before you make the crisp, in a small saucepan over medium heat, combine the dried cherries with enough water and/or wine to cover by 2 inches. Bring the mixture to a simmer, then remove from the heat and let cool. Let the cherries soak overnight (or for at least 8 hours) in the refrigerator so that they are plump and soft. Drain the cherries, reserving the juice.

In a large bowl, combine the pears, drained cherries, and ¹⁄₄ cup of the granulated sugar and toss well. Mix in ¹⁄₂ cup of the cherry soaking liquid (or whatever cherry soaking liquid is left plus enough water to make ¹⁄₂ cup). Let stand for 30 minutes.

Meanwhile, preheat the oven to 375 degrees.

tip

FOR TIMES when you find yourself with a windfall of apples or berries, here's a simple formula for the crispest of crisps passed on to us by Pacific Northwest chef Greg Atkinson, who got it from Marion Cunningham, who got it from Sharon Kramis, who apparently got it from a ten-year-old neighbor, Willie. Combine 1 cup each flour and sugar. Stir in 1 teaspoon each salt and baking powder. Make a well in the center and add 1 beaten large egg. Stir to make a crumbly mixture. Put 6 cups apples (peeled and thinly sliced) or berries in an ungreased 8-inch square baking dish. Toss with 1/2 cup sugar (we sometimes use less) and 2 tablespoons flour. Sprinkle the dry mixture over the top. Melt 8 tablespoons (1 stick) butter and drizzle evenly over the top. Bake until the topping is golden brown, about 40 minutes. Serve warm with ice cream (cinnamon is especially good).

In a large bowl, whisk together the remaining 1/4 cup sugar, the flour, almonds, brown sugar, cinnamon, and nutmeg. Slowly drizzle in the butter and stir with a fork until the mixture is crumbly and all the flour is incorporated. Do not let the mixture come together in a ball. Break up any large crumbs with your fingers: the crumbs should be smaller than 1 inch (otherwise they won't cook all the way through).

Spoon the fruit mixture into eight 8-ounce ramekins and place them on a baking sheet. (To bake one large crisp, see note.) Evenly sprinkle the crumbs on top of the fruit. Bake until the fruit is bubbling and the topping is browned, about 40 minutes. Serve hot or warm.

notes from our test kitchen

- If you don't want to bake this in individual 8-ounce ramekins, use a 2-quart baking or gratin dish instead and bake for 45 to 50 minutes. It works beautifully and still serves 8.
- If you make this crisp with water and not wine, you'll still get the deep burgundy color from the cherries, but you'll lose a bit of the complexity of flavor.

skillet blueberry cobbler

❊

COOK   Ezra Stovall

SOURCE   Gang e-mail

This is one of those word-of-mouth recipes that made its way from kitchen to kitchen on its own merits. The original comes from the late Ezra Stovall, who lived in the Blue Ridge Mountains of North Carolina. She passed it along to her grandson, Brad, who related it to his wife, Daphne Zepos (a Manhattan cheese consultant), who eventually told her friend Cindy Major, who is co-owner of Vermont Shepherd, one of the best cheesemakers in the country.

All you have to do is melt a stick of butter in a cast-iron skillet, add the berries and let them cook a bit, blob on the batter, and bake. The cobbler comes out with a juicy layer of buttery fruit under a golden, tender biscuit top. ❧

notes from our test kitchen

- You can make this dessert with frozen blueberries, blackberries, or peaches. Let the fruit thaw at room temperature first.
- If you don't have a cast-iron skillet, any ovenproof skillet will work.
- The cobbler is best served warm directly from the pan. If you have leftovers, scrape the cobbler into a nonreactive container.

8 **tablespoons (1 stick) butter**
4 **cups blueberries (see note)**
3/4 **cup plus 2 tablespoons sugar**
2 **tablespoons water, if needed**
1 **cup self-rising flour**
1 **teaspoon baking powder**
1/4 **teaspoon salt**
3/4 **cup milk**
   Whipped cream or vanilla ice cream for serving (optional)

serves 6 to 8

Preheat the oven to 400 degrees.

Melt the butter in a large cast-iron skillet (10- to 12-inch is good). Add the blueberries and 2 tablespoons of the sugar. Stir gently and cook just until the berries begin to soften. If the mixture seems at all dry, add the water.

Meanwhile, whisk together the flour, the remaining 3/4 cup sugar, the baking powder, and the salt in a medium bowl. Add the milk and stir to make a thick batter. Spoon the batter onto the fruit. Drag a spatula or spoon through the batter to make streaks of white and blue. Don't mix thoroughly.

Bake until a tester inserted in the biscuit top comes out clean and the fruit is bubbling around the edges, about 20 minutes. Serve warm with whipped cream or ice cream, if desired.

santa rosa plum galette

✳

SOURCE *San Francisco Chronicle*   STORY BY Janet Fletcher

COOK Mary Jo Thoresen after Jacques Pépin

California pastry chef Mary Jo Thoresen, a veteran of Chez Panisse, is now co-owner of Jojo in Oakland, where she specializes in fruit desserts. Her favorite is this seductive plum galette, a free-form tart baked directly on a baking sheet. It's the best we've ever tasted.

The pastry is part of the reason this galette is so good. It's the creation of Jacques Pépin, who spent a week cooking at Chez Panisse and forever changed the way the restaurant's chefs make their pastry. The Pépin pastry makes a rustic tart that doesn't even need to be perfectly round when you roll it out, so it's ideal for a beginner. If you're nervous about artfully arranging plum slices on top, no problem. The galette looks just as gorgeous with the plums dropped in helter-skelter. ❧

dough

- 1 cup all-purpose flour
- 1/2 teaspoon salt
- 8–12 tablespoons (1–1 1/2 sticks) cold unsalted butter (see note)
- Ice water

filling

- 8–10 firm, ripe Santa Rosa or other plums (about 1 1/4 pounds)
- 2–3 tablespoons all-purpose flour, depending on the juiciness of the plums
- 5 tablespoons sugar, or more depending on the sweetness of the plums, plus more for sprinkling
- Melted butter for brushing
- French vanilla ice cream for serving

serves 6 to 8

To make the dough: Combine the flour and salt in a medium bowl. Cut the butter into small pieces and add to the flour. Work in the butter with a mixer or by hand until the pieces are the size of tiny peas. Add ice water 1 tablespoon at a time, tossing and mixing gently by hand until the dough is moist but not sticky.

Wrap the dough in plastic wrap and flatten into a disk. Refrigerate for at least 1 hour or preferably overnight.

On a floured surface, roll out the dough to a 12-inch-diameter circle. Don't worry if it's not perfectly round.

WASHINGTON POST food columnist Robert Wolke writes that it's silly to pay lots of money for pastry brushes, which often need replacing. He buys small bristle brushes at the hardware store for a fraction of the cost and tosses them when they start looking frowsy. To clean brushes, just swish them in warm soapy water, rinse very well, and let air-dry. Another option: use silicone pastry brushes, which can go right in the dishwasher.

notes from our test kitchen

- The amount of butter is up to you. Use the higher amount for a rich crust.
- If you don't have a rimless baking sheet, use this tip from Bay Area baker David Lebovitz: just turn over your rimmed baking sheet and bake the galette on the bottom.
- If you make the galette several hours ahead, slide it back into a low oven to warm just a bit before serving.

Line a pizza pan or rimless baking sheet (see note) with parchment paper. Transfer the dough to the pan, cover with plastic wrap, and refrigerate briefly.

Preheat the oven to 400 degrees.

To make the filling: Halve and pit the plums. Cut each half into 5 or 6 slices.

Remove the dough from the refrigerator. Leaving a 2-inch border, sprinkle the surface of the dough with the flour and 1 tablespoon of the sugar.

Place the plum slices on the dough, maintaining the 2-inch border. You can arrange them artfully or scatter them; either way, the galette will look lovely. Sprinkle the plums with the remaining 4 tablespoons (or more) sugar.

Carefully draw up the dough from the sides and fold it over to form the rim. Make sure there are no cracks where juices can run out during baking. Brush the rim of the dough with melted butter and sprinkle generously with sugar.

Bake until well browned and bubbly, about 40 minutes, rotating as needed so the galette browns evenly. Slide the galette off the paper and onto a wire rack so the bottom crust doesn't get soggy. Use a pastry brush to dab the plums with some of the cooked plum juices to glaze them while still hot.

Serve the galette warm with a scoop of ice cream.

souffléd lemon custard

COOK Gordon Hamersley after Craig Claiborne

This super-lemony dessert has been on the menu at Gordon Hamersley's eponymous Boston restaurant, Hamersley's Bistro, since it opened twelve years ago. All efforts to take it off the menu are greeted with outrage by Hamersley's customers, so he's finally given in and shared the recipe with the rest of us.

Although it seems to have vanished from contemporary cookbooks, versions of this southern dessert appear in many old American cookbooks. This particular variation is based on a recipe by Craig Claiborne, but it's much richer and has four times as much fresh lemon. What all these desserts have in common is their airy, cakey top and custardy bottom, which turns into a sort of sauce. ☙

notes from our test kitchen

- Depending on the eggs, you may have more custard than will fit in the cake pan, especially if it's shallow. In that case, bake the custard in a 2-quart soufflé dish.
- You can bake the custard several hours ahead and hold it at room temperature until ready to serve.

8 tablespoons (1 stick) unsalted butter, softened

1 1/2 cups sugar

6 large eggs, separated

1/4 teaspoon grated lemon zest

1 cup fresh lemon juice

2/3 cup all-purpose flour, sifted

2 cups milk

1 cup heavy cream

1/2 teaspoon salt

Fresh mint leaves or berries for garnish

serves 8

Preheat the oven to 350 degrees.

In a large bowl, with an electric mixer on medium speed, cream the butter and sugar until fluffy.

Add the egg yolks one at a time. Add the lemon zest, lemon juice, and flour, stirring until just barely combined. Stir in the milk and cream until smooth.

In a separate large bowl, beat the egg whites until they hold soft to medium peaks, adding the salt halfway through. Fold into the custard mixture. Pour the custard mixture into a 10-inch round cake pan and set into a larger pan filled with 1 inch water.

Bake for about 50 minutes, or until the custard is just set. Let cool to room temperature.

Serve garnished with mint leaves or berries.

lemon posset

✳

SOURCE *À la Carte with Lee White* (WICH-1310 AM, Norwich, Connecticut)

COOK James O'Shea

With just three ingredients and perhaps 5 minutes of your precious time, you can have a dessert that will be the talk of your dinner party. This airy confection, a cross between a pudding and a mousse, is a classic British dessert (albeit transmitted by an Irish chef).

You may be tempted to add lemon zest to the cream, which is fine, but you don't need it, because there's plenty of lemon flavor in the juice and you save the extra step of straining out the zest. ❧

tip

MOST PLASTIC WRAP is pretty disappointing in terms of its ability to cling tightly or seal anything. It's also often a nightmare to use, since it sticks to everything else. Try this tip we learned recently: keep the plastic wrap in the fridge. It will seal much better and not get all tangled up.

2 cups heavy cream
¾ cup sugar
Juice of 2 lemons
Raspberries (see note) and confectioners' sugar for garnish

serves 6

Bring the cream and sugar to a boil in a medium, heavy nonreactive saucepan, stirring constantly.

Reduce the heat to a simmer and stir vigorously for 2 to 3 minutes, or until thickened. Off the heat, whisk in the lemon juice. Pour the cream into small cups or glasses, let cool slightly, cover with plastic wrap, and refrigerate until set, about 4 hours. Serve slightly chilled or at room temperature, garnished with raspberries and a dusting of confectioners' sugar.

---

notes from our test kitchen

- The posset looks best presented in cut glass. Chill the cups or glasses first so the dessert will set up faster.
- Lime posset is wonderful, too, made exactly the same way.
- The posset will keep overnight in the refrigerator. Let it sit for a while at room temperature before serving so that it's not too cold.
- Raspberries (both golden and red) are just one of the fruits you can use to top the posset. Diced mango is another option. You also can use blackberries, heated gently in a saucepan just to the point they give up their juice. Add a little sugar and pour the cooled berries over the posset, then garnish with a sprig of mint, preferably variegated.

butterscotch custard

SOURCE *Chef Interrupted* by Melissa Clark

COOK Karen DeMasco

Imagine all that's good about butter-scotch pudding and then double or triple that. It's creamy, dense, and velvety smooth, with the richest, most intense butterscotch flavor we've ever tasted. The mastermind behind this recipe is Karen DeMasco, the pastry chef from Craft and Craftbar in New York City. De-Masco doesn't rely on just brown sugar (the key ingredient in most butter-scotch); she makes a caramel for a much bolder flavor. Her other secret weapon? Salt. Not enough to make the custard taste salty, but just enough to perk up your taste buds. ✑

tip

TO CLEAN A PAN that's coated with caramel, Mediterranean cooking expert Paula Wolfert suggests boiling an inch of water in the pan and letting the caramel liquefy in the hot water.

2 **cups heavy cream**

1 **cup whole milk**

1/4 **cup packed dark brown sugar**

3/4 **cup sugar**

1/4 **cup water**

6 **large egg yolks, lightly beaten**

1 **teaspoon pure vanilla extract**

3/4 **teaspoon coarse salt**

serves 8

Preheat the oven to 300 degrees.

In a medium saucepan over medium heat, bring the cream, milk, and brown sugar to a simmer, stirring until the sugar dissolves.

Combine the sugar and water in another saucepan over medium-high heat. Simmer, swirling the pan occasionally, until the mixture is a golden caramel, 10 to 12 minutes. Slowly whisk some of the cream mixture into the caramel to stop the cooking (stand back; the liquid may spit), then con-tinue to whisk over low heat to dissolve any caramel bits that have hardened. Whisk the caramel into the rest of the cream mixture.

Whisk the warm caramel cream into the egg yolks along with the vanilla and salt. Pour the mixture through a fine-mesh strainer set over a bowl (see note).

Pour the custard into eight 5-ounce ramekins or into an 8-or 9-inch glass loaf pan, then place the custard(s) in a large

tip

MELISSA CLARK notes that even if you've never made caramel before, it's not really any harder than melting butter. Besides, sugar is cheap enough that if you do mess up (usually by overcooking the caramel), you can make it again. Clark, who has learned an untold number of culinary tricks from coauthoring several cookbooks with famous chefs, wisely recommends using a light-colored pan (such as stainless steel) when making the caramel so that you can monitor its progress. A black-bottomed pan makes it very hard to tell how dark the caramel is getting. If you don't have a light-colored pan, Clark recommends periodically taking the pan off the heat and spooning some syrup onto a white plate to check the color. For the custards, you want only a golden caramel, so stop before it gets too dark.

roasting pan. Place the roasting pan in the oven, then pour enough very hot tap water into the pan to come about halfway up the sides of the ramekins or loaf pan.

Cover the pan with aluminum foil and bake until the custard is just set around the edges, 30 to 45 minutes for individual custards or 40 to 50 minutes for one large custard. Lift a corner of the foil after 15 and 30 minutes to vent the steam, then reclose the foil. Transfer the ramekins or loaf pan to a wire rack and let cool to room temperature. Refrigerate until set, at least 4 hours. The custard will keep in the refrigerator for up to 4 days (see note). Serve cold.

notes from our test kitchen

- If you have a large (1-quart or larger) spouted measuring cup, strain the custard into that. It will make filling the ramekins much easier.

- Fill the ramekins only about three-fourths full, or you won't have enough custard for all 8.

- A teapot makes neat work of filling the roasting pan with very hot water.

- The cooking time will depend on the shape and depth of your dishes. Check for doneness by jostling them. The custard is done when it is firm around the edges and still slightly jiggly in the middle.

- If we're keeping the custards for more than a day, we like to cover them individually with plastic wrap to ensure that they don't take on any off flavors from the refrigerator.

mocha fudge pudding

SOURCE *Food & Wine*

COOK Jan Newberry

Food & Wine selected this insanely simple and completely decadent mocha pudding as one of its best recipes ever. It's the recipe we turn to when we need a knockout dessert for a cooking demonstration or impromptu dinner party. It's so quick and mindless that people are always amazed by how good it tastes. Not unlike the center of a good truffle, this pudding is dense, dark, and divine. We wouldn't think of serving it without a little puff of lightly sweetened whipped cream, and if you're feeling festive, add a few chocolate curls.

The recipe comes from Jan Newberry, food editor at *San Francisco* magazine, who says the original idea came from Ann Hodgman, who says she got it off a Nestlé's package. As is often the case, truly good recipes do live on. 🙰

tip

TO WHIP UP this pudding just before your guests arrive and have it ready by dessert, Jan Newberry suggests this shortcut. Begin by freezing the ramekins. When the pudding mixture is ready, pour it into the frozen dishes, return the ramekins to the freezer, and freeze for 20 minutes. Voilà — instant pudding without a box.

1/2 cup heavy cream

2 teaspoons instant espresso powder

6 ounces bittersweet chocolate, coarsely chopped

1/2 cup sugar

1 large egg, at room temperature

1 teaspoon pure vanilla extract

Pinch of salt

Lightly sweetened whipped cream and chocolate curls for garnish (optional)

serves 4

In a small saucepan, bring the cream and espresso powder to a boil over high heat, stirring.

Meanwhile, in a food processor, combine the chocolate and sugar and pulse until the chocolate is finely ground. Add the egg, vanilla, and salt and pulse to a paste. With the machine on, add the hot cream in a steady stream and blend until smooth and silky, about 1 minute.

Transfer the pudding to small (6-ounce) ramekins and refrigerate until firm, at least 1 hour or overnight. Garnish, if you like, with whipped cream and chocolate curls.

---

notes from our test kitchen

- The quality of the pudding has everything to do with the quality of the chocolate. Look for a brand with at least 60 percent cocoa solids.

- Be sure to start with evenly chopped chocolate. Big pieces can result in lumps in the otherwise silky pudding.

brown butter dream cookies

SOURCE *San Francisco Chronicle*

COOK Nancy Kux

Anytime you need an instant but intriguing cookie made from staples you always have on hand, make this recipe. Created by California pastry chef Nancy Kux, they have an appealing sandy texture, not unlike sand tarts. The nutty, rich fragrance of the butter browning is a delight in itself. It's easy to be creative; we almost always add some cardamom seeds and salt (see notes). Not only are the cookies great keepers, but they actually improve in flavor for up to 2 weeks. ❧

notes from our test kitchen

- We love a little salt on or in these cookies. Either add it along with the flour to the dough or sprinkle sea salt over the cookies as they come out of the oven.
- For cardamom cookies, add a rounded teaspoon of cardamom seeds to the cookie dough and blend well.

16 **tablespoons (2 sticks) unsalted butter**
 1 **cup sugar**
 1 **teaspoon pure vanilla extract**
 2 **cups unsifted all-purpose flour**
 1/2 **teaspoon baking soda**
 1/4 **teaspoon salt (optional; see note)**

makes 5 dozen cookies

Preheat the oven to 350 degrees and set a rack in the lower-middle level. Line a large baking sheet with parchment paper or use a Silpat baking mat.

Melt the butter in a small saucepan over medium heat, then let it brown, stirring constantly. Watch it like a hawk; you want the butter to turn brown, not black. Let cool and transfer to a large bowl. Scrape out the pan, if necessary, to get all the delectable little browned bits. Add the sugar and vanilla in 3 additions, stirring after each addition. Whisk the flour, baking soda and salt, if using, together in a small bowl and add to the butter mixture in 3 additions, blending well after each addition. Using about 1 1/2 teaspoons of dough, roll into balls. Place on the baking sheet 2 inches apart.

Bake for 12 to 14 minutes, or until the cookies are golden on the bottom and crack a bit on top.

Let cool in the pan on a wire rack for 5 minutes, then slide the paper with the cookies on it onto the rack. Let cool completely. Store in a tin for up to 2 weeks.

frozen lemon cream sandwiches

✳

SOURCE *Food & Wine*

COOK Grace Parisi

Let's face it — our pantries have changed quite a bit in the past decade, and we think for the better. With higher-quality ingredients available in jars, cans, boxes, and tubs, it's easier than ever to get things like real crème fraîche, jarred lemon curd, and buttery Danish cookies, the three key ingredients in this impressive dessert. Combining lemon curd and crème fraîche to create a filling for a frozen dessert sandwich is a smart idea. Once frozen, the lovely pale yellow filling remains soft and creamy, with a flavor that is slightly sweet, plenty rich, and a little tart with a bright shot of lemon.

Our advice: double the recipe. Everyone will want two. ❧

1 **7-ounce container cold crème fraîche**
¼ **cup lemon curd (see note)**
   Finely grated zest of 1 lemon
12 **crisp butter waffle cookies (see note)**
¼ **cup finely chopped unsalted pistachios**

makes 6 sandwiches

Line a small baking sheet with waxed paper.

Beat the crème fraîche, lemon curd, and lemon zest in a chilled bowl with a handheld mixer until firm peaks form.

Arrange half the cookies on the baking sheet and spoon the lemon cream onto the centers, letting it ooze gently to the edges. Top with the remaining cookies, pressing down very gently. Transfer the baking sheet to the freezer and freeze until the sandwiches are firm, at least 4 hours.

Spread the nuts on a plate and roll the edges of the sandwiches in them. Serve at once. The cookies can be frozen in an airtight container for up to 1 week.

notes from our test kitchen

- *Food & Wine* staffers recommend Wilkin & Sons Tiptree Lemon Curd as "the creamiest, most lemony" brand they tried. Surprisingly, it's less expensive than other brands. Most well-stocked supermarkets carry it, or you can find it at Todaro Bros.: todarobros.com or (877) 472-2767.
- Jules Destrooper Crisp Butter Wafers are available in the fancy cookie section of most supermarkets. They are best, because they won't become brittle when frozen.

italian shortbread with almonds and jam

※

SOURCE *Desserts: Mediterranean Flavors, California Style* by Cindy Mushet

COOK Cindy Mushet

We've completely fallen in love with this recipe. Not only is the almond short-bread delicious, but it's also a great emergency dessert, since its made from pantry ingredients, it smells heavenly as it bakes, and it's so gorgeous it makes you look like a genius pastry chef. You don't even have to grease the pan!

The shortbread tastes best the day after it's baked — if any remains — and leftovers will keep well, wrapped in foil or stored in an airtight tin. Serve the shortbread with ice cream or with a glass of vin santo or other sweet after-dinner wine. It's also lovely with coffee. ☙

12 **tablespoons (1½ sticks) unsalted butter, softened**

½ **cup sugar**

¼ **teaspoon pure almond extract**

1½ **cups unbleached all-purpose flour**

⅛ **teaspoon salt**

¼ **cup low-sugar apricot jam (preferably Smucker's), grapefruit marmalade, or other not-too-sweet jam (see note)**

⅓ **cup sliced almonds**

Confectioners' sugar for serving (optional)

serves 6 to 8

Preheat the oven to 350 degrees and set a rack in the middle level. Have ready a 9-inch ungreased fluted springform pan (see note).

Beat the butter and sugar on medium speed in a stand mixer (or with a handheld mixer; it will just take a little longer) for 3 to 4 minutes, or until very light, scraping down the sides of the bowl and the paddle from time to time. Add the almond extract and beat on medium speed for 30 seconds more to blend well.

In a small bowl, whisk the flour and salt together. Add to the butter mixture and beat on low speed, just until the dough is thoroughly blended, 30 to 40 seconds. (The dough will be stiff.) Remove ½ cup of the dough and spread it on a small plate in a thin layer; place it in the freezer.

Press the remaining dough evenly into the pan — it can be a little higher at the edge, but the center shouldn't be ele-

notes from our test kitchen

- If you don't have a 9-inch springform pan or one with a removeable bottom, don't let that stop you. Bake the shortbread in a 9-inch pie pan. If it doesn't come out of the pan in one piece, break it into serving pieces and pile them on a serving platter.

- You can skip the jam, if you'd like. Just press all the dough into the pan and top it with the almonds. You might want to add the grated zest of a lemon to the dough along with the almond extract.

- You can make the shortbread, unbaked, up to 1 month ahead. Wrap it twice in plastic wrap and freeze it on a flat surface. To bake the shortbread, unwrap it and set it frozen in the oven. Allow a few extra minutes of baking time.

vated. Spread the jam evenly over the dough to within an inch of the edge. Retrieve the remaining dough from the freezer and crumble it over the jam, allowing some of the jam to peek through. Sprinkle the almonds evenly over the top.

Bake for 40 to 50 minutes, or until golden brown. Remove from the oven and let cool completely on a wire rack. Stand the pan on a heavy can to remove the sides — the rim will just fall away. Transfer the shortbread, still on the pan bottom, to a platter, or use a spatula to remove it from the pan.

To serve, dust with confectioners' sugar, if desired, and either break into serving pieces or let your guests break off pieces as they like.

peanut butter cookies

✳

SOURCE *Gourmet*

COOK **Mom-Mom Fritch**

Amy Fritch's grandmother always made these peanut butter cookies, which were her father's favorite — and so good she decided to share them with *Gourmet*'s readers. Simple, intense, and flourless, they were the best peanut butter cookies the editors had ever tasted.

This is a good recipe to keep in your head: there are just four common ingredients that almost everyone has on hand and just one of everything.

Although you can use either creamy or chunky peanut butter, the recipe works best with the commercial creamy variety. Organic nonhydrogenated peanut butter — just ground peanuts — will work, too, and it will taste delicious, but be prepared for some serious crumbling. The hydrogenated commercial product is also sweetened, which may affect the taste of these already quite sweet cookies, so we like to add a little salt (see note). ✎

1 **cup creamy or chunky peanut butter**

1 **cup sugar**

1 **large egg**

1 **teaspoon baking soda**

makes about 5 dozen cookies

Preheat the oven to 350 degrees and set a rack in the middle level. Grease two baking sheets or line them with parchment paper.

In a large bowl, with an electric mixer, beat the peanut butter and sugar until well combined. In a small bowl, lightly beat the egg, then beat it into the peanut butter mixture along with the baking soda until well combined.

Roll level teaspoons of dough into balls and arrange them about 1 inch apart on the baking sheets. With the tines of a fork, flatten the balls to about 1½ inches in diameter, making a crosshatch pattern. Bake the cookies in batches until puffed and pale golden, about 10 minutes.

Let cool on the baking sheets for 2 minutes, then transfer with a metal spatula to wire racks to cool completely. Store in an airtight container up to 5 days.

note from our test kitchen

These cookies are especially tasty with ½ teaspoon salt added with the baking soda. We also like to press a whole roasted salted peanut into the center of each cookie, Chinese almond cookie style.

mayan mystery cookies

SOURCE Fleet Bank postcard mailing
COOK Pat Tillinghast

These cookies first appeared in a lunch-time cookie basket at New Rivers restaurant in Providence and quickly rocketed to local fame. Their creator offered a free cookie basket to whoever could guess the mystery ingredient. Only two people (one of them Julia Child's associate, Nancy Verde Barr) ever did. As you can see, it's cayenne pepper, partnered with its alluring companion of Mexican origin, chocolate.

Chef Bruce Tillinghast says that every other item on the menu changes from time to time, but not the cookies. They were created by his late wife, Pat. ☙

¾ **cup (1½ sticks) unsalted butter, softened**
¾ **cup sugar, plus more for rolling**
1½ **cups all-purpose flour**
1½ **teaspoons baking powder**
¼ **teaspoon salt**
1 **teaspoon ground cinnamon**
½ **teaspoon finely (and freshly) ground black pepper**
¼ **teaspoon ground allspice**
⅛ **teaspoon cayenne pepper**
¾ **cup unsweetened cocoa powder**
1 **large egg**
1½ **teaspoons pure vanilla extract**
    Semisweet chocolate chips

makes about 5 dozen cookies

Preheat the oven to 350 degrees. Line two baking sheets with parchment paper or Silpat baking mats.

Cream the butter and the ¾ cup sugar in a food processor. Sift the flour, baking powder, salt, spices, and cocoa in a medium bowl and add to the butter mixture. Add the egg and vanilla and mix until the batter is uniform.

Refrigerate the dough for at least 1 hour.

Using your hands, roll the dough into balls about the width of a quarter. Tuck about 5 chocolate chips into the center of

THE 150 BEST AMERICAN RECIPES

296

each one. Put some sugar on a flat plate and roll the balls in the sugar to cover lightly.

Place the balls on the baking sheets. Bake for 8 minutes, being careful not to overbake; the cookies should be delicate and soft in the center. Let cool on the baking sheets.

Store the cookies in an airtight container, separating the layers with sheets of waxed paper.

chewy chocolate chip cookies

---

*

SOURCE *New York Times Magazine*

COOK Amanda Hesser

We've conducted our fair share of chocolate chip cookie bake-offs over the years, and if we've learned anything, it's that almost everyone has their own image of the ultimate cookie. Some tasters claim to prefer them thick and gooey, others defend a soft cakey texture, and still others insist on something crisp and delicate. But anytime we put out a plate of these cookies, they are gobbled up faster than any others.

What makes these so special is a combination of factors. They get a sweet caramel edge from the generous amount of butter and light brown sugar in the dough. Their flavor is emboldened by a full tablespoon each of kosher salt and vanilla (most recipes stay in the tamer range of ½ to 1 teaspoon). And finally, the dough is refrigerated before shaping and the cookies are baked at a lower temperature than normal, so they come out chewy in the center and lightly crisp on the edges. ❧

- 2 **cups all-purpose flour**
- 1 **tablespoon kosher salt**
- 1¼ **teaspoons baking soda**
- 16 **tablespoons (2 sticks) unsalted butter, softened (see note)**
- 1½ **cups packed light brown sugar**
- ¼ **cup sugar**
- 2 **large eggs**
- 1 **tablespoon pure vanilla extract**
- 2 **cups chopped bittersweet chocolate, chunks and shavings (see note)**
- 2 **cups chopped toasted walnuts (optional)**

makes 30 to 35 cookies

Preheat the oven to 325 degrees with racks in the lower- and upper-middle levels. Line two baking sheets with parchment paper or Silpat baking mats.

Sift together the flour, salt, and baking soda.

With a stand mixer fitted with a paddle (or in a large bowl using a handheld mixer), cream together the butter and sugars until fluffy, about 3 minutes. Add the eggs one at a time, then add the vanilla. Add the flour mixture all at once and blend until a dough forms. Fold in the chocolate and the walnuts, if using. Refrigerate the dough for at least 1 hour (see note).

Roll 2½-tablespoon lumps of dough into balls, then place them on the baking sheets. Flatten with your hand to

tips

EVEN THOUGH Silpat baking mats are sold rolled up like scrolls, we learned recently that they are best stored flat. Over time, rolling the mats can break the fiberglass filaments inside the mats. The easiest way to store them flat is to stack them directly on your baking sheets.

FRAN BIGELOW, a world-class chocolatier who runs Fran's Chocolates in Seattle, stresses the importance of buying the very best chocolate when making desserts. Bigelow explains that inferior chocolate produces inferior results, no matter how good your technique or formula is. She encourages reading labels and purchasing only pure chocolate. Sugar, cocoa, butter, vanilla, and lecithin are the only other allowable ingredients. Eschew any chocolate listing vegetable fats as an ingredient. Recommended brands are Callebaut, Valrhona, El Rey, Michel Cluizel, and Scharffen Berger, most of which are available in gourmet stores and online.

½-inch-thick disks, spacing them 2 inches apart. Refrigerate the bowl of dough between batches.

Bake until the edges are golden brown, 14 to 16 minutes. Let cool slightly on the baking sheets, then transfer to a wire rack to cool completely.

notes from our test kitchen

- Be sure to use unsalted butter, or the cookies will be too salty.
- Use only pure vanilla extract. The artificially flavored stuff just won't cut it.
- We recommend using good-quality chocolate with at least 60 percent cocoa solids. You'll need 12 ounces to get 2 cups chopped. Use a heavy kitchen knife to chop the chocolate, and be sure to scrape up all the shavings along with the chunks.
- For best results, refrigerate the cookie dough for a good hour before baking. This means that you won't need to preheat the oven or prepare the baking sheets quite so early.

perfect brownies

❋

SOURCE *The Perfect Recipe* by Pam Anderson

COOK Pam Anderson

What *is* the perfect brownie? That may be an unanswerable question—or at least an excuse to keep trying every brownie recipe that looks the least bit interesting, as we have done for years.

Here's what we know: We're not interested in a tarted-up brownie or a milk chocolate brownie or pseudofudge. We're going for a plain, old-fashioned, bittersweet chocolate brownie—deeply chocolate, not too sweet, with moist more-cake-than-fudge insides and a crackly top.

One cook who shares our view is Pam Anderson, who created a brownie—not without a lot of kitchen angst, mind you—that could be all things to all people, a recipe she calls Fudgy, Chewy, Cakey Brownies. You can add nuts or not—your call—or even chocolate chips, caramel bits, toffee, mint flavoring, M&M's or, Lord knows, hashish. The point is you'll have a delicious basic brownie—the one you know you tasted somewhere but, until now, have never been able to duplicate. ❧

²/₃ **cup all-purpose flour**

¹/₂ **teaspoon salt**

¹/₂ **teaspoon baking powder**

4 **ounces bittersweet or semisweet chocolate**

2 **ounces unsweetened chocolate**

10 **tablespoons (1 stick plus 2 tablespoons) unsalted butter**

1¹/₄ **cups sugar**

2 **teaspoons pure vanilla extract**

3 **large eggs**

³/₄ **cup chopped walnuts, pecans, macadamia nuts, or peanuts, toasted (optional)**

makes 16 brownies

Preheat the oven to 325 degrees and set a rack in the lower-middle level. Spray an 8-inch square baking pan with non-stick cooking spray. Fit an 8-x-16-inch sheet of aluminum foil into the pan and up and over two sides, so you can use the foil overhang as handles to pull the cooked brownie out of the pan. Spray the foil with nonstick cooking spray.

Whisk together the flour, salt, and baking powder in a small bowl. Set aside.

Melt the chocolates and butter in a medium bowl over a pan of simmering water (or in a double boiler). Remove from the heat and whisk in the sugar and vanilla. Whisk in the eggs one at a time, fully incorporating each one before adding the next. Continue to whisk until the mixture is completely smooth and glossy. Add the dry ingredients and whisk until just incorporated. Stir in the nuts, if using.

tips

TO TOAST chopped nuts, put them on a baking sheet in a single layer. Bake at 325 degrees until they smell good, about 10 minutes. Stir them a couple of times during the toasting.

IF YOU'RE USING nonstick cooking spray on the baking sheets, how do you avoid getting an oily film on your countertops as well? CleverChef.com had a very clever solution: open the dishwasher and spray the sheet while it's resting on the dishwasher door. Any sprayed oil will get washed away with the next load of dishes.

Pour the batter into the prepared pan, smoothing the top. Bake until a cake tester or toothpick inserted in the center comes out with wet crumbs, 35 to 45 minutes. (*Important: if the toothpick comes out clean, the brownies are overcooked.*)

Cool the brownies in the pan on a wire rack for 5 minutes. Use the foil handles to pull the one big brownie out of the pan and turn it out on the rack upside down to cool completely, at least 3 hours.

Cut the brownie into 16 squares and serve. If not serving immediately, wrap the whole brownie in plastic wrap, then aluminum foil, and refrigerate for up to 5 days or freeze for up to 2 months.

tuscan rosemary and pine nut bars

SOURCE *Short & Sweet* by Melanie Barnard

COOK Melanie Barnard

Essentially, these Italian-inspired bars are elegant shortbreads and so good that we now automatically double the recipe. Because they keep so well, it's not a bad idea to whip up a batch or two in any off moment—they take about 10 minutes to assemble. A tin of these in the kitchen will always be good to go. ❧

⊰ VARIATION ⊱

You can use chopped walnuts instead of pine nuts. Rosemary and walnuts have a remarkable affinity.

¼ **cup pine nuts**

8 **tablespoons (1 stick) unsalted butter, cut into 10 pieces**

½ **cup confectioners' sugar**

1 **tablespoon chopped fresh rosemary or 2 teaspoons dried**

1 **cup all-purpose flour**

makes 16 cookies

Preheat the oven to 350 degrees and set a rack in the middle level.

Spread the pine nuts on a baking sheet and place in the oven. Toast, stirring once or twice to prevent burning, until they are a shade darker and fragrant, about 5 minutes. Watch carefully; pine nuts can burn easily. Remove from the sheet and set aside.

Meanwhile, in a medium saucepan, melt the butter over medium heat. Remove from the heat and stir in the confectioners' sugar, rosemary, and pine nuts. Then stir in the flour to make a stiff dough.

Spread and pat the dough evenly into an ungreased 8-inch square baking pan. Bake until the bars are golden and firm at the edges, about 20 minutes. Let cool in the pan on a wire rack for about 2 minutes, then use a sharp knife to cut into 16 squares. Let cool in the pan for at least 10 minutes before removing the bars with a small spatula. The bars can be stored, tightly covered, for up to 5 days or frozen for up to 1 month.

matzo buttercrunch

SOURCE *Los Angeles Times*

COOK Marcy Goldman

We were skeptical, but this candy really is delicious. It has great crunch, a rich buttery flavor, and chocolate on top. It's much like standard buttercrunch or butter-toffee bark, but the matzos add a little something extra—like bread with chocolate, they're a good counterpoint to the richness of the toffee and chocolate.

We like the unusual technique, too. Instead of cooking the butter-sugar mixture on the stovetop all the way, you pour it over the single layer of matzos and let it bubble away in the oven for 15 minutes. It works like a charm.

Serve this as a dessert or treat, or pack it into tins to give as gifts at the holidays. In an airtight container, it will keep for days. ❧

4–6 **unsalted matzos, preferably regular, but you can use egg**

16 **tablespoons (2 sticks) unsalted butter or Passover margarine**

1 **cup firmly packed brown sugar, light or dark**

3/4 **cup coarsely chopped semisweet chocolate or chocolate chips**

Toasted slivered almonds for garnish (optional)

serves 6 to 8

Preheat the oven to 350 degrees. Stack two rimmed baking sheets together (this will insulate the buttercrunch so it won't burn in the oven). Line the top sheet with aluminum foil, then with parchment paper.

Arrange the matzos as evenly as possible in a single layer on the baking sheet, cutting the squares into pieces as needed to fill any gaps. Set aside.

In a medium heavy saucepan, heat the butter or margarine and brown sugar, whisking to combine. Bring to a medium boil for 2 to 4 minutes. Remove from the heat and pour over the matzos. Pour as evenly as possible, but if you miss any spots, use a spatula to spread the mixture to cover all the matzos.

Bake for about 15 minutes, watching that the edges don't get too dark.

Remove from the oven and sprinkle the chocolate over the top. Let stand for 5 minutes, then smear the top with a metal

notes from our test kitchen

- A 6-ounce bag of chocolate chips will give you the ¾ cup you need.

- Although the cook says the toasted almonds are optional, we can't imagine making this without them.

- During baking, keep an eye out for any areas of exposed matzos to be sure they don't burn.

- Use a light touch when you smear the chocolate so that you don't mess up the buttercrunch, which has not set completely.

- If you can't fit the baking sheet in your freezer, you can just refrigerate it for a longer time. For that matter, it will eventually set up at room temperature, too.

- Be careful when you freeze the buttercrunch not to let any ice or freezer frost drip onto it. Any water will cause it to weep and melt.

spatula to spread the chocolate evenly. Sprinkle on the slivered almonds, if using. Slide the entire baking sheet into the freezer (see note) and freeze until firm, 1 hour or less. Break the buttercrunch into pieces, squares, or odd shapes and serve.

brown sugar sour cream cheesecake

brown sugar sour cream cheesecake

✳

SOURCE *Sweet Stuff* by Karen Barker

COOK Karen Barker

Karen Barker, the James Beard Foundation Award–winning pastry chef at Magnolia Grill in Durham, North Carolina, takes familiar desserts and joyfully revitalizes them. This cheesecake, for instance, has the standard elements of any New York–style cheesecake, but Barker adds a few down-home southern accents, adding a bit of cornmeal to the graham cracker crust, sweetening the cream cheese filling with molasses and brown sugar, and adding a bit of peach brandy (or bourbon or orange juice) to the sour cream topping.

Barker also introduced us to a novel way of baking cheesecake. She eliminates the nuisance of a water bath (hallelujah!) and instead has us lower the oven temperature at 20-minute intervals. This descending heat keeps the cake smooth, satiny, and completely crack-free. ❧

crust

- 1½ **cups graham cracker crumbs**
- ½ **cup yellow cornmeal, preferably stone-ground**
- 2 **tablespoons sugar**
- 6 **tablespoons (¾ stick) unsalted butter, melted**

filling

- 1½ **pounds cream cheese, at room temperature**
- 8 **tablespoons (1 stick) unsalted butter, softened**
- 1¼ **cups lightly packed light brown sugar**
- 2 **tablespoons molasses**
- 2 **teaspoons pure vanilla extract**
- ½ **cup sour cream**
- ¼ **cup heavy cream**
- 4 **large eggs**

topping

- 1½ **cups sour cream**
- 2 **tablespoons lightly packed light brown sugar**
- 1½ **tablespoons peach brandy, bourbon, or orange juice**

serves 12

To make the crust: Preheat the oven to 350 degrees. For a gas oven, place a rack in the lower level. For an electric oven, place a rack in the middle level. Butter a 10-inch springform pan, line the bottom and sides with parchment paper, and butter the parchment paper.

Combine the graham cracker crumbs, cornmeal, sugar, and melted butter in a bowl. Mix with a fork until the crumbs are

tips

KAREN BARKER offers these precautions for avoiding cheesecake cracks:

- Have all your ingredients at room temperature.
- Don't overbeat the filling.
- Line the sides and bottom of the pan with parchment paper.
- Don't overbake: Overbaking is the most common cause of cracking.
- Cool the cake completely on a wire rack before refrigerating.
- If the surface still cracks, decorate it with berries!

notes from our test kitchen

- For tamping down the crust, Karen Barker recommends using the bottom of a metal ¼-cup measuring cup. This produces a smoother crust than you can get using your fingers.
- The timing for the final baking in the low oven differs widely from one oven to another. The only way to be sure is to nudge the cake and check that the edge is set and the center is just jiggly. This takes anywhere from 20 to 40 minutes.
- The topping may take longer than 3 minutes to set. How long depends on how quickly your oven reheats. Don't leave the cake in too long, however. You want the topping to barely set, usually 5 to 10 minutes.

evenly moistened. Press the crumbs into the bottom and ½ inch up the sides of the pan (see note). Bake for about 8 minutes, or until the crust just starts to pick up a bit of color around the edge. Remove from the oven and let cool. Leave the oven on.

To make the filling: Combine the cream cheese, butter, and brown sugar in the bowl of a stand mixer fitted with the paddle attachment (or in a large bowl with a handheld mixer) and mix until very smooth, scraping down the sides of the bowl as necessary. Add the molasses and vanilla and mix. Add the sour cream and mix. Add the heavy cream and mix just to blend. Add the eggs one at a time and mix just to incorporate. Scrape the bowl, making sure the filling is well mixed. Pour into the prepared crust.

Bake for 20 minutes, then turn the oven down to 300 degrees.

Bake for 20 minutes more and turn the oven down to 250 degrees. Bake for 20 minutes more and turn the oven to low (or 225 degrees). Continue baking until the cake looks set around the edge but just a bit jiggly in the very center (see note).

To make the topping: Meanwhile, whisk together the sour cream, brown sugar, and brandy (or bourbon or orange juice).

As soon as the cake is done, remove it from the oven and turn the oven up to 350 degrees. Slowly and evenly pour the sour cream topping over the cake. You can use an offset spatula to help spread it into an even layer.

Bake for 3 minutes, or until the topping is just set. Let cool completely in the pan on a wire rack. Refrigerate for several hours or overnight before serving.

intense chocolate torte

SOURCE **Palace Market flyer (Point Reyes, California)**

COOK **Gloria Pedilla**

This is one of those sensational recipes that travel quickly from hand to hand by e-mail, fax, and scribbled note. Part of the reason it's so over-the-top delicious is an entire pound of chocolate and a cup of cream barely held together by eggs and the tiniest amount of flour. But that's just the filling. There's also a pecan graham cracker crust to give it a homey crunch. Cooks also love this torte because it's so easy to make—even a tenderfoot in the kitchen will have no problems.

This dessert is so rich that you should serve only skinny slices, with espresso, if possible. ❧

crust

1 **cup pecans, toasted and coarsely chopped**

1 **cup graham cracker crumbs (about 10 double crackers)**

2 **tablespoons sugar**

4 **tablespoons (½ stick) unsalted butter, melted, plus more if needed**

filling

1 **pound semisweet chocolate, chopped**

1 **cup whipping cream**

6 **large eggs, beaten**

¾ **cup sugar**

⅓ **cup all-purpose flour**

serves 16

To make the crust: Preheat the oven to 325 degrees.

In a medium bowl, combine all the ingredients, using more melted butter, if needed, to make the crust stick together. Press the mixture onto the bottom and 1½ inches up the sides of a 9-inch springform pan.

To make the filling: In a medium saucepan, heat the chocolate and cream over low heat until the chocolate melts. Remove from the heat and set aside. In a stand mixer or large bowl, combine the eggs, sugar, and flour. Beat for 10 minutes (less if you're beating by hand), or until thick and lemon-colored. Fold one quarter of the egg mixture into the chocolate mixture, then fold the chocolate mixture

notes from our test kitchen

- Obviously, the better the chocolate, the better the torte, but this recipe also works with plain old chocolate chips from the supermarket.
- You may get a few cracks on top of the torte as it cools, but don't worry; it will still be delicious.

into the remaining egg mixture. Pour the filling into the crust.

Bake for about 45 minutes, or until puffed around the edge and halfway to the center. Let cool on a wire rack for 20 minutes, then remove the sides of the pan.

Let cool for 4 hours before serving.

grandmother's creamy chocolate cake

* * *

SOURCE *Paris Sweets* by Dorie Greenspan

COOK Robert Linxe

The grandmother here belongs to Robert Linxe, the master chocolatier of La Maison du Chocolat in Paris. But the minute Dorie Greenspan, the Franco-phile food writer, tasted this sensational chocolate cake, she thought of her own American grandmother and the simple, deeply chocolaty cakes she used to make in a saucepan with just a few in-gredients. We wish we had those grand-mothers, but we're overjoyed to have this recipe. It's serious comfort food that also manages to be quite sophisticated, never mind simple.

This cake is sort of a cross between a brownie and fudge — dense, not too sweet, and incredibly moist and smooth. It has a single drawback — it's not pretty — so it's best served in bowls. And al-though *grand-mère* probably wouldn't have dreamed of it, we like it *à la mode Américaine* — topped with vanilla ice cream.

16 **tablespoons (2 sticks) unsalted butter, cut into 16 pieces**

8 **ounces bittersweet chocolate, finely chopped**

3/4 **cup sugar**

4 **large eggs, at room temperature**

1/4 **cup all-purpose flour**

Whipped cream, crème fraîche, or vanilla ice cream for serving (optional)

serves 8

Preheat the oven to 300 degrees and set a rack in the middle level. Butter an 8-inch square baking pan and line it with aluminum foil.

Melt the butter, chocolate, and sugar in a medium heavy saucepan over medium-low heat, stirring almost constantly until well blended. Remove the pan from the heat and let stand for 3 minutes.

One by one, whisk in the eggs. Sift the flour over the mixture and stir in. Rap the saucepan on the counter to deflate any air bubbles and pour the batter into the prepared pan.

Put the baking pan inside a larger pan and fill the larger pan with enough hot water to come halfway up the sides of the baking pan.

Bake for 35 to 40 minutes, or until the cake is set on top and a knife inserted in the center comes out streaky but not wet. Lift the baking pan out of the water bath and place it on a

tip

DORIE GREENSPAN has a great idea for leftovers: cut them into tiny cubes and freeze them. They won't actually freeze completely, just turn a bit chewy. When you're serving vanilla ice cream for dessert (or chocolate or coffee, we think) soften it slightly in the microwave, then stir in these little tidbits.

wire rack. Let cool to room temperature. Refrigerate for at least 1 hour before unmolding.

When the cake is cold, gently turn it over onto a serving platter, lift off the pan, and carefully remove the foil. The cake is meant to be served upside down, with its sleeker side facing the world. It can be served cold or at room temperature with whipped cream, crème fraîche, or ice cream, if you like.

note from our test kitchen

The baking time may be as much as 10 to 15 minutes longer. Rely on the knife test to be sure it's done.

double-chocolate layer cake

double-chocolate layer cake

SOURCE *Gourmet*

COOK **Ed Kasky**

For chocolate lovers, this is *the* birthday cake.

It's the one served at the Los Angeles restaurant Engine Co. No. 28 when Ed Kasky was chef. Kasky used some fancy chocolate in his cake—Callebaut semisweet for the cake and Guittard French Vanilla semisweet dark chocolate for the frosting—but we've had great results using less noble brands. Any good semisweet chocolate will deliver the goods.

You can make it up to 3 days ahead, another big plus. ✍

cake

- 3 ounces good-quality semisweet chocolate, finely chopped
- 1½ cups hot brewed coffee
- 3 cups sugar
- 2½ cups all-purpose flour
- 1½ cups unsweetened cocoa powder (not Dutch-process)
- 2 teaspoons baking soda
- ¾ teaspoon baking powder
- 1¼ teaspoons salt
- 3 large eggs
- 1½ cups buttermilk, shaken well
- ¾ cup vegetable oil
- ¾ teaspoon pure vanilla extract

frosting

- 1 cup heavy cream
- 2 tablespoons light corn syrup
- 2 tablespoons sugar
- 1 pound good-quality semisweet chocolate, finely chopped
- 4 tablespoons (½ stick) unsalted butter, cut into small pieces

serves 12

To make the cake: Preheat the oven to 300 degrees and set a rack in the middle level. Grease two 10-inch round cake pans. Line the bottoms with rounds of waxed paper and grease the paper.

In a small bowl, combine the chocolate and coffee and let stand, stirring occasionally, until the chocolate is melted and smooth.

In a large bowl, sift together the sugar, flour, cocoa powder, baking soda, baking powder, and salt. In another large bowl, with an electric mixer, beat the eggs until slightly thickened and lemon-colored, about 3 minutes with a stand mixer or 5 minutes with a handheld mixer. Slowly add the buttermilk, oil, vanilla, and melted chocolate mixture to the eggs, beating until well combined. Add the sugar mixture and beat on medium speed until just combined. Divide the batter between the pans and bake until a cake tester inserted in the center comes out clean, 60 to 70 minutes.

Let cool completely in the pans on wire racks. Run a thin knife around the edges of the pans and invert the layers onto the racks. Carefully remove the waxed paper and let cool completely. The cake layers may be made up to 1 day ahead and kept at room temperature, wrapped well in plastic wrap.

To make the frosting: In a medium saucepan, bring the cream, corn syrup, and sugar to a boil over medium-low heat, whisking until the sugar is dissolved. Remove from the heat and add the chocolate, whisking until the chocolate is melted. Add the butter, whisking until smooth.

Transfer the frosting to a medium bowl and let cool, stirring occasionally, until it's spreadable. (Depending on the chocolate, it may be necessary to refrigerate the frosting to bring it to spreadability.)

Spread the frosting between the cake layers and over the top and sides. The cake will keep, covered and refrigerated, for 3 days. Serve at room temperature.

walnut and prune cake périgord style

✳

SOURCE *The Walnut Cookbook* by Jean-Luc Toussaint

COOK Jean-Luc Toussaint

You might walk right by this unassuming little cake and not give it a second glance. Big mistake: it's luscious and as elegant and all-purpose as a Chanel black dress. The recipe originated in the Périgord region of France (where walnuts and prunes thrive), and it's best eaten as the French do: anytime. The nuts keep the cake incredibly moist, which means it won't get stale for several days, making it an ideal token to offer a weekend host.

For dessert, serve it in thin slices with scoops of ice cream — walnut, honey, or coffee. It's also fine all by itself, with cognac or Sauternes. Or bake it in a square pan, cut it into squares, and serve it as a breakfast or tea cake. Our advice is to make two at a time: one for now, one for the freezer. ❧

9 **tablespoons (1 stick plus 1 tablespoon) unsalted butter, softened**

$1^1/_4$ **cups sugar**

5 **large eggs**

$^2/_3$ **cup finely ground almonds**

Scant $^2/_3$ cup sifted all-purpose flour (sift before measuring)

$^1/_2$ **teaspoon baking powder**

2 **tablespoons cognac or other brandy**

1 **cup walnut pieces, finely chopped**

1 **cup pitted prunes, cut into $^1/_4$-inch pieces**

serves 6 to 8

Preheat the oven to 350 degrees and set a rack in the lower-middle level. Grease and flour a 9-inch round or square cake pan.

Beat the butter in a large bowl with an electric mixer until smooth. Gradually add the sugar and beat until creamy. Add the eggs one at a time, beating continuously. Add the ground almonds. Combine the flour and baking powder and sift them onto the batter, beating until smooth. On low speed, beat in the cognac or brandy.

Stir the walnuts and prunes into the batter. Pour the batter into the prepared pan, smoothing the top.

notes from our test kitchen

- For ⅔ cup ground almonds, you'll need 3 ounces or ¾ cup whole almonds. Grind them by pulsing in a food processor. If the almonds start to turn to nut butter before they are evenly ground, add ¼ cup of the sugar called for in the cake batter. When creaming the butter and sugar together, add only the remaining 1 cup of sugar.

- If you're serving the cake to people who turn up their noses at the mention of prunes, don't mention them. The dried fruit keeps the cake moist but doesn't dominate.

Bake for about 45 minutes, or until the top is rounded and golden. Let cool in the pan for 10 minutes. Loosen the cake by running a knife around the sides of the pan. Turn the cake out onto a wire rack with a quick jerk. Immediately reverse the cake and let it cool right side up.

Well wrapped, the cake will keep at room temperature for 2 days or in the refrigerator for 3 days. To freeze, wrap the cake in plastic wrap, then foil. It will keep in the freezer for a month or so.

almond cake with
strawberry rhubarb compote

※

SOURCE *Bouchon* by Thomas Keller with Jeffrey Cerciello
COOK Thomas Keller

Lots of people think that Thomas Keller is the best chef in America, and anyone who has dined at the French Laundry restaurant in the Napa Valley or Per Se in New York City might agree. Although he made his name in the world of haute cuisine, Keller also loves simple food, and that's what this almond cake is. It gets a triple-almond whammy from almond paste, sliced almonds, and amaretto.

You don't need to serve it with the strawberry rhubarb compote, but it's a wonderful companion and so easy to make that you really ought to try it. If strawberries and rhubarb aren't in season, serve the cake with fresh raspberries and a dollop of whipped crème fraîche. ❧

1   7-ounce package almond paste (not marzipan)
¼   cup sugar
8   tablespoons (1 stick) unsalted butter, cut into small pieces and chilled
2   tablespoons honey
3   large eggs
2   tablespoons amaretto, plus more for brushing
⅓   cup all-purpose flour, sifted
    Kosher salt
⅓–½ cup sliced almonds, toasted (see note)
    Confectioners' sugar for dusting
    Strawberry Rhubarb Compote (recipe follows)
¼   cup crème fraîche, whipped to soft peaks

serves 8

Preheat the oven to 350 degrees. Butter the bottom of an 8-inch round cake pan and butter and flour its sides. Line the bottom with parchment paper.

Cream the almond paste and sugar in a stand mixer or in a large bowl with a handheld mixer. Start on low speed to break up the almond paste, then increase the speed to medium for about 2 minutes, or until the paste is broken into fine particles. Add the butter and mix for 4 to 5 minutes, or until the mixture is light in color and airy, scraping down the sides of the bowl as necessary. It's important to mix it long enough, or the cake will have a dense texture. Mix in the honey, then add the eggs one at a time, beating

notes from our test kitchen

- You can buy tiny bottles of amaretto at the liquor store. They're useful to have on hand.
- To toast the almonds, put them on a rimmed baking sheet in a 350-degree oven and toast, shaking the pan occasionally, just until they smell toasty, 8 to 10 minutes.

until each one is incorporated before adding the next. Add the amaretto, flour, and a pinch of salt and mix just to combine. Scrape the batter into the prepared pan and smooth the top.

Bake for about 25 minutes, or until the cake is golden and springs back when pressed. Let cool in the pan on a wire rack.

Invert the cooled cake onto the rack, remove the parchment paper, and invert the cake again so that the top is facing up. Brush the top of the cake with amaretto and sprinkle with the almonds. Dust with confectioners' sugar.

Cut the cake into 8 wedges and serve with the compote and a dollop of whipped crème fraîche. The cake will keep, well wrapped, at room temperature for up to 2 days.

strawberry rhubarb compote

✳

1 pound strawberries, rinsed and hulled

1 pound rhubarb, trimmed

1 lemon

³/₄ cup sugar

This compote is also delicious for breakfast, especially with crème fraîche. ❧

Select about 4 ounces (3/4 cup) of the smallest strawberries. Cut them lengthwise into quarters and set aside.

Cut the remaining strawberries into halves or quarters of about the same size. Place them in a medium saucepan.

With a paring knife, pull away and discard the strings that run the length of the rhubarb stalks. Cut the stalks into ³/₄-inch pieces and add to the saucepan.

Use a fine grater or Microplane zester to zest the lemon. Add 1 teaspoon of the zest to the pan. Squeeze 1 tablespoon juice from the lemon and add to the pan. Add the sugar and stir.

Cook over medium-high heat, stirring often to dissolve the sugar. By the time the sugar has dissolved, the fruit will have released a lot of juice. Boil for about 4 minutes to reduce the liquid somewhat, then reduce the heat and simmer for 2 minutes more, or until the rhubarb is soft. Don't worry if some of the rhubarb falls apart.

Remove from the heat and stir in the reserved strawberries. Let cool to room temperature, then refrigerate in a covered container until cold. Any extra compote will keep for 2 weeks in the refrigerator.

cashew cake with maple frosting

✳

SOURCE *Seasoned in the South: Recipes from Crook's Corner and from Home* by Bill Smith

COOK Bill Smith

Crook's Corner in Chapel Hill, North Carolina, is the kind of casual restaurant where you walk in and feel happy. Partly that's a result of the constantly changing art on the walls and the high spirits, but mostly it comes from knowing that you're going to have some great food. The late Bill Neal founded the restaurant in the 1980s as a venue to raise southern food to national prominence. Bill Smith does a brilliant job of honoring that commitment while giving the southern fare his own spin with dishes such as this monumental cashew cake.

This is one of those towering southern layer cakes — each of the two layers is more than three inches high — and it's also airy and light, made from ground cashews, lots of egg whites, and only a small amount of flour. It's impressive to behold and unbelievably delicious. Smith says it's perfect for entertaining. ❧

2   tablespoons butter, softened, for the pans

1½ pounds raw cashews

3   cups sugar

    Grated zest of 1 large orange

¾   cup sifted all-purpose flour (sift before measuring)

2   teaspoons cider vinegar

1   teaspoon salt

2   cups egg whites (about 16 eggs; save the yolks for the frosting)

¼   teaspoon cream of tartar

    Maple Frosting (recipe follows)

makes 1 very tall layer cake

Preheat the oven to 350 degrees and set a rack in the middle level. Butter two 9-inch springform pans (see note) and line them with parchment paper. Butter and flour the parchment.

Grind the cashews coarsely with 1½ cups of the sugar and the orange zest in a food processor. Cashews are very oily, so be sure not to grind them so much that they begin to form a paste. Toss with a little of the flour to help keep the nut meal separate. Put the nut mixture in a large bowl.

Rinse a large bowl with the vinegar. Swirl in the salt. Shake the bowl over the sink to empty, but don't wipe it out. In the bowl, using an electric mixer, beat the egg whites with the cream of tartar and the remaining 1½ cups sugar. Beat until soft peaks form. Fold the egg whites into the nuts by thirds

notes from our test kitchen

- Regular cake pans are too shallow for this impressive cake. If you don't have two springform pans, you'll need to divide the batter into 3 or even 4 ordinary layer cake pans. Expect them to bake more quickly.

- A stand mixer is a big help when making this cake, although a handheld electric mixer will do.

and with the last third gently include the remaining flour. Divide the batter between the two pans.

Bake until the cakes are pretty and browned and a toothpick, broom straw, or cake tester inserted in the center comes out clean, about 1 hour. Let cool in the pans on wire racks for at least 1 hour before removing the sides of the pan.

Each cake will be a layer. The cake layers must be completely cooled before they can be frosted. The cake layers may be made ahead and kept at room temperature, well wrapped in plastic. Frost the layers with the maple frosting, spreading it between the two layers and over the top and sides. The cake will keep, covered and refrigerated, for up to 2 days. Serve at room temperature.

⇥ VARIATION ⇤

Smith says he often makes this cake with other nuts besides cashews, such as pecans, almonds, pistachios, or hazelnuts.

tip

OBVIOUSLY, this is a very sweet cake. For a lighter, less sugary dessert, Bill Smith sometimes puts barely sweetened whipped cream between the layers and on top of the cake and uses the frosting only on the sides. The extra frosting will keep well, tightly wrapped in plastic, in the refrigerator for up to 5 days. It must be softened very slowly at room temperature before using. Serve the whipped cream–filled cake the same day you make it.

note from our test kitchen

Grade B maple syrup is darker and more robust than Grade A, which is what most people prefer on their pancakes. It's easiest to find Grade B in places where they make maple syrup, such as Vermont and New Hampshire. Trader Joe's stores usually carry it. If you can't find Grade B, the regular stuff will do.

maple frosting

❋

8   **large egg yolks**

$^3/_4$ **cup sugar**

$^1/_2$ **cup pure maple syrup, preferably Grade B (see note)**

1   **pound (4 sticks) unsalted butter, cut into small bits and softened**

makes 2 cups frosting, enough for a 2-layer cake

Beat the egg yolks with a stand mixer on high speed, preferably with the whisk attachment, for about 10 minutes, or until pale yellow. Meanwhile, combine the sugar and maple syrup in a saucepan and bring to a boil that can't be stirred down, about 3 minutes.

Reduce the mixer speed to medium and slowly drizzle the maple syrup mixture in a thin steam into the egg yolks. Try not to hit the whisk and sling the hot sugar out into the room. Add all the syrup. Turn off the mixer and scrape down the bowl with a spatula. Return the mixer to high speed. The egg yolks will be fairly hot. Continue to beat until the mixture has cooled to room temperature. Don't cheat: the eggs must be cool enough that the butter doesn't melt when added to them. When the side of the mixing bowl feels cool, add the butter, bit by bit, until it is all absorbed.

You will have enough frosting to put between the cashew layers and to ice the outside of the cake.

ginger mascarpone icebox cake

✳

SOURCE *Fine Cooking*

COOK Heather Ho

This no-bake dessert is a legacy from Heather Ho, the brilliantly talented young pastry chef who was at work at Windows on the World the morning of 9/11. It has some of the charm of tiramisù, with the zing of ginger and the voluptuousness of mascarpone. It's a great holiday sweet, for times when oven space is at a premium. Icebox cakes are almost by definition unpretentious, and this one uses plain old gingersnaps as its base.

More virtues: it must be made a day ahead, it travels well (as long as you keep it chilled), and there probably won't be any leftovers to fuss with. It's as good in the summer as it is for the holidays and pairs well with blueberries, mangoes, or peaches. ❧

- 12 **ounces gingersnap crumbs (about 2¼ cups, from about 40 Nabisco gingersnaps)**
- 5 **tablespoons unsalted butter, melted**
- 1 **8-ounce package cream cheese, at room temperature**
- ½ **cup plain low-fat yogurt**
- ⅔ **cup sugar**
- ½ **teaspoon pure vanilla extract**
- ½ **cup minced crystallized ginger**
- 1 **pound mascarpone cheese**
- ⅓ **cup heavy cream**

serves 12

Spray a 9-inch springform pan with nonstick cooking spray or butter it lightly. Dust the pan with a little sugar and shake out any excess.

In a medium bowl, combine the gingersnap crumbs and butter, rubbing them together with your fingertips to combine thoroughly. Sprinkle half of the crumbs over the bottom of the pan and pat down evenly; reserve the rest.

In a large bowl, with an electric mixer, whip together the cream cheese, yogurt, sugar, vanilla, and ginger until smooth, scraping down the sides of the bowl. Add the mascarpone and cream and whip until the mixture is thoroughly combined and just holds peaks. Don't overwhip, or the mixture may separate.

Carefully spoon half of the mixture over the crust, spreading it evenly to the edge of the pan. Sprinkle half of the remaining crumbs over the mascarpone mixture in the pan. Top with the remaining mascarpone mixture and finish with the remaining crumbs. Gently tap the pan on the counter to eliminate any air bubbles. Cover with plastic wrap and refrigerate overnight. Serve cold.

sticky toffee pudding with chocolate chips and toffee sauce

sticky toffee pudding
with chocolate chips and toffee sauce

SOURCE Gang e-mail from *Gourmet* staffers

COOK Andrew Blake

Sticky toffee pudding is nothing new to Brits and Aussies, and it has recently begun to take hold on our shores. There are now even a few Web sites devoted to this famous cake, one exclaiming that "sticky toffee pudding isn't a dessert, it's a phenomenon." To the uninitiated, it helps to understand that the word "pudding" here evokes the British use, meaning dessert, and this extravagant confection is what we call a cake. But it's a rich cake, flavored with dates and served warm with a thick, gooey toffee sauce. This wicked version takes tradition one step further, adding chopped bittersweet chocolate.

This recipe originally came from Sydney, Australia. Somewhere along the line, it was picked up by *Gourmet*'s executive food editor, Zanne Stewart, who sent it to a few people, and before you could say "sticky toffee pudding," it was the recipe everyone had to have. Now it's yours. ❧

sauce

- 1½ cups packed dark brown sugar (see note)
- 8 tablespoons (1 stick) butter
- ½ cup heavy cream

pudding

- 6 ounces pitted dates (8 ounces unpitted)
- ¼ teaspoon baking soda
- ¾ cup boiling water
- 6 tablespoons (¾ stick) butter, softened (see note)
- ½ teaspoon salt, if using unsalted butter
- ¾ cup packed dark brown sugar
- 2 teaspoons pure vanilla extract
- 2 large eggs, beaten
- 1¼ cups all-purpose flour
- 2 teaspoons baking powder
- 7 ounces bittersweet chocolate, coarsely chopped
- 2 teaspoons instant espresso powder (optional)
- Crème fraîche for serving (optional)

serves 12 to 14

Preheat the oven to 350 degrees. Butter a 9-inch round cake pan with 2-inch sides and line the bottom with a round of parchment paper.

To make the sauce: Combine the brown sugar, butter, and cream in a small saucepan over medium heat. Stir until the sugar has completely dissolved and the sauce is bubbling.

notes from our
test kitchen

- For the best toffee flavor, you must use dark brown sugar.
- Use either salted or unsalted butter for the pudding. Just be sure to include the ½ teaspoon salt if using unsalted.
- The technique of soaking the dates in boiling water with baking soda may surprise you. In the brief soak, the dates melt into marvelous sweet, sticky bits that then get stirred into the batter.
- For individual puddings, use eight 3-inch ramekins. Bake for only about 25 minutes.
- The pudding can be made 1 day ahead and kept in an airtight container. To serve, cut into wedges, top with a little sauce, and reheat quickly in a hot oven.

Pour half of the sauce into the prepared cake pan and set aside the rest to serve with the pudding.

To make the pudding: Put the dates and baking soda in a small bowl and add the boiling water. Set aside.

Cream the butter (add the salt if using unsalted butter), brown sugar, and vanilla together in a large bowl until white and fluffy. Beat in the eggs a little at a time, sprinkling in 1 tablespoon of the flour when you have added about half the beaten eggs (this helps stop the batter from curdling). Mix in the dates and their soaking water. Sift the remaining flour and the baking powder over the mixture, then fold in gently but thoroughly. Stir in the chopped chocolate and the espresso powder, if using.

Pour the batter into the pan. Bake until the top is golden and firm and the sides have shrunk away slightly from the pan, 50 to 60 minutes. Let cool in the pan on a wire rack for 15 minutes. Run a knife around the edge of the pudding and turn it out onto a serving plate.

Reheat the remaining sauce until bubbling. Cut the warm pudding into wedges, spoon the sauce over the pudding, and serve with a dollop of crème fraîche, if you like.

tip

TO DEAL WITH hardened brown sugar, according to Robert L. Wolke, the kitchen science guy who solves cooking conundrums for the *Washington Post* food section, you need to rehydrate the molasses that makes it brown. To do that, put the hardened sugar in a sealable container, place a layer of plastic wrap over it, add a damp paper towel, and seal tightly. Leave overnight – or all day – then remove the paper towel. The sugar should be soft and will stay that way for a while, unlike the highly touted microwave method, which warms the molasses only for a few minutes.

almond flan

SOURCE *Fonda San Miguel* by Tom Gilliland and
Miguel Ravago with Virginia B. Wood

COOK Ana Maria

For thirty years, Mexican-food lovers in Austin, Texas, have had the huge pleasure of dining at Fonda San Miguel, a spectacular restaurant filled with a major collection of Mexican paintings. In the early days of the restaurant, a loyal customer named Ana Maria shared her heirloom family recipe for almond flan. At the time, flan was exotic in Texas, even in other Mexican restaurants. This one quickly became a classic at the restaurant.

This gorgeous flan is unusually dense and creamy and has a little almond crust that magically appears on the bottom of the pan. It only improves when it's made a day ahead. The recipe, which is dead easy, comes from the state of Guanajuato in Mexico. ❧

$3/4$ **cup sugar**

$2/3$ **cup blanched slivered almonds**

$1^1/2$ **14-ounce cans Eagle Brand sweetened condensed milk**

1 **cup whole milk**

3 **large eggs, plus 3 large egg yolks**

1 **teaspoon Mexican vanilla extract (see note)**

serves 8 to 12

Preheat the oven to 350 degrees and set a rack in the middle level.

Put the sugar in a round 9-x-3-inch metal cake pan. Place the pan directly over medium heat on the stovetop to caramelize the sugar. (Use heavy oven mitts or tongs to handle the pan.) Heat until the sugar liquefies, 3 to 5 minutes, stirring occasionally with a wooden spoon. Do not touch the sugar, which is extremely hot. When the sugar is golden brown, remove the pan to a rack and let cool and harden.

Combine the remaining ingredients in a blender and process on medium speed until well blended. Pour the custard mixture over the prepared caramel. Place the cake pan in a larger, deeper pan and pour about an inch of hot water around the cake pan to make a water bath. Cover the flan loosely with an aluminum foil tent and place the larger pan in the oven.

notes from our test kitchen

- If you don't have Mexican vanilla, which is especially heady, ordinary pure vanilla extract will be fine.
- When making the caramel, it's best not to stir the sugar any more than you have to, or it may seize up and harden.
- A 2-inch-deep cake pan will also work here and makes it slightly less likely that the flan will fall apart on its slide to the serving platter.
- You can also make the flan in a springform pan. Just be sure to wrap the outside of the pan tightly with aluminum foil so that no water seeps in.

Bake for 1¼ hours, or until the flan is set in the center and no longer jiggles. Let cool to room temperature on a wire rack. Refrigerate until well chilled, at least 1 hour.

To serve, run a knife or thin spatula around the edge of the pan to loosen the flan. Put a platter 10 inches in diameter (or more) over the pan and gently invert it, so that the flan is left on the serving platter. Scrape up any caramel left on the bottom of the pan and pour it over the flan. Cut into triangular wedges and serve.

bitter orange ice cream

SOURCE *Nigella Bites* by Nigella Lawson

COOK Nigella Lawson

Even if you've never dreamed of making ice cream and have no ice cream maker, you can make this one. It takes only a few minutes to put together and a few hours to freeze. Not quite ice cream, not quite mousse, this is a cloudlike frozen confection with a velvety texture.

The intensely flavorful Seville orange (bitter orange) is the primary ingredient in British marmalade. It's not yet common in the United States, but like other once exotic fruits, you see it more often every year — especially just after Christmas. In the meantime, orange and lime mixed together give a good approximation, and lime all by itself also is great. ❧

3 **Seville oranges or 1 navel orange plus 2 limes**
1 **cup plus 2 tablespoons confectioners' sugar**
2½ **cups heavy cream**
    Wafer cookies for serving (optional)

serves 6

If you're using Seville oranges, grate the zest of 2 of them. Squeeze the juice out of all 3 and place it in a large bowl with the zest and sugar. If using the navel orange and limes, grate the zest of the orange and 1 lime. Juice the orange and both limes and add to the zest and sugar as before. Stir to dissolve the sugar, then add the heavy cream.

Whip everything until it holds soft peaks. (A stand mixer is perfect for this job, but a handheld mixer will do.) Turn the mixture into a shallow airtight container with a lid (see note). Cover and freeze until firm, 3 to 5 hours. Remove from the freezer to soften for 15 to 20 minutes (30 to 40 minutes in the refrigerator) before serving. Serve in bowls, in cones, or sandwiched between wafer cookies.

---

notes from our test kitchen

- For the all-lime option, use 4 limes, zesting 2 of them.
- This is the place to use those disposable plastic food-storage containers. Two 25-ounce containers will hold the ice cream perfectly.
- Lawson uses giant pizzelle-like wafers, which she refers to as "cookie wafers," for ice cream sandwiches.

credits
and index

credits

Charred Tomatillo Guacamole with Seeded Tortilla Triangles. Originally published in *Gourmet*. Copyright © 2000 by Mary Sue Milliken and Susan Feniger. Reprinted by permission of Mary Sue Milliken and Susan Feniger.

Sweet and Spicy Pecans. From *New Tastes from Texas* by Stephan Pyles. Copyright © 1998 by Stephan Pyles. Reprinted by permission of Stephan Pyles.

Cheddar Walnut Crisps. Originally published in *Sainsbury's Magazine*. Copyright © 1998 by Lorna Wing. Reprinted by permission of Lorna Wing.

Phyllo Cheese Straws. From *Patrick O'Connell's Refined American Cuisine* by Patrick O'Connell. Copyright © 2004 by Patrick O'Connell. Reprinted by permission of Little, Brown and Co., Inc.

Pancetta Crisps with Goat Cheese and Pear. Originally published in *Bon Appétit*. Copyright © 2004 by Condé Nast Publications. Reprinted by permission of Condé Nast Publications.

Salsa-Baked Goat Cheese. From *El Mundo de Frontera* newsletter by Rick Bayless. Copyright © 2002 by Rick Bayless. Reprinted by permission of Rick Bayless.

Parsi Deviled Eggs. Originally published in the *San Francisco Examiner*. Copyright © 1998 by Niloufer Ichaporia King. Reprinted by permission of Niloufer Ichaporia King.

Vodka-Spiked Cherry Tomatoes with Pepper-Salt. Originally published in *Gourmet*. Copyright © 2001 by Condé Nast Publications. Reprinted by permission of Condé Nast Publications.

Crimped Shrimp. Originally published in the *Los Angeles Times*. Copyright © 2000 by Michael Roberts. Reprinted by permission.

Smoked Salmon Rolls with Arugula, Mascarpone, Chives, and Capers. From *In the Hands of a Chef* by Jody Adams and Ken Rivard. Copyright © 2002 by Jody Adams and Ken Rivard. Reprinted by permission of HarperCollins Publishers.

Roasted Asparagus with Panko Bread Crumbs. From *The Way We Cook* by Sheryl Julian and Julie Riven. Copyright © 2003 by Sheryl Julian and Julie Riven. Reprinted by permission of Houghton Mifflin Co.

Mini Frittatas with Wild Mushrooms. Originally published in Macy's De Gustibus handout. Copyright © 1999 by Eileen Weinberg. Reprinted by permission of Eileen Weinberg.

Manly Meatballs. Originally published on www.thefoodmaven.com by Arthur Schwartz. Copyright © 1998 by Arthur Schwartz. Reprinted by permission of Arthur Schwartz.

Savory Fig Tart. Originally published in the Winter 2003 *Whole Foods Holiday Entertaining Guide* by Whole Foods Market. Copyright © 2003 by Whole Foods Market. Reprinted by permission.

Pea Soup with Crispy Pancetta, Bread, and Sour Cream. From *Jamie's Kitchen* by Jamie Oliver. Copyright © 2003 by Jamie Oliver. Reprinted by permission of Hyperion/Buena Vista Books, Inc.

Carrot Ginger Soup with Lime Crème Fraîche. From *Simply Elegant Soup* by George Morrone with John Harrisson. Copyright © 2004 by George Morrone and John Harrisson. Reprinted by permission of Ten Speed Press, Berkeley, CA. www.tenspeed.com.

Yellow Pepper and Pine Nut Soup. Originally published in *Marie Claire*. Copyright © 2000 by Han Feng. Reprinted by permission of Gillian Duffy.

Fresh Corn Soup. From *The Essential Cuisines of Mexico* by Diana Kennedy. Copyright © 2000 by Diana Kennedy. Reprinted by permission of Clarkson Potter/Publishers, a division of Random House, Inc.

Italian Pumpkin Soup. Originally published in a Palio Restaurant press release. Copyright © 1999 by Maria Pia. Reprinted by permission of Maria Pia restaurant.

Roasted Butternut Squash Soup with Bacon. Originally published as Butternut Squash Soup with Minced Bacon in *Tom Valenti's Soups, Stews, and One-Pot Meals* by Tom Valenti and Andrew Friedman. Copyright © 2003 by Tom Valenti and Andrew Friedman. Reprinted by permission of Scribner, an imprint of Simon & Schuster Adult Publishing Group.

Garlic Soup with Ham and Sage Butter. From *Between Bites* by James Villas. Copyright © 2002 by James Villas. Reprinted by permission of Wiley Publishing Inc., a subsidiary of John Wiley & Sons, Inc.

Senegalese Peanut Soup. From *The Daily Soup Cookbook* by Leslie Kaul, Bob Spiegel, Carla Ruben, and Peter Siegel with Robin Vitetta-Miller. Copyright © 1999 by Leslie Kaul, Bob Spiegel, and Peter Siegel. Reprinted by permission of Hyperion/Buena Vista Books, Inc.

Crab Soup with Sweet Spices and Ginger Juice. From *Raji Cuisine* by Raji Jallepalli. Copyright © 2000 by Raji Jallepalli. Reprinted by permission of HarperCollins Publishers.

Tortilla Soup with Chicken and Avocado. Originally published in *Fine Cooking*. Copyright © 2002 by The Taunton Press, Inc. Reprinted by permission of Taunton Press, Inc.

Roasted Mushroom-Leek Soup with Crispy Pancetta. From *Stonewall Kitchen Harvest* by Jim Stott, Jonathan King, and Kathy Gunst. Copyright © 2004 by Jim Stott, Jonathan King, and Kathy Gunst. Used by permission of Clarkson Potter/Publishers, a division of Random House, Inc.

The Lentil Soup. From *A Mediterranean Feast* by Clifford A. Wright. Copyright © 1999 by Clifford A. Wright. Reprinted by permission of HarperCollins Publishers/William Morrow.

Malaysian Noodle Soup. From Ramekins Sonoma Valley Culinary School handout. Copyright © 2001 by John Ash. Reprinted by permission of John Ash.

Smoky Shrimp and Halibut Stew. Originally published in *Bon Appétit*. Copyright © 2002 by Bruce Aidells. Reprinted by permission of Bruce Aidells.

Wild Rice and Turkey Soup. Originally published in the *Atlanta Journal-Constitution*. Copyright © 1998 by Kathie Jenkins. Reprinted by permission of Kathie Jenkins.

Alice Waters's Coleslaw. Originally published in the *New York Times Magazine*. Copyright © 2004 by The New York Times Syndication Sales Corp. Reprinted with permission.

Crunchy Cucumber, Celery, and Red Bell Pepper Salad with Cumin and Fresh Mint. From *Once Upon a Tart . . .* by Frank Mentesana and Jerome Audureau with Carolynn Carreño. Copyright © 2003 by Frank Mentesana and Jerome Audureau. Used by permission of Alfred A. Knopf, a division of Random House, Inc.

Green Bean Salad with Cream. From *Guy Savoy: Simple French Recipes for the Home Cook* by Guy Savoy. Copyright © 2004 by Guy Savoy. Reprinted by permission of Harry N. Abrams/Stewart, Tabori & Chang.

Heirloom Tomato and Watermelon Salad. Originally published in *New York* magazine. Copyright © 2001 by *New York*. Reprinted by permission of Gillian Duffy.

Carrot, Parsley, and Pine Nut Salad with Fried Goat Cheese. Originally published on www.formaggio kitchen.com. Copyright © 2001 by Ana Sortun. Reprinted with permission of Ana Sortun.

Cherry Tomato Salad with Olives. From *The Naked Chef Takes Off* by Jamie Oliver. Copyright © 2001 by Jamie Oliver. Reprinted by permission of Hyperion/Buena Vista Books, Inc.

Tomato, Avocado, and Roasted Corn Salad. Originally published in *Food & Wine*. Copyright © 2000 by Elizabeth Falkner. Reprinted by permission of Elizabeth Falkner.

Tomato Salad with Cumin. Originally published as *Ajotomate* — Tomato Salad (Murcia) in *The Cuisines of Spain* by Teresa Barrenechea. Copyright © 2005 by Teresa Barrenechea. Reprinted by permission of Ten Speed Press, Berkeley, CA. www.tenspeed.com.

Beet Salad with Horseradish and Fried Capers. Originally published in the *New York Times Magazine*. Copyright © 2004 by The New York Times Syndication Sales Corp. Reprinted with permission.

Sicilian Slow-Roasted Onion Salad. First published in *Food & Wine*. Copyright © 2001 by Paula Wolfert. Reprinted by permission of Paula Wolfert.

Fennel, Red Pepper, and Mushroom Salad. Originally published on www.Martha-Rose-Shulman.com.

index

Page numbers in *italics* refer to photographs.

green, –potato gratin, 207
green, Tex-Mex macaroni and cheese with, 112–13
peeling, 249
removing seeds from, 128
roasting, 207, 249
chile verde, pork, with posole, *177*, 178–79
chive pasta, cremini mushrooms with, 108–9
chocolate
cake, grandmother's creamy, 313–14
chip cookies, chewy, 298–99
chips and toffee sauce, sticky toffee pudding with, *329*, 330–31
double-, layer cake, *315*, 316–17
high quality, buying, 299
matzo buttercrunch, *304*, 305–6
Mayan mystery cookies, 296–97
mocha fudge pudding, 288
perfect brownies, *300*, 301
torte, intense, *310*, 311–12
cilantro
Alice Waters's coleslaw, 67
arroz verde, 221
and cream, zucchini with, 216
relish, 155
smoky bacon, and lime, mussels with, 126–28, *127*
Tex-Mex macaroni and cheese with green chiles, 112–13
cinnamon buns from heaven, *265*, 266–67
cobbler, skillet blueberry, 279
coconut (dried)
sesame orange granola, 231–32
coconut (milk)
laksa paste, 57
and lime, stir-fried chicken with, 129
Malaysian noodle soup, *56*, 57–58
coleslaw, Alice Waters's, 67
Colicchio, Tom, 197
compote, strawberry rhubarb, 323
Conte, Anna del, 190

cookies and bars
brown butter dream cookies, 289
chewy chocolate chip cookies, 298–99
Italian shortbread with almonds and jam, *292*, 293–94
Mayan mystery cookies, 296–97
peanut butter cookies, 295
perfect brownies, *300*, 301
Tuscan rosemary and pine nut bars, 303
cooking odors, eliminating, 61
coriander seeds, cracking, 73
corn
double-, polenta, *202*, 203–4
roasted, adding to guacamole, 79
roasted, tomato, and avocado salad, 77–79, *78*
soup, fresh, 37
tortilla soup with chicken and avocado, 48–51, *50*
corn bread
with sage leaves and feta, 258–59
salad with grilled sausage and spicy chipotle dressing, 91–92, *93*
skillet, preparing, 259
cornmeal
corn bread, skillet, preparing, 259
corn bread with sage leaves and feta, 258–59
double-corn polenta, *202*, 203–4
crab
cakes with scallions and jalapeños, 121–23, *122*
soup with sweet spices and ginger juice, 46–47
cranberry(ies)
pecan bread, 268–69
wild mushroom stuffing, 150–51
crème fraîche
and arugula, tagliatelle with, 102–3

frozen lemon cream sandwiches, 290, *291*
green bean salad with cream, 71
lime, 34–35
crisps
apple, preparing, 278
berry, preparing, 278
pear, with dried sour cherries, *276*, 277–78
cucumber(s)
celery, and red bell pepper salad, crunchy, with cumin and fresh mint, *68*, 69–70
English, about, 70
Kirby, about, 70
slicing tool for, 209
tomato, avocado, and roasted corn salad, 77–79, *78*
cumin seeds, toasting and grinding, 70
Cunningham, Marion, 235, 263
custard, butterscotch, 286–87
custard, souffléd lemon, 283

dates
sticky toffee pudding with chocolate chips and toffee sauce, *329*, 330–31
Del Grande, Robert, 112, 206
DeMasco, Karen, 286
dip. *See* guacamole
Douglas, Tom, 146
duck
Asian flavorings for, 144
roast, the amazing five-hour, 142–44, *143*
Dunaway, Suzanne, 107

eggs
baked, in maple toast cups, *242*, 243
cracking, tip for, 243
with crunchy bread crumbs, 244–45
deviled, Parsi, *14*, 15
green chile cheese puff, 249
hard-cooked, preparing, 15
mini frittatas with wild mushrooms, 24

eggs (cont.)
smoked salmon hash, *246*, 247–48

Falkner, Elizabeth, 77
Feniger, Susan, 4, 178
fennel
red pepper, and mushroom salad, *86*, 87
seeds, grinding, 107, 191
smoky shrimp and halibut stew, 59–61, *60*
fig spread, buying, 27
fig tart, savory, *26*, 27
Finamore, Roy, 210
fish
cooking odors, eliminating, 61
halibut and shrimp stew, smoky, 59–61, *60*
salmon, kippered, about, 248
salmon fillets, sear-roasted, with lemon ginger butter, 124–25
smoked salmon hash, *246*, 247–48
smoked salmon rolls with arugula, mascarpone, chives, and capers, 19–21, *20*
tuna, canned, buying, 111
tuna sauce, spaghettini with, 110–11
white anchovies, about, 111
flan, almond, 332–33
flaxseeds
buying, 5
seeded tortilla wedges, *3*, 4
Flay, Bobby, 215
Fleming, Claudia, 277
Foster, Sara, 255
French toast, pecan praline, *237*, 238–39
frittatas, mini, with wild mushrooms, 24
frosting, maple, 326

galette, Santa Rosa plum, *280*, 281–82
garlic
allioli, 133

oil, preparing, 220
peeling, tip for, 206
soup with ham and sage butter, 43
Germon, George, 169, 203
ginger
and apple cider, sweet potatoes with, 215
carrot soup with lime crème fraîche, 34–35
chard with, 201
crystallized, buying, 257
juice, buying, 47
juice, preparing, 47
laksa paste, 57
lemon butter, sear-roasted salmon fillets with, 124–25
mascarpone icebox cake, 327–28
oil, 34–35
Glezer, Maggie, 268
Goin, Suzanne, 114
Gold, Rozanne, 188, 215
Goldstein, Joyce, 198
Granger, Bill, 153
granola, sesame orange, 231–32
grapes and sausages, roasted, 169–70
gratin, potato–green chile, 207
gratin, pumpkin and goat cheese, 218–19
Gray, Rose, 102
green bean(s)
braised, with tomato and fennel, 190–91
roasted, with garlic, 189
salad with cream, 71
greens. *See also* arugula
arroz verde, 221
chard with ginger, 201
gremolata, roasted broccoli florets with, 192–93
grits
buying and storing, 120
shrimp and, 118–20, *119*
guacamole
charred tomatillo, with seeded tortilla wedges, *3*, 4–5
grilling avocados for, 92
Gunst, Kathy, 52

halibut and shrimp stew, smoky, 59–61, *60*
ham
Monte's, 180
and sage butter, garlic soup with, 43
savory fig tart, *26*, 27
sugar snap pea and prosciutto salad, 90
wild rice and chickpea salad, 88–89
Hamersley, Gordon, 283
hash, smoked salmon, *246*, 247–48
hazelnuts
nutty roasted cremini, 205
toasting and husking, 205
wild mushroom stuffing, 150–51
Henderson, Fergus, 217
herb(s). *See also* basil; cilantro; rosemary; sage
chicken thighs baked with lemon, sage, rosemary, and thyme, *132*, 133–34
fresh, roasted potato crisps with, *208*, 209
salad, 116
Tuscan herbed salt, 172
Hesser, Amanda, 82, 298
Ho, Heather, 327
Husbands, Andy, 274

ice cream, bitter orange, 334

Jallepalli, Raji, 46
Jordan, Michele Anna, 175
Julian, Sheryl, 209

Kasky, Ed, 316
Katzen, Mollie, 240
Kaul, Leslie, 44
Keller, Thomas, 321
Kelley, Jeanne Thiel, 213
Kennedy, Diana, 37
Killeen, Johanne, 169, 203
King, Jonathan, 52
King, Niloufer Ichaporia, 15, 201
Kummer, Corby, 190
Kux, Nancy, 289

sweet potatoes
  with ginger and apple cider,
    215
  whipped chipotle, 215

tarts
  onion, bacon, and ricotta,
    114–16
  Santa Rosa plum galette, *280*,
    281–82
  savory fig, *26*, 27
Taylor, John Martin, 259
Thoresen, Mary Jo, 281
toffee sauce, 330–31
tofu, adding to peanut soup, 45
tomatillo(s)
  charred, guacamole with
    seeded tortilla wedges, *3*,
    4–5
  pork chile verde with posole,
    177, 178–79
tomato(es)
  and bread casserole, Sardin-
    ian, 224–25
  canned, buying, 111
  cherry
    James Beard's drunken, 17
    salad with olives, 76
    slow-roasted, basil, and
      Parmesan cheese,
      spaghetti with, *104*,
      105–6
    vodka-spiked, with pepper-
      salt, 16–17
  and fennel, braised green
    beans with, 190–91
  fresh, storing, 76
  peeling, 81
  salad
    avocado, and roasted corn,
      77–79, *78*
    cherry, with olives, 76
    with cumin, 80–81

heirloom, and watermelon,
    72, 73
  salsa, 178–79
  spaghettini with tuna sauce,
    110–11
torte, intense chocolate, *310*,
  311–12
tortilla(s)
  corn, warming, 176
  slow-roasted chipotle pork,
    175–76
  soup with chicken and avo-
    cado, 48–51, *50*
  strips, crispy, 51
  Tex-Mex macaroni and cheese
    with green chiles, 112–13
  wedges, seeded, *3*, 4
Toussaint, Jean-Luc, 318
Tower, Jeremiah, 43
Traunfeld, Jerry, 258
tuna
  canned, buying, 111
  sauce, spaghettini with, 110–11
turkey
  broth, 152
  buying, tip for, 148
  carcass, storing, 63
  roasting, in hot oven, 149
  Sloppy Joes, 145
  spice-rubbed, with sage gravy
    and wild mushroom stuff-
    ing, 146–52, *147*
  and wild rice soup, 62–63

Valenti, Tom, 41
vodka
  James Beard's drunken cherry
    tomatoes, 17
  -spiked cherry tomatoes with
    pepper-salt, 16–17

waffles
  amazing overnight, 240, *241*

keeping warm, 240
  made from pancake batter, 236
walnut(s)
  cheddar crisps, *8*, 9
  chewy chocolate chip cookies,
    298–99
  cinnamon buns from heaven,
    265, 266–67
  fillet of beef with Roquefort
    sauce and mixed nuts,
    156–57
  Kona Inn banana muffins,
    263–64
  and pecorino, roasted Brussels
    sprouts with, *194*, 195
  perfect brownies, *300*, 301
  and prune cake Périgord style,
    318–19
  in rosemary bar cookie recipe,
    303
  salsa-baked goat cheese, 13
watermelon and heirloom tomato
  salad, 72, 73
Waters, Alice, 67
Weinberg, Eileen, 24
Weir, Joanne, 90
wild rice
  buying, 63
  and chickpea salad, 88–89
  and turkey soup, 62–63
Willan, Anne, 275
Willinger, Faith, 99
wine, opened, storing, 141
Wolfert, Paula, 84, 156

Yorkshire pudding, 160

Zakarian, Geoffrey, 73
zucchini
  with cilantro and cream, 216
  Malaysian noodle soup, *56*,
    57–58
  mushy, 217